The Ethics of Animal Shelters

T0352866

The Ethics of Animal Shelters

Edited by

Valéry Giroux
Angie Pepper
and
Kristin Voigt

OXFORD
UNIVERSITY PRESS

Oxford University Press is a department of the University of Oxford. It furthers
the University's objective of excellence in research, scholarship, and education
by publishing worldwide. Oxford is a registered trade mark of Oxford University
Press in the UK and certain other countries.

Published in the United States of America by Oxford University Press
198 Madison Avenue, New York, NY 10016, United States of America.

CIP data is on file at the Library of Congress

ISBN 978-0-19-767864-0 (pbk.)
ISBN 978-0-19-767863-3 (hbk.)

DOI: 10.1093/oso/9780197678633.001.0001

Printed by Marquis Book Printing, Canada
Hardback printed by Bridgeport National Bindery, Inc., United States of America

Contents

Acknowledgments

The publication of this collected volume was made possible thanks to the trust of Peter Ohlin of Oxford University Press. The project that led to it was born from the enthusiasm of Élise Desaulniers, who convinced us of its interest and graciously accepted to collaborate with us. We would like to thank her dearly, as well as the other employees of the Montreal SPCA who took time out of their busy schedules to discuss with us the ethical dilemmas they face in their daily work. We are especially grateful to Amélie Martel and Sophie Gaillard, who patiently answered our many questions and helped us avoid numerous misinterpretations, to Frédéric Côté-Boudreau and Hosanna Galea for their invaluable assistance throughout this project, and to Michelle Picard-Aitken for helping us secure financial support for this work. We would finally like to thank the Social Sciences and Humanities Research Council (SSHRC), which funded this project, and the Group of Environmental and Animal Ethics (GRÉEA) and the Center for Research in Ethics (CRÉ), under whose auspices we were able to carry it out.

Above all, we wish to acknowledge the extraordinary work of the staff of the Montreal SPCA and all the other people who devote themselves tirelessly to improve the lives of animals. We are full of admiration for the perseverance, commitment, and selflessness they bring to their work. We sincerely hope that this book will offer them support and perhaps even alleviate some of the countless challenges they face on a daily basis.

Contributors

Frédéric Côté-Boudreau is Professor at Collège de Maisonneuve in Montréal, Canada, and a member of the Animals in Philosophy, Politics, Law, and Ethics (APPLE) research group.

Nicolas Delon is Associate Professor of Philosophy and Environmental Studies at New College of Florida, Sarasota.

Sue Donaldson is Research Associate in the Department of Philosophy, Queen's University (Kingston), and co-convenor of the Animals in Philosophy, Politics, Law, and Ethics (APPLE) research group.

Valéry Giroux is Associate Director of the Centre for Research in Ethics (CRÉ). She is also an adjunct professor at the Law Faculty, at Université de Montréal.

François Jaquet is Lecturer in Ethics at the Université de Strasbourg, France.

Will Kymlicka is Canada Research Chair in the Department of Philosophy, Queen's University (Kingston).

Angela Martin is Assistant Professor of Philosophy at the University of Basel, Switzerland.

Angie Pepper is Lecturer in Philosophy at the University of Roehampton, London.

Agnes Tam is Assistant Professor at the University of Alberta, Calgary.

Kristin Voigt is Associate Professor at McGill University, jointly appointed in the Institute for Health and Social Policy and the Department of Philosophy. She is also Co-Director of the Centre for Research in Ethics (CRÉ).

Introduction

Exploring the Ethics of Animal Shelters

Valéry Giroux, Angie Pepper, and Kristin Voigt

I.1 Background

A vast number of companion animals live in shelters. Precise numbers are hard to come by, but the fragments of information we have suggest that globally the figure is in the millions. Mars Petcare has devised a State of Pet Homelessness Index which estimates that, across the United States, United Kingdom, India, Mexico, Germany, Russia, South Africa, China, and Greece, there are 224 million homeless dogs and cats, with 20 million of those animals currently being housed in shelters (Mars Petcare 2021). In the United States alone it is estimated that about 5.4 million animals enter shelters each year (Mars Petcare 2021); the American Society for the Prevention of Cruelty to Animals puts this number at 6.5 million (ASPCA 2022). And Humane Canada reports that, in 2019, Canadian SPCAs and humane societies took in about 78,000 cats and 28,000 dogs as well as 11,000 animals of other species (Humane Canada 2020).

As these numbers suggest, cats and dogs represent a large proportion of the shelter population but many shelters also house less common companion animals such as rabbits, as well as exotic animals such as turtles and parrots. Some shelters also take in animals saved from farms or research laboratories, and some also care for orphaned, injured, and sick wild animals. Many shelters are part of larger animal protection organizations that seek to contribute to

Valéry Giroux, Angie Pepper, and Kristin Voigt, *Introduction* In: *The Ethics of Animal Shelters*. Edited by: Valéry Giroux, Angie Pepper, and Kristin Voigt, Oxford University Press. © Oxford University Press 2023.
DOI: 10.1093/oso/9780197678633.003.0001

broader social change for animals, for example by seeking changes in legislation governing the "use" of animals. In some contexts, such as several Canadian provinces, animal protection organizations not only run shelter and advocacy programs but also monitor individuals' and corporations' compliance with animal welfare legislation.

The everyday operations of animal shelters and animal protection organizations involve a large number of ethical decisions, arising at different levels of the organization. The most challenging ethical decisions involve the treatment of animals in need of rescue and animals who reside within the shelter. For example, given the resource and space constraints that shelters struggle with, a recurring ethical question is whether specific animals should be killed.[1] Particularly difficult cases involve individuals who have medical conditions that can be treated but only at significant cost to the shelter and individuals who are healthy but unlikely to be adopted because they are unpopular or because they have complex needs that are more difficult for potential adopters to meet. Similarly, difficult decisions must be made about shelter adoption policy, quality-of-life assessments, palliative care provision, shelter animal diets, and the termination of pregnancies, among many others.

In addition to making decisions about shelter animals, animal protection organizations must also determine how to interact within and toward the wider social and institutional environment in which nonhuman animals are routinely exploited. For example, most, if not all, shelters operate in social and legal contexts that typically regard animals as property and not persons. In such contexts, large-scale factory farming is widely accepted and continues to expand, as does the use of animals in biomedical research, and animals are frequently kept captive and used for human entertainment and labor purposes. How explicit a stance should such organizations take against such practices? On the one hand, an organization concerned with protecting the welfare of nonhuman animals should arguably address the welfare of *all* animals, not just companion animals. On the other hand, if shelters express strong public opposition to such practices, that could alienate donors who are primarily concerned with companion animals—not, for example, farmed animals, laboratory animals, zoo animals, or law enforcement animals—and thereby reduce the resources available to the organization.

This last point is important. Most animal protection organizations are charities and therefore rely heavily on successful fundraising and the goodwill of donors. This means that the public image of such organizations is crucial to their capability, success, and longevity. This adds a further layer of complexity to decision-making in animal shelters. Since decisions made by animal protection organizations can be subject to public scrutiny, how such decisions will be received by the public must also be considered. If members of the public perceive shelter decisions as problematic, this can lead to public criticism, reduced public trust, and decreases in donations. A prominent example of this occurred when animal rights advocacy group People for the Ethical Treatment of Animals (PETA) was found to kill large numbers of animals in its shelter. This was met with severe criticism from both the public and other animal protection organizations. PETA defended its approach, arguing that many animals arrive at the shelter in such poor condition that ending their suffering is the only thing that can be done for them and that while "no-kill" policies might be feasible in shelters that can simply turn down animals when they are at capacity, they are not appropriate for open-admission shelters such as the one operated by PETA.[2] Controversies such as this can do significant damage to the reputation of animal protection organizations.

The ethical dimension of the decisions that must be taken in shelters and the complexity of the ethical questions at hand are, of course, not lost on these organizations. The UK's Royal Society for the Prevention of Cruelty to Animals (RSPCA), for example, recently outlined some of the ethical challenges it faces in an article, "Difficult Decisions," noting that "the RSPCA has to grapple with a number of ethical dilemmas on a daily basis" (RSPCA 2010). Despite the prominence of ethical questions in the operation of animal shelters, there is very little philosophical work that investigates these questions. While there is some work on veterinary ethics (e.g., Rollins 2006; Wathes et al. 2011; Linzey and Linzey 2017) and the ethical guidelines published by veterinary organizations, such as the American Veterinary Medical Association (AVMA 2019) and the Canadian Veterinary Medical Association (CVMA 2004), this work typically does not speak to the very distinct situation of animal shelters, which face a very different set of circumstances than, say, veterinarians in private surgeries. Work on shelters (e.g., Miller and Zawistowski 2013; Weiss et al. 2015) addresses various aspects of shelter management but for the most part does not address the ethical questions that are important to this work. Finally, to the extent that ethical questions are identified and discussed in these literatures, they typically fail to challenge problematic ideas about the status of nonhuman animals. For example, Rollins (2006) does not explicitly oppose the use of animals for food, nor does he challenge the idea that companion animals have "owners." Our goal in this volume is to speak to the ethical challenges faced by animal shelters, many of which are created or complicated by the particularities of the shelter environment, and to do so in a way that is consistent with nonhuman animals' moral status.

This volume is the outcome of a collaboration between a team of animal ethicists and representatives and employees of an animal shelter, the Montreal Society for the Prevention of Cruelty to Animals (Montreal SPCA). Our objective was to identify the most pressing questions that animal shelters face and to offer recommendations on how to respond to these questions, taking into account the many constraints that shelters must operate under. Importantly, these recommendations were to be informed by and consistent with a commitment to taking seriously the moral status of nonhuman animals. The recommendations developed as part of this project are reproduced in Part I of this collection. Part II brings together a set of chapters that explore in more detail some of the ethical questions involved in everyday animal shelter operations.

While our primary audience for this volume is shelter employees, we also hope that it can create and contribute to debates among philosophers and animal ethicists. Philosophers' work, even in the field of "applied philosophy," is all too often far removed from the messy complexity of the real world, focusing instead on highly abstract questions on the basis of a range of idealizing assumptions.

Working with people who must navigate ethical questions in the real world gives us a better appreciation of the many factors and considerations that fall out of the picture when we engage in the kind of abstraction philosophers are used to and of how we might make philosophical work useful for practical contexts.

With this introduction, we hope to provide some more information about this project. We begin by offering some details about the Montreal SPCA so that readers can get a sense of its mission, structure, and range of responsibilities (Section I.2). We then describe some of the practical steps we took in developing this project (Section I.3). This is important for understanding the context of our practical recommendations and the particularities of the Montreal SPCA, which will help readers who work in shelters get a sense of where their own organizations differ in ways that require adaptation of the recommendations offered here. Section I.4 describes the "practitioner-driven" methodology that informed the project. This methodology was central to the project, and we hope that it can be helpful for philosophers who are also planning or considering collaborations with practitioners. Section I.5 discusses our hope that the guidelines can be useful for animal shelter staff, including staff at shelters whose work differs substantially from that of the Montreal SPCA. We offer some thoughts on which aspects of our recommendations can easily be extended to other shelters and some suggestions on those that may need to be adapted if they are to be suitable for different shelter environments. In Section I.6, we identify and discuss some of the themes that will come up, implicitly or explicitly, in the chapters included in Part II. The final section briefly summarizes the practical guidelines included in Part I and the individual chapters that constitute Part II of this collection.

I.2 About the Montreal SPCA

Founded in 1869, the Society for the Prevention of Cruelty to Animals (SPCA) was the first animal welfare organization in Canada. Now known as the Montreal SPCA, it is still one of Canada's most prominent animal rescue organizations and carries out a wide range of activities, such as sheltering abandoned animals and arranging adoptions, providing veterinary care for companion animals and urban wildlife, investigating and enforcing violations of animal welfare legislation, and undertaking advocacy work. The official mission of the Montreal SPCA is to protect animals from neglect, abuse, and exploitation; represent their interests and ensure their welfare; promote public awareness; and help foster compassion for all sentient beings.

A detailed account of the history of the Montreal SPCA was published in 2019, the organization's 150th anniversary (Simoneau-Gilbert 2019). This book recounts the transformations undergone by the organization from its creation to the present day as the sociocultural, technological and economic realities of the city of Montreal have shaped the presence and use of animals on its territory.

Simoneau-Gilbert explains that the Montreal SPCA has not always defended the rights of all animals: it began by focusing primarily on the neglect and abuse of horses and then came to focus almost exclusively on companion animals. In addition, while the welfare of companion animals was at the heart of its mission, it is only recently, through the leadership of Alanna Devine, who acted as the organization's interim executive director between 2008 and 2011, that significant efforts were made to reduce the number of cats and dogs brought to the shelter to be killed by encouraging the adoption and spaying/neutering of these animals. Along with this, there has been significant lobbying to strengthen animal protection laws and extend their application to laboratory animals, animals raised for their fur, and farmed animals. Increasingly concerned about the fate of farmed animals, the Society also decided in 2012 to adopt a policy requiring that food served at its events be plant-based. Other measures aimed at discouraging the consumption of food from animals raised in factory farms and improving the fate of farmed animals have been put forward. Among those was the "Truth in Labelling" campaign designed to convince the Canadian Food Inspection Agency (CFIA) to regulate the use of animal welfare labels, which are too often misused. There was also the investigation led by the

Montreal SPCA after the broadcasting of images illegally filmed in a Quebec milk-fed calf farm, which led to the conviction of an employee and the "Transport Reform" campaign aimed at improving Canadian legislation concerning the transportation of farmed animals from the farm to the slaughterhouse.

While the Society has historically been relatively conservative, the examples given above show that the past few decades have seen it take on more ambitious goals. Shortly after Élise Desaulniers—a leading figure for veganism in Quebec who has published several books on the subject (Desaulniers 2011, 2013, 2016) and frequently speaks about it in the media—took over the direction of the Montreal SPCA in 2017, the "AniMAL" campaign was launched to raise awareness of the plight of farmed animals and to obtain better protection for their well-being. If the Society's positions are still essentially welfarist, in the sense that it is first and foremost the way in which animals are treated that is its main focus, one can feel an abolitionist and anti-speciesist trend emerging: its positions in favor of the abolition of certain practices, such as carriage rides or fur farming, as well as its promotion of veganism through the publication of a book of entirely plant-based recipes, clearly show this. Indeed, this latest phase of the Montreal SPCA's evolution now means that it is widely considered to be more progressive and ambitious than most other humane societies in Canada.

I.3 The Stages of the Project

This project began in 2017, with an informal conversation between Élise Desaulniers, who had just been appointed Executive Director of the Montreal SPCA, and two of the co-editors of this volume, Valéry Giroux and Kristin Voigt. Desaulniers described the many ethical challenges the organization faces and noted that the Montreal SPCA's existing policies provided little or no guidance on responding to these challenges. These conversations helped us see the important role that philosophers—especially animal ethicists—could play in filling the gap in the Montreal SPCA's policies and guidelines. We began to develop a plan for what a collaboration between philosophers and shelter staff might look like and what it might achieve. We then assembled a team of philosophers who we knew would be interested in being involved in a project with such a practical focus and organized our first team meeting in October 2018. The meeting was held on the premises of the Montreal SPCA, not only to make it easy for staff to join us for (parts of) the meeting but also to allow the researchers to gain an understanding of the physical space of the organization and its various departments. The sounds of the shelter provided a powerful backdrop for our conversations.

The aim of this meeting was to identify the major normative issues and questions that arise in the SPCA's day-to-day work, which of these are considered most urgent or pressing by staff, how these challenges are experienced by staff, how SPCA employees currently respond to them, and which constraints—resources, time, etc.—affect their work. We also wanted to get a sense of how precisely philosophers could make a helpful and meaningful contribution to this work. Based on the conversations at this meeting, we wrote a discussion paper that summarized the questions identified as well as the Montreal SPCA staff members' accounts of the constraints they face in dealing with them.

Over the next few months, we began drafting both the Guidelines as well as a number of papers that would allow the ethicists to engage in more detail with specific questions arising in the shelter context. We met again at the Montreal SPCA in March 2019, to present the Guidelines with the staff, get feedback on our proposals, and allow for discussions among the entire team—practitioners as well as philosophers. On the basis of this feedback, several rounds of further revisions were made to arrive at the final version.

I.4 Methodology

While philosophers are increasingly trying to apply their expertise to real-world problems, even "applied" or "real-world" philosophy often proceeds from various idealizing assumptions. This approach, however, often makes the conclusions philosophers draw less useful for practical purposes than they might be if they tackled the "messiness" of the real-life situations head-on. We hope that our project can provide one example of how to engage directly with practitioners facing difficult ethical challenges to make philosophical work more relevant for the real world.

In this project, we started from the assumption that philosophers can contribute meaningfully to real-world questions such as those arising in animal shelters only if they engage in dialogue with practitioners in the field. For this reason, we relied on what we called a "practitioner-driven" methodology. There were a number of components to this approach. First, rather than having the ethicists identify the ethical questions that they wanted to investigate, we wanted to hear from practitioners which questions or problems *they* thought were most pressing or difficult in their work. The questions to be addressed in this project were driven by practitioners' understanding of the ethical challenges they face and their assessment of which of these are the most urgent and/or most timely to address. This method allowed our team of researchers to look at issues that they would never have identified were it not for interviews with Montreal SPCA employees. For example, our team members were surprised to learn that the staff working in the shelter division were concerned about the amount of resources the enforcement team would spend on individual animals rescued from situations of criminal neglect or serious abuse. One of the recommendations we made in response to this problem was to separate the budget among different units so that different divisions of the organization could make their own decisions about how to allocate their resources without this reducing the amount available for other activities. This particular suggestion has been the subject of deeper reflection, the results of which are presented in detail by Sue Donaldson and Will Kymlicka (Chapter 7, this volume). Another of our recommendations that addresses this concern is the creation of an Ethics Board, which the Montreal SPCA can ask to investigate specific questions and offer advice on particularly challenging cases or issues. This suggestion is explored in more detail in Angela Martin's chapter (Chapter 3, this volume).

Second, we understood that for our proposals to be a valuable tool for staff, they must be consistent with the constraints that shape what shelters can and cannot do. We used our conversations with the Montreal SPCA staff to get as much insight as possible on the limitations and considerations that shape how they can respond to the problems they are facing. Knowing which solutions would fail immediately because they relied on resources that the shelter did not have was crucial to the project. While, of course, financial and space constraints loom large for the Montreal SPCA, as they do for many animal shelters, it was important to learn about other, less obvious considerations as well. For example, the fact that the shelter relies on donations from pet food companies might restrict what changes can be made with respect to the food fed to shelter residents. Another example of such constraints arose in considering whether the Montreal SPCA should aim to retain its powers to investigate complaints of animal cruelty or neglect: while there are good reasons for these powers to be exercised by the police, police officers will—at least in the short term—lack the competencies, means, and motivation that Montreal SPCA employees currently bring to this task. Or consider the question of who should create decision trees that would aid staff in making particularly challenging ethical choices: if these are left to employees to design, hierarchies within the organization could allow those with more authority to have disproportionate influence on the outcome, at the expense of other perspectives that must also be considered. While such practical considerations and constraints are typically not considered by philosophers, it is clear that they must inform what practitioners should do, all things considered, so it was crucial that they inform our analyses.

Third, while it was important for the success of the project that we had as much input as possible from the Montreal SPCA, it was also important to recognize that shelter staff are already overburdened and overworked. This means that we had to find a balance between, on the one hand, getting staff input wherever possible and, on the other, not creating unnecessary work for the employees. In addition to the open discussions we had with staff from different departments, we also followed up with individual staff members when we had specific questions. At the same time, however, we also made sure that we had done our "homework" before contacting the staff, for example, by locating relevant research ourselves or going over documents available on the organization's website.

Perhaps the most important consideration to keep in mind is that, while philosophers typically remain emotionally detached from the questions they're engaging with, staff and practitioners on the ground do not have the luxury of detachment: they are in a situation where they have to make decisions and see the results of those decisions, good and bad, up close. In a context where resources are often so scarce that many animals simply cannot be given all the care one would like to provide for them, even the "right" choice can involve significant suffering and, often, death. The knowledge that one is making the "right" decision given the (terrible) circumstances often does little to attenuate the sense that one is deeply implicated, perhaps even complicit, in harming the very beings one is seeking to protect. In our conversations, staff were often in tears as they told us about animals they had not been able to help or situations that continued to haunt them. The emotional burden that the staff face became an explicit consideration as we developed our proposals and recommendations (see especially Chapter 2, this volume). For example, the fact that staff often become attached to specific animals under their care is something that must be taken into account in shelters' decision-making processes, rather than dismissed (see section 8 of the Guidelines).

While we believe that this kind of practitioner-driven approach offers many advantages, it is also important to acknowledge its shortcomings. By having staff guide us to the research questions, other, equally important issues were undoubtedly overlooked. Some questions may not have been raised by staff because they were uncomfortable discussing them with outsiders or because they didn't want to create conflict within the organization or between specific colleagues. Other questions may not have emerged in our discussions with staff at the Montreal SPCA simply because they were not ethical issues that they experienced. Not all animal shelters are the same, and the unique context of each shelter will make a difference to the kinds of challenges that they face. Think, for instance, of the sexism and racism that can characterize employee relations or emanate from the policies adopted by an organization's management. This type of issue, which is as serious as it is widespread, did not come up in interviews with Montreal SPCA employees.

It should also be noted that our researchers did not entirely limit themselves to addressing the issues raised by the Montreal SPCA employees. Some ethical issues that were not recognized as such by the interviewed employees seemed sufficiently pressing within the organization that our team nevertheless chose to address them. For example, we thought it morally important to bring some clarity and precision to the use of the term "euthanasia" and make a clear distinction between animals killed because they have a serious, terminal illness and/or are enduring unbearable suffering with little prospect of alleviation or recovery and those who are killed for other reasons, such as a lack of resources.

I.5 The Guidelines and Recommendations: Hopes and Limits

The first part of this volume sets out the guidelines and recommendations that the authors developed in response to our conversations with staff of the Montreal SPCA. This document does several key things. First, it identifies, explains, and clarifies the ethical challenges that shelter staff face. Second, it makes recommendations for how staff should respond to those challenges. Third, it provides a reasoned defense of those recommendations.

The reasoning given for each recommendation is rooted in the ethical framework laid out at the beginning of the document. What makes this document distinctive in the arena of animal shelter policy is that the progressive framework endorsed promotes the protection of a wide range of interests for *all* sentient animals.

The framework makes it clear that all sentient animals matter for their own sakes and that they have morally significant interests in not suffering, continued life, positive experiences, having control over the shape of their lives, and, where they so desire, caring and respectful relationships with humans. Recognizing that animals have a broad range of interests raises the stakes in terms of what ethical animal protection looks like. For instance, acknowledging that animals have significant interests in continued life makes killing healthy animals morally problematic. Similarly, recognizing the importance of animals' agency interests cautions against overly paternalistic policies that deny animals the freedom to shape their own lives. And recognizing that *all* animals have these interests raises challenges for how to feed shelter animals: it is inconsistent to think that shelter animals have an interest in continued life that ought to be protected while at the same time feeding them the bodies of other sentient animals who also had that interest.

It is important to stress that the ethical framework set out in the Guidelines reflects the Montreal SPCA's own commitments (and, we believe, the commitments of many animal protection organizations). It was crucial for the success of the project that we did not impose values and commitments on the SPCA that they did not already endorse. So, while we have teased out and laid bare implicit assumptions and developed the commitments into a philosophically defensible and internally consistent framework, we have also worked to make sure that the framework is not at odds with the Montreal SPCA's expressed commitments. The end result is a framework that is progressive in many respects but that nonetheless rests on quite minimalist assumptions that we hope will resonate with the sheltering community.

Given the genesis of this project, the recommendations and guidelines developed are specifically tailored for the Montreal SPCA. This means that not all of our recommendations will be relevant for all shelters, and, therefore, the document does not necessarily translate neatly on to the practices of other sheltering organizations. For example, not all shelters are involved in inspections work, which means that certain sections of the guidelines will not apply to them. Similarly, we developed a range of recommendations in response to the possibility that the Montreal SPCA might be able to open a second site outside of Montreal; this is an opportunity that is unlikely to be open to many shelters.

Despite our focus on the Montreal SPCA, we are confident that many of our general recommendations address issues that arise in animal shelters of different kinds. For example, ethical questions around ending animal lives, shelter animals' diets, resource allocation, and disagreement among shelter staff are a mainstay of everyday shelter operations. Other recommendations, even if they do not apply in the exact same way to other shelters, may be adaptable to different circumstances. For example, the adoption criteria we recommend (Section 6.C) take into account the fact that the space and resources available at the Montreal SPCA are insufficient to meet the needs of all the animals that end up in the shelter. An organization that does not have the mission to take in all animals in need may be able to offer its residents better living conditions and could therefore apply more restrictive criteria for selecting adoptive families. In such a context, animals may not be as significantly harmed or disadvantaged by a longer stay in the shelter, so there may be less reason to forego a more demanding selection.

However, it's important to urge caution. In some cases, the exact circumstances of an individual shelter may be so different that we would not make the same recommendation. For instance, whereas the Montreal SPCA can provide a home for some exotic animals that require special provisions, a shelter with significantly more constrained resources may not be able to provide homes for exotic animals, and our recommendations would have to change to reflect that. In light of this, we strongly recommend that shelters reading these guidelines adopt the policy set out in Section 3.B of creating an Ethics Board comprised of shelter staff, ethicists, lawyers, and other relevant experts. This Board will be available to offer advice in relation to complex ethical decisions that must be made by the organization, including decisions about policy and more time-sensitive matters regarding individual cases.

We should also keep in mind that not all of the recommendations are things to implement right away. A recurring theme throughout this project was the conflict between, on the one hand, a desire, shared by the shelter workers and the philosophers, to adopt a more ambitious, anti-speciesist stance and, on the other hand, a recognition that adopting too radical an animal rights agenda could alienate actors on whom the organization depends (in particular donors but also government and industry actors), which in turn would undermine the organization's capacity to act. Our recommendations respond to this tension by identifying, where appropriate, the "short-term" goal that we think the Montreal SPCA should pursue as well as the more ambitious stance that we think the organization should ultimately adopt. These more "aspirational" goals may not be things that can be achieved in the near future, but they are nonetheless objectives that we believe that the Montreal SPCA and similarly situated shelters should work toward.

One final note on the Guidelines is that this work should not be regarded as the final say on these matters. Rather, while we hope that the current document offers practical advice for the here and now, it is open to revision and amendment. This means that if circumstances change, new empirical evidence comes to light, or overlooked questions are raised, then the existing Guidelines can be revised to accommodate these developments. The incompleteness of the Guidelines is also noted by Élise Desaulniers in the afterword to this volume, where she suggests that shelters need guidance in addressing the ethical dimensions of their community work, including shelters' role in helping impoverished, politically marginalized, and victimized humans care for their animal companions. Addressing this gap will involve thinking about the relationship and interconnections between the social injustice manifest in systems of race, class, and gender and the injustice done to nonhuman animals. This is important work that must be firmly integrated into the future research agenda in animal ethics and underscores the need for further work in this area.

I.6 The Philosophical Chapters: Aims and Themes

The second part of the volume is composed of seven philosophical chapters that unpack some of the arguments presented in the Guidelines. Each of the chapters tackles one of the key ethical challenges facing shelter workers and shows how philosophy can help us to navigate these difficult circumstances.

There are several recurrent themes addressed by the philosophical chapters.

I.6.1 Operating in Non-Ideal Conditions

It was evident from talking with shelter staff at the Montreal SPCA that the source of many of their problems is that they must operate within *non-ideal conditions*. What we mean by this is that many features of the context in which they operate make it difficult for them to fully realize the moral commitments outlined in their mission statement and the ethical framework which guides their decision-making. If the shelter were operating in *ideal* conditions, then many of the moral problems that they face would not arise.

To see more clearly how non-ideal conditions can impact a shelter's ability to fulfill its mission and moral commitments, consider the following factors. First, the shelter frequently finds itself underresourced and understaffed. This makes it difficult for shelter staff to rescue and provide adequate care to all animals in need. Second, the shelter must operate in a context in which animals are regularly abandoned, mistreated, and abused. This means that there is more demand for shelter services than they can cope with. Third, the shelter must operate in a context where animals are widely regarded as property and where speciesist assumptions are deeply entrenched. This regrettable social fact poses numerous challenges. It makes the pursuit of a fully just agenda unfeasible because such an agenda is at odds with public opinion and the views of other actors with whom the SPCA must interact. It also creates a tension in the

Montreal SPCA's own commitments: on the one hand, the SPCA is committed to protecting and rescuing all animals in need, and, on the other hand, they must engage with animal farmers who raise animals to be killed. Additionally, shelter staff are not themselves immune to speciesist assumptions, which makes consensus difficult to achieve and disagreement a persistent feature of workplace relations. Fourth, since shelters are chronically underfunded and understaffed, shelter staff are typically stressed and there are high levels of burnout within the profession.

Many of the philosophical contributions to this volume make use of a common distinction in philosophy between *ideal* and *non-ideal theory*. In short, ideal theory offers a view of what an ideally just society looks like and thereby gives us something to aim toward. Non-ideal theory, on the other hand, specifies what justice requires in the actual circumstances in which we find ourselves.

Since we want our recommendations to be action-guiding, many of the philosophical contributions in this volume are works in non-ideal theory (see especially Chapters 2, 3, and 4). They take seriously the very non-ideal conditions that shelters like the Montreal SPCA must work in and offer an account of what shelter workers are morally required to do in the here and now. What this means in practice is that the recommendations are not always perfectly just and they would have no place in a perfectly just interspecies society.

I.6.2 Hope and Possibility

Though many of the contributions focus on the everyday reality that shelter workers must negotiate, others take a more positive stance by thinking about how shelters might play an important role in bringing us closer to the ideal interspecies society (see Chapter 7). These works take the ideal society as their starting point and suggest ways that shelters might play a role in getting us there.

The importance of ideal theory should not be overlooked. Without hope of a better future and something to strive for, it is very easy to become disillusioned, depressed, and ground down by what seems like relentless failure, grief, and disappointment. Indeed, many of the shelter staff expressed frustration at not being able to do more good by tackling the broader structural and systemic issues that cause so many animals to be in need of rescue and protection.

The need for hope and possibility is accommodated in the Guidelines and some of the philosophical chapters by discussion of more aspirational goals. These are things that cannot (because of non-ideal conditions) be implemented now but that specify what an ideally just interspecies society would require and thus give shelters clear long-term objectives. For example, we suggest that the Montreal SPCA should be committed to the long-term goal of eliminating animal agriculture (section 2.B), changing animals' legal status as property (section 2.C), and having two physical locations in order to more effectively serve the widely divergent dimensions of its mandate. None of those goals will be achieved any time soon, and many of them will require coordinated efforts beyond the animal shelter community. However, these long-term goals are crucial to making shelter work more hopeful and for showing how shelter staff have an important role to play in the realization of a just interspecies society.

I.6.3 Disagreement, Negotiation, and Compromise

Many of the philosophical contributions in some way address the challenges of disagreement in the context of shelter work. Disagreement occurs at multiple levels and between multiple stakeholders and adds additional stress to already overburdened shelter staff. For example, shelter staff may disagree with one another on a range of issues from what to do with an individual animal to issues of general policy, such as how the SPCA should interact with the animal agriculture industry. Additionally, there are deep disagreements within the wider shelter community about which policies to pursue, and shelters frequently criticize others with different policies. We have seen this most keenly in regard to no-kill policies, open adoption policies, and return-to-field policies.

One of the key challenges is to determine when shelters should compromise on their core ethical commitments in order to bring about the most good or most effectively satisfy their mission objectives. Shelters have to think carefully about what policies to pursue not just in terms of how those policies will affect the animals, but also in terms of how those policies will be received by the media, public, and, most importantly, their donors. Shelter organizations occupy a unique position in animal advocacy and have the potential to play a crucial role in realizing justice for animals, but it is difficult for them to play that role if they always bend to public opinion (see Chapter 7). Moreover, bending to public opinion will often force shelters to compromise on their core commitments and lead to internally inconsistent policies that further perpetuate injustice for animals. Thus, one of the key overarching issues for animal shelters in operation today is how to remain true to their commitments and fulfill their role as advocates of justice for animals while at the same time not alienating or angering those upon whom they depend for support.

The philosophical contributions address disagreement in two important ways. First, some try to facilitate the resolution of disagreement by carefully showing how some options are morally inadequate (see, for example, Chapters 1, 2, 4, and 6). Careful consideration of policies around killing, plant-based diets, and adoption, for example, show that even in non-ideal conditions some options are morally prohibited and some options are preferable to others. Second, some of the contributions make practical suggestions for how disagreement might be undercut and managed in the future. For instance, implementation of an Ethics Board, similar to those currently employed in human hospitals, is recommended by Angela Martin, and Agnes Tam and Will Kymlicka defend a new form of advocacy that will help to undercut speciesist group norms and enable shelters to pursue more progressive agendas.

I.7 Chapter Summaries

Part I contains the main outcome of this project: a practical policy document that sets out the recommendations we developed in response to the ethical challenges faced by the Montreal SPCA. Based on an ethical framework detailed in the document, these recommendations respond to ethical challenges arising across the organization's activities, including its internal structure; shelter operations; dealing with the public, animal industry, and governmental agencies; and work that focuses on feral animals.

Part II contains a set of chapters that engage, in more detail than was possible or desirable in the context of the practical recommendations, various aspects of the organization's work that raise ethical challenges. These chapters offer philosophical analyses of the ethical challenges that animal shelters face in their day-to-day operations, including issues such as how shelters should decide whether or not to kill specific animals; how to approach decision-making procedures in the organization; which conditions to apply when it comes to adoption of shelter animals; and how shelters can contribute to a larger, transformative practice. These chapters are informed by close collaboration with SPCA staff and are sensitive to the difficulties and constraints that shape the work of animal protection organizations; at the same time, the chapters also provide more detailed discussion of the ethical questions that we addressed in our recommendations.

Perhaps one of the most difficult and pressing issues that shelters have to deal with is the question of when individual animals should be killed. This complex matter is addressed from different angles by several contributions in this volume. Nicolas Delon, in Chapter 1, addresses the philosophical questions around the *value* and *harm* of animal death. In order for us to think about when killing might be morally wrong, morally permissible, or morally required, we need to know whether and why death is bad for animals and whether and why death might sometimes be valuable for animals. Delon defends a deprivation account of the badness of death for animals: death is bad for them because it deprives them of valuable future life. The flipside of this view is that death can sometimes be good for animals if it prevents a future life of suffering and misery. Delon argues that deprivationism implies that euthanasia is either forbidden (because the individual's life still has value for them) or obligatory (because, on balance, the individual's life is not one worth living), and he makes some suggestions as to how shelter workers might determine an individual animal's *optimum life span* so that death is neither induced too early or too late.

While shelter workers should only kill animals when life no longer has value for those animals, one of the challenges facing open-admission shelters is that they frequently find themselves in situations where they have more animals than they can provide adequate care for. In light of the challenges facing many open-admission shelters, Angie Pepper, in Chapter 2, brings philosophical theory on the ethics of killing to bear on the practice of ending lives in animal shelters. Pepper distinguishes between three types of killing that may occur in animal shelters: genuine euthanasia, injustice-dependent justified killing, and absolutely unjustified killing. The central aim of her chapter is to show how under the very non-ideal circumstances that many open-admission shelters are forced to operate, shelter workers may sometimes be permitted to kill healthy or potentially adoptable animals. Though the shelter workers may have justification for killing animals who have a right not to be killed, Pepper argues that this kind of killing nonetheless wrongs the animals in question. Moreover, she suggests that the wrong is not perpetrated by the shelter workers—who do the morally best thing in tragically non-ideal conditions—but rather it is the state and the political community more generally who are responsible for the distributive injustice that creates the moral tragedy.

In an ideally just world, the rights and moral status of all sentient animals would be acknowledged and upheld. While the first few chapters focus on the financial and institutional barriers to achieving justice for shelter animals, the injustice of non-ideal circumstances goes far beyond matters of resource distribution. Sadly, we live in a time where many animals are legally and socially regarded as property, where animals are afforded different moral status depending on what humans use them for, and where farmed animals are typically regarded as mere food as opposed to thinking, feeling creatures.

Angela Martin starts Chapter 3 by acknowledging the highly nonideal circumstances that shelters currently operate in. For Martin, many animal shelters fulfill the conditions that make triage protocols necessary: they operate with a limited financial budget, limited space, limited medical resources, limited time, and limited staff. Martin argues that the guiding principles that have shaped human healthcare triage protocols can be fruitfully extended and applied to the context of animal shelters. Martin maintains that the establishment of triage protocols for shelters will make the decision-making process less arbitrary, fairer, and more transparent. One important benefit of this approach is that it will help to reduce and manage disagreement among shelter staff and alleviate some of the emotional and practical costs of deep conflict. To this end, Martin further defends the creation of an external Ethics Board that can help analyze and potentially resolve some of the ethical issues that shelter staff are uncertain about or unable to settle by themselves.

François Jaquet's contribution to this volume (Chapter 4) looks at the impact of entrenched speciesism on shelter practices and considers what shelter workers can reasonably be expected to do in non-ideal conditions. Jaquet examines three especially ethically challenging dimensions of shelter operations: killing healthy shelter animals for lack of resources, building partnerships with animal agriculture, and feeding meat to shelter animals. He argues that, in ideal conditions, none of these practices would be permissible. Yet since shelters must operate in non-ideal circumstances, we need to assess shelter practices according to different standards, standards specially designed for non-ideal conditions. Specifically, Jaquet argues that current shelter policies must meet three desiderata of non-ideal theory: they must be feasible, permissible, and effective. With this framework in place, Jaquet argues that killing healthy shelter animals because of a lack of resources and cooperating with animal agriculture are both morally acceptable practices in non-ideal conditions. However, Jaquet finds that feeding meat to shelter animals is unacceptable even in non-ideal conditions because, although feasible, it is neither morally permissible nor does it effectively help us to transition toward a more just world.

We know that progressive animal shelters frequently find themselves at odds with widely held public views that deny moral status to all sentient nonhuman animals. This can make it difficult for shelters to pursue more progressive agendas—which would better approximate what justice requires—without alienating those private donors who provide shelters with their main source of income. This raises the question of how shelters should negotiate the challenge of doing what's right without being the victims of a costly public backlash. In Chapter 5, Agnes Tam and Will Kymlicka examine this tension by considering the question of feeding plant-based food to shelter residents. A Los Angeles shelter that sought to make this move was met with a big backslash from the local community. Tam and Kymlicka draw on evidence and arguments from a range of fields—psychology, sociology, philosophy—to diagnose the problem facing animal protection organizations looking to pursue progressive agendas. Their main finding is that public resistance to progressive agendas stems from human beings' strong orientation toward group norms or what they call "we-reasons." The central upshot of their view is that shelters will be unlikely to secure and mobilize support for progressive agendas that are backed by clear and compelling arguments and scientific evidence. The reason for this is that progressive agendas tend to conflict with "we-reasons," and these norms are a powerful dimension of social life, indeed, they make group life possible. Consequently, Tam and Kymlicka argue that animal protection organizations must try to wield the power of "we-reasoning" to mobilize public support for their progressive agendas, and they show how the Los Angeles Animal Services might have achieved a different result for the vegan shelter campaign if they had followed the logic of "we-reasoning."

One of the ways in which animal shelters interact with the general public is through the adoption process: local residents frequently visit shelters with the intention of adopting an animal. How precisely should the adoption process be designed? Chapter 6, by Valéry Giroux and Kristin Voigt, takes on this question. A number of high-profile animal protection organizations have recently advocated for an "open adoption" policy, which focuses on engaging would-be adopters in a conversation with the aim of finding them a "match" among adoptable animals. Central to the open adoption approach is that criteria that, on earlier adoption policies, might have led to adoption applications being denied (e.g., absence of a fenced yard) are no longer exclusion criteria. The open adoption approach emphasizes that would-be adopters should be trusted rather than approached with suspicion. Giroux and Voigt agree that the traditional approach has significant flaws but also raise concerns about the open adoption approach. This approach rests on shakier empirical grounds than advocates suggest and, importantly, may undermine the long-term goal of signaling to would-be adopters—and the general public more broadly—that animals matter for their own sakes. Giroux and Voigt offer some practical suggestions on how shelters can design the adoption process in a way that takes into account the goal of finding good and suitable homes for their residents while also challenging problematic social norms about animals' moral status.

Many of our contributors have focused primarily on what animal protection organizations should do in the here and now given the incredibly challenging conditions they must negotiate. In contrast, in Chapter 7, Sue Donaldson and Will Kymlicka approach the project from a different angle by first considering what animal protection organizations would look like in a just interspecies society. This project eschews the limitations of pessimism and offers a much more hopeful vision of the future, which is a much needed tonic for those who work on the front line of animal protection. For Donaldson and Kymlicka, there will be a place for animal protection organizations in a just interspecies society, and they can be part of the transformative movement that is seeking to change the ways that human–animal relations are defined and instantiated. By imagining what animal protection organizations would look like and how they might operate in a better world, Donaldson and Kymlicka show us how such organizations might pursue a prefigurative political agenda that recognizes animals as embodied agents who are full members of a shared society with humans. By imagining what animal protection organizations could look like, Donaldson and Kymlicka invite us to think not just about what we do now, but about where we want to go.

Notes

1. While this type of killing would normally be called "euthanasia," we reserve that term for cases where it is in the animal's best interest to be killed; see Chapter 2 for a more detailed discussion.
2. See, for example, Winerip (2013). PETA has responded to this issue (e.g., PETA, "Why We Euthanize" and "Animal Rights Uncompromised: 'No-Kill' Shelters").

References

American Veterinary Medical Association (AVMA) (2019) "Principles of veterinary medical ethics of the AVMA." https://www.avma.org/resources-tools/avma-policies/principles-veterinary-medical-ethics-avma, last accessed on May 2, 2022.

American Society for the Prevention of Cruelty to Animals (ASPCA) (2022) "Pet statistics." https://www.aspca.org/animal-homelessness/shelter-intake-and-surrender/pet-statistics, last accessed on May 2, 2022.

Canadian Veterinary Medical Association (CVMA) (2004, revised 2018) "Principles of veterinary medical ethics of the CVMA." https://www.canadianveterinarians.net/about-cvma/principles-of-veterinary-medical-ethics-of-the-cvma/, last accessed on May 2, 2022.

Desaulniers, É. (2011) *Je mange avec ma tête: Les conséquences de nos choix alimentaires*. Montreal: Stanké.

Desaulniers, É. (2013) *Vache à lait: Dix mythes de l'industrie laitière*. Montreal: Stanké.

Desaulniers, É. (2016) *Le défi végane 21 jours*. Montreal: Trecarré.

Humane Canada (2020) "2019 animal shelter statistics." Ottawa: Humane Canada, https://humanecanada.ca/wp-content/uploads/2020/11/Humane_Canada_Animal_shelter_statistics_2019.pdf, last accessed May 3, 2022.

Linzey, A., and C. Linzey (eds.) (2017) *Animal Ethics for Veterinarians: Common Threads*. Urbana, Illinois: University of Illinois Press.

Mars Petcare (2021) "State of Pet Homelessness Index." https://endpethomelessness.com/, last accessed on May 2, 2022.

Miller, L., and S. Zawistowski (eds.) (2013) *Shelter Medicine for Veterinarians and Staff*. 2nd ed. Oxford: Wiley-Blackwell.

People for the Ethical Treatment of Animals (PETA) (2018) "Why We Euthanize." https://www.peta.org/blog/euthanasia/, published February 1, 2018, last updated January 27, 2022, last accessed on May 2, 2022.

People for the Ethical Treatment of Animals (PETA) (n.d.) "Animal Rights Uncompromised: 'No-Kill' Shelters." https://www.peta.org/about-peta/why-peta/no-kill-shelters/, last accessed on May 2, 2022.

Rollin, B. (2006) *An Introduction to Veterinary Medical Ethics: Theory and Cases.* 2nd ed. Oxford: Blackwell.

Royal Society for the Prevention of Cruelty to Animals (RSPCA) (2010) "Difficult decisions." https://www.rspca.org.uk/documents/1494939/7712578/Diffic ult+decisions+%282010%29+%28PDF+146KB%29+%5Bfeatured+in+Ani mal+Life%5D.pdf/d442aa0a-fc3a-4763-6f4e-e1bcb165b817?t=1555430474 715&download=true, last accessed on May 2, 2022.

Simoneau-Gilbert, V. (2019) *Au nom des animaux : L'histoire de la SPCA de Montréal (1869–2019).* Montreal: Somme Toute.

Wathes, C., S. A. Corr, S. A. May, S. P. McCullock, and M. C. Whiting (eds.) (2011) *Veterinary & Animal Ethics: Proceedings of the First International Conference on Veterinary and Animal Ethics.* Hertfordshire: Universities Federation Animal Welfare, Animal Welfare book series.

Weiss, E., H. Mohan-Gibbons, and S. Zawitowski (eds.) (2015) *Animal Behavior for Shelter Veterinarians and Staff.* Oxford: Wiley-Blackwell.

Winerip, M. (2013) "PETA finds itself on receiving end of others' anger." *The New York Times,* July 6, "https://www.nytimes.com/2013/07/07/us/peta-finds-itself-on-receiving-end-of-others-anger.html, last accessed on May 2, 2022.

PART I

The Ethics of Animal Shelters

Guidelines and Recommendations

Valéry Giroux, Angie Pepper, Kristin Voigt, Frédéric Côté-Boudreau, Nicolas Delon, Sue Donaldson, François Jaquet, Will Kymlicka, Angela K. Martin, and Agnes Tam

Introduction

These recommendations are based on discussions between staff at the Montreal SPCA and the authors. Shelter staff shared their views on the ethical problems they face in their work and their own responses to these problems. They also offered valuable insights on the various parameters that constrain how they can respond to these problems, such as resource and space limitations, or concerns about donor responses.

In this policy document, we describe what struck us as the most urgent and challenging ethical problems arising in the day-to-day operations of the Montreal SPCA and offer recommendations on how these problems might be addressed given the various constraints and challenges under which the organization operates. The first part of the policy document summarizes these recommendations; the second part explains, in more detail, the reasoning behind these recommendations.

As became clear from our conversations, the difficult ethical challenges that characterize the daily work of shelter staff take a heavy emotional toll on already overworked and overburdened staff. The goal of this document is to help lighten this load. With this in mind,

Valéry Giroux, Angie Pepper, Kristin Voigt, Frédéric Côté-Boudreau, Nicolas Delon, Sue Donaldson, François Jaquet, Will Kymlicka, Angela Martin, and Agnes Tam, *The Ethics of Animal Shelters* In: *The Ethics of Animal Shelters*. Edited by: Valéry Giroux, Angie Pepper, and Kristin Voigt, Oxford University Press.

the "guidelines" we put forward should not be understood as an exacting set of standards that shelter staff must comply with. Rather, we have developed these recommendations with the hope that they will help shelter staff navigate the complex demands of their work and the many dilemmas they encounter on a daily basis. Moreover, the recommendations we make here may need to be adjusted or even abandoned if circumstances at the shelter change. Context is everything, and the concrete realities that shelter staff face—including the political and legal context, as well as the availability of resources—are variable, which means that recommendations made now might not always be feasible or desirable in the future. Nonetheless, we hope to have provided some guidance and foundations for thinking through some of the difficult decisions that are sadly an inevitable feature of shelter life.

The importance of context also affects the extent to which our suggestions may be helpful for shelters or organizations that find themselves in a very different set of circumstances. While our recommendations are informed by our conversations with staff at the Montreal SPCA, many of the fundamental ethical questions this organization faces also apply to other animal shelters, in Canada and beyond. For example, the questions of when to end animal lives or how to deal with overpopulation in an open-admission shelter, are sadly far from unique. Other questions, such as how to interact with governmental agencies or how to respond to challenges arising in the context of legal enforcement, may be more specific to the social and legal context of the Montreal SPCA and less directly applicable to other organizations. Even here, however, our recommendations could provide a helpful starting point for deliberations about the ethical issues at stake and how best to respond to them.

Recommendations

1 Ethical Framework

The following commitments, which we believe are fully in line with the Montreal SPCA's commitments, underlie this document:

- The recognition that animals matter for their own sakes, irrespective of whether or not they bring benefit to humans;
- The recognition of the importance of *all* sentient beings, including those who live in farms, factories, and laboratories; in our towns and cities; and in the wild;
- The recognition of the value of animals' lives and the importance of protecting their lives and well-being more generally;
- The recognition that animals have morally significant capacities for agency;
- The recognition that animals are entitled to relationships with humans that are characterized by care and respect;
- The recognition that humans have duties of protection toward animals.

2 Overarching Issues and Objectives

2.A Shaping Norms Around Our Relationships with Animals
We recommend that the SPCA explicitly include the shaping of social norms among its objectives. Ways to shape relevant social norms include featuring farmed animals prominently on promotion materials and adopting language that reflects animals' moral status.

2.B Language Surrounding Animals
We recommend that the SPCA adopt language and terminology that reflect the moral status of nonhuman animals.

2.C Position on Animal Exploitation and Farmed Animals
We recommend that the Montreal SPCA explicitly oppose all exploitation of animals, including animal agriculture.

2.D Property Status
We recommend that the Montreal SPCA take the position that nonhuman animals should not be property and that their legal status must change to accurately reflect their moral status.

2.E The Value of Animal Life

The SPCA's work should be guided by a commitment to the view that most sentient animals have an interest in continued existence and that therefore death is bad for them.

Assessments of animals' well-being should consider not only their physical health but also factors that affect their psychological well-being, such as boredom or loneliness. Well-being assessments should, where feasible, allow for differences between individual animals rather than making assessments purely on the basis of species membership.

The organization should recognize that staff are likely to have different intuitions about animal death and that life-or-death decisions can be distressing for staff.

3 Internal Structure and Decision-Making

3.A Relationship Between Departments and Respective Budgets

Given the wide range of responsibilities assumed by different departments of the Montreal SPCA, staff may not always agree on which aspects of the organization's work should be prioritized. We offer two recommendations:

(1) Separate the Montreal SPCA into two physical locations. Site A would focus on activities with a faster "turnover" track, such as adoption of companion animals, feral cat programs, and liminal animal rehab. Site B would have space for activities with a slower turnover track (e.g., housing large animals, dogs who require longer-term training for behavioral issues, indefinite accommodation for exotics and injured animals who cannot [or should not] be released or adopted, and animals held in limbo during criminal proceedings).

(2) Organize the Montreal SPCA into subunits that have discretion over their own budgets, rather than being in ongoing competition for limited resources with several other units.

3.B Decisions About Controversial Issues

We recommend that the Montreal SPCA add an Ethics Board to its structure, which would offer advice on particularly complex ethical decisions and could also develop decision aids to help with ethically charged, day-to-day decisions.

3.C Ethical Commitments of Staff

We recommend that the Montreal SPCA be explicit about its values in its Mission Statement and that it consider making a commitment to these values a consideration in hiring and appointment procedures for staff at the Montreal SPCA as well as for its Board.

4 Relationship with the Public, Donors, Industry, and Government

4.A Public Perception

We recommend that the Montreal SPCA explicitly oppose all animal exploitation and defend the interests of farmed animals.

4.B Relationship with Industry

We recommend that the SPCA seek dialogue with the animal industry only when this is very likely to deliver concrete, significant benefits for animals. We recommend that the SPCA prioritize collaborations with distributors and restaurant chains over those with producers.

4.C Relationship with Government

We recommend that the SPCA not refrain from presenting ambitious demands for improving animal welfare legislation and not hesitate to criticize governmental agencies for failing to implement stronger animal protection legislation and enforce existing legislation. The SPCA could also encourage politicians to include animal concerns in their campaigns.

We recommend that the SPCA not constrain its activities in opposition to animal agriculture, even if that risks undermining relationships with governmental agencies, such as the ministère de l'Agriculture, des Pêcheries et de l'Alimentation du Québec (MAPAQ, Quebec Ministry of Agriculture, Fisheries and Food). Public criticism should especially be favored over collaboration when evidence of MAPAQ's failure to prevent animal abuse can be used in media campaigns.

5 Law Enforcement

Staff need to reach a democratically informed decision over whether the Montreal SPCA should seek to retain its law enforcement and inspection powers. We recommend that any such efforts should not come at the cost of compromising core activities and commitments. In addition, the Montreal SPCA should lobby for the enforcement of provincial animal welfare legislation to be transferred from the MAPAQ to the Ministry of Justice or a new ministry devoted to animal issues. It should also consider offering training for police officers, as they may ultimately be charged with enforcing animal welfare legislation.

6 Shelter Operations

6.A Plant-Based Food for Shelter Residents
We recommend that, where appropriate, the Montreal SPCA transition its shelter animals to plant-based food, beginning with dogs. Public justification for this move should emphasize that the SPCA mandate extends to farmed animals and that dogs can thrive on a plant-based diet.

6.B Overpopulation and Living Environment in the Shelter
We recommend that the Montreal SPCA direct all the animals surrendered to the society by their guardians to its shelter. All stray animals who are brought or reported to the SPCA by community members should be evaluated: those who are not sterilized

or considered to be at risk should also be directed to the shelter.[1] Animals who appear to be lost should be listed on a website to help reunite them with their guardians. Friendly animals who are not claimed after a few days at the shelter should be, like those who were surrendered, sterilized, medically attended to, and put up for adoption.

We recommend that the Montreal SPCA continue to pursue strategies that reduce the number of animals who need to be admitted and kept at the shelter, like education about the necessity to sterilize companion animals and lobbying to prohibit breeding and selling companion animals.

In addition, we recommend that the Montreal SPCA ask their Ethics Board to determine (a) the maximum number of animals who can be housed at the SPCA while maintaining a decent quality of life for each and (b) the "ideal" number of animals at the SPCA. During emergency periods, it may be necessary to go above the maximum number; when this is the case, it may also be appropriate to temporarily relax certain principles that normally govern shelter operations.

6.C Abortions

We recommend that the Montreal SPCA continue to pursue strategies that reduce the need for abortions, such as the trap, neuter, release, and maintain (TNRM) program and public education about sterilization. For pregnancies that cannot be prevented through these efforts, aborting embryos and fetuses can be morally justified under current circumstances.

6.D Ending Animal Lives

It is crucial to distinguish between two kinds of cases. First, in cases of *euthanasia*, the animal has a serious, terminal illness and/or is enduring unbearable suffering with little prospect of alleviation or recovery. Ending the life of the animal in such cases is meant to end their suffering.

In contrast, there are instances where an animal has the prospect of a decent life but is unlikely to be rehomed. Animals who are difficult to rehome are a significant burden on SPCA resources and often experience diminished quality of life the longer they reside in the shelter. In such non-ideal conditions, there are likely to be cases in which killing is the only appropriate course of action. Ending the life of an animal in such cases constitutes an act of regrettable but nonetheless *morally permitted non-euthanasia killing*.

We also recommend that, in its internal discussions as well as public documents, the SPCA clearly distinguish between genuine cases of euthanasia and killing for other reasons.

Decisions about euthanasia: While some cases of euthanasia will be clearly justified and, indeed, required, other cases may be more difficult to judge. We recommend that the Ethics Board devise a decision tree to help staff make decisions about euthanasia. Items included in the decision tree should be empirically verifiable as indicators of good or diminished quality of life and sensitive to species as well as individual differences.

Decisions about morally permitted non-euthanasia killing: In cases where an animal is unlikely to be rehomed (or will only be suitable for rehoming after significant expense), killing the animal can sometimes be the only morally appropriate course of action. We maintain that:

- In the first instance, the SPCA should introduce measures that reduce the need for killing (e.g., funding rehabilitation programs for animals with behavioral problems). While this recommendation is necessary for the non-ideal conditions that the SPCA finds itself in, the organization must always act with a view to realizing the ideal goal of never killing an animal who could have a minimally decent life if time and resources were no issue.
- The Montreal SPCA should also ask the Ethics Board to devise a decision tree to distinguish impermissible from permissible killings.
- Instead of a no-kill policy, the SPCA should set its ideal "live release rate" and make its goal—and its strategy for achieving that goal—public.

6.E Palliative Care

We recommend that the Montreal SPCA keep its palliative care program in place for animals for whom palliative care is in their best interest.

6.F Exotic Animals

We recommend that the Montreal SPCA seek to find homes for exotic animals whose needs can be met in human homes or sanctuaries. For exotic animals with specific needs and requirements, staff must determine what quality of life these animals can realistically have. If no option can be found that ensures that the animal has a life worth living, it may be required to end their life.

6.G Adoption Process

We recommend that the adoption process include a conversation between the prospective adopter and a staff member to ensure that adopters are committed to meeting the needs of the animal. We encourage resisting an "open adoption" approach and keeping some basic selection criteria. This commitment can be formalized through an adoption form signed by the adopter. A member of staff should follow-up with a phone call after the adoption.

We also caution against the implementation of promotional adoption campaigns and similar events that can undermine the message that animals and their well-being matter. During periods of overpopulation, events like "Adoption Days" may be appropriate, but their tone must always reflect the seriousness of adoption.

We recommend that the Montreal SPCA offer as much information as possible to the adoptive families, as well as educational classes and animal training courses and/or online advice on how to address behavioral problems.

6.H Information About "Breeds"

The Montreal SPCA should not seek to determine or keep on record the "breeds" of specific animals, such as "Siamese" for cats or "Golden Retriever" for dogs. In general, staff should decline requests from adopters for specific breeds. SPCA staff should educate prospective adopters about problematic breeding practices and resulting health problems for animals.

6.I Dangerous Animals and Behavioral Issues

We recommend that the Montreal SPCA emphasize that behavioral issues affect individual animals and resist the idea that certain breeds of dogs are inherently dangerous.

The Montreal SPCA should continue to partner with therapists and vets who can treat dogs with behavioral problems so as to maximize the number of animals who can be successfully treated.

The Montreal SPCA should not put up for adoption animals for whom there is a risk that they could be a danger for other animals or for humans.

Site B discussed in Section 3.A could be a long-term home for dogs who are not suitable for rehoming with an adoptive family but can live good lives if given specialized care in an environment adapted to their needs. Animals who remain a danger to others even under those circumstances might be candidates for morally permitted non-euthanasia killing.

7 Animals in the Community

7.A Community Cats and the TNRM Program

All healthy, unclaimed animals who are friendly and able to live with humans should be put up for adoption. With regard to lost animals, the Montreal SPCA should develop effective practices to reunite those animals and their human caregivers.

Any community cats who are feral (and therefore not adoptable) and who seem able to survive in the community without being placed in a home, after having been spayed and neutered, medically examined and treated, and ear-tipped (i.e., a small portion of the animal's ear is removed to indicate that they have been sterilized), should be returned to the area where they were found as part of a TNRM program, extended to apply not only to colony cats but also to individual free-roaming cats. A "return to field" practice is often appropriate in those cases, under the condition that a caregiver is designated as responsible for the animals. In collaboration with the city of Montreal, the Montreal SPCA should support the citizens responsible for providing those animals with shelter, food, water, and medical assistance.

We also recommend that the Montreal SPCA continue its efforts to convince municipalities of the benefits of the TNRM program and get them to facilitate its operations by different means, such as making it legal to install temporary shelters in public places and encouraging citizens to get involved and take responsibility for community cats.

In addition, less invasive methods of contraception should be employed if/when available, and the possibility of expanding the programs to other liminal animals (raccoons, squirrels, rats, etc.) should be explored.

7.B Veterinary Care for Companion Animals Outside the Shelter

We recommend that the SPCA investigate the possibility of providing low-cost veterinary care for animals who have been adopted from the SPCA, for families on low incomes. Free services of capture, transportation, and veterinary care should also be offered to community cat caregivers under the TNRM program.

8 Issues for Staff

We recommend that the SPCA directly incorporate the staff's psychological well-being into its goals and projects. This includes acknowledging that staff will have emotional responses to certain cases and form attachments to individual animals, adopting programs that can support staff in reducing the burden of emotional labor, and allowing for exceptions to standard procedures when this enables staff to cope and continue in their work.

The Recommendations in Detail: Explanation and Justification

1 Ethical Framework

The Montreal SPCA's objectives, as described in its by-laws, are to "provide effective means for the prevention of cruelty to animals and to strive for continued improvement in the way animals are treated by human beings, through public education, advocacy, inspection, shelter services, legislation, and working with allied organizations."[2] The organization's mission—of "protecting animals from neglect, abuse and exploitation; representing their interests and ensuring their well-being; and last but not least, raising public awareness and helping develop compassion for all sentient beings"[3]—provides further clarification of the Montreal SPCA's goals and its underlying commitments.

The enormity of the SPCA's task can hardly be overstated. We live in a world in which exploitation and abuse of animals are ubiquitous. Animals[4] are all too often treated as objects that can be used for our benefit, however minimal, with little regard for their interests or well-being. Despite occasional attempts to curb the suffering animals experience at our hands (such as the adoption of legislation that seeks to reduce animals' suffering in industries in which they are used), the idea that animals' interests are always secondary to our own remains a widely shared norm that is only rarely challenged.

This context highlights the importance of the work that animal protection organizations such as the Montreal SPCA do: we see this work as an important part of a broader social justice movement that calls attention to and seeks to challenge the way we treat sentient beings. At the same time, the context in which organizations such as the SPCA work severely constrains what they can achieve: limited resources (financial, but also physical and emotional), laws that fail to recognize the interests of animals and sanction their exploitation, and a public that often does not recognize the claims of animals— these are all factors that stand in the way of organizations such as the Montreal SPCA achieving its aims.

As philosophers, we are committed to a number of assumptions that, we think, are fully in line with the Montreal SPCA's commitments and may even strengthen them. Specifically, this includes:

- The recognition that animals have moral status: they matter for their own sakes, irrespective of whether or not they bring benefit to humans.
- The recognition of the importance of *all* sentient beings, including not only members of those species that typically share our homes, such as cats, dogs, and rabbits, but also those who live on farms, in factories, and laboratories, in our towns and cities, and in the wild.
- The recognition of the value of animals' lives and the importance of protecting their lives and well-being. Most animals have an interest in staying alive and in living good lives. This is consistent with cases of genuine euthanasia (i.e., instances where an animal has a serious, terminal illness and/or is enduring unbearable suffering with little prospect of alleviation or recovery), but not with the killing of animals for human convenience or lack of space or resources.
- The recognition that animals have morally significant capacities for agency. This means that they have an interest in having some degree of control over the shape and content of their lives.
- The recognition that animals are entitled to relationships with humans that are characterized by care and respect, to the extent that they desire such relationships.
- The recognition that humans have duties of protection toward animals, especially when these animals are in a vulnerable position or when they have been harmed or made vulnerable by humans.

The Montreal SPCA is uniquely positioned among animal protection organizations because of its size, reputation, and experience. We believe that this offers the opportunity to be at the forefront of the movement and take more risks than other, smaller organizations. In addition, while organizations such as the SPCA must direct much of their energy and attention toward the prevention and alleviation of harm, they can also play a more positive role by facilitating and supporting the kinds of relationships between humans and nonhumans that would exist in a more just world.

2 Overarching Issues and Objectives

2. A Shaping Norms Around Our Relationships with Animals

One of the problems the Montreal SPCA faces in its work is that the general public does not share many of the commitments the organization stands for. At the same time, the Montreal SPCA can take an important role in shaping how people see their relationships with animals and their understanding of animals' moral status.

Recommendation: We recommend that the SPCA explicitly include the shaping of social norms among its objectives. This includes norms around the moral status of animals and the importance of all sentient beings, including farmed animals and wild animals. Possible ways of shaping social norms include:

- Featuring farmed animals prominently on promotion materials (as the Montreal SPCA already does);
- Considering ways of arranging living space in the shelter so that those seeking to adopt a companion animal also cross paths with farmed or wild animals or urban wildlife (as the Montreal SPCA already does with its resident pigeons);
- Adopting language that reflects the moral status of animals in its promotion materials as well as internal documents and in interactions with the public (see Section 2.B).

2.B Language Surrounding Animals

Much of the language we employ to talk about animals reflects our failure to recognize their moral status and plays an important role in sustaining problematic attitudes toward them.

Recommendation: We recommend that the Montreal SPCA adopt terminology that is consistent with the moral status of animals. We recommend that the SPCA review its communications with the public (including website, press releases, etc.) but also internal documents, and revise the language where appropriate. Particularly important examples include:

- "Companion animal" and "guardian" instead of "pet" and "owner."
- "Farmed animals" instead of "farm animals."
- "Animal flesh" instead of "pork," "beef," etc.
- Limiting the term "euthanasia" to genuine instances of euthanasia (i.e., when an animal's life is ended to relieve their pain and suffering). Cases where an animal is killed because of behavioral problems or resource constraints are not cases of euthanasia and should not be referred to as such. (See discussion in Section 6.D.)
- Reference to individual animals as "them," "she" or "he," rather than "it."
- Use of the term "nonhuman animals" rather than "animals" because it challenges the idea that there is a clear moral distinction between animals and humans. While it is typically too cumbersome to use the term "nonhuman animals" in all instances, even occasional use, especially in communication with the public, can help challenge problematic assumptions.

While changing the language the SPCA uses may seem inconsequential, it offers an important opportunity to challenge problematic assumptions and norms surrounding animals as well as humans' relationship with them.

2.C Position on Animal Exploitation and Farmed Animals

While the Montreal SPCA is traditionally associated primarily with companion animals such as cats, dogs, and rabbits, its mandate includes "compassion for all sentient beings." This means that all sentient animals, including those used in various industries and businesses and for scientific and academic research, fall within the remit of the Montreal SPCA's mandate. Of particular concern are farmed animals (i.e., those animals who are used within animal industries, such as the meat, egg and dairy industries). From an ethical perspective, the interests of farmed animals are no less important than those of companion animals. This, we think, gives the Montreal SPCA reasons to promote the interests of farmed animals in their internal practices and their external advocacy.

This could be done in more or less ambitious ways. At a minimum, the Montreal SPCA could seek to ensure it does not contribute to the denigration and instrumentalization of farmed animals; more ambitiously, it could proactively seek to change laws and public opinion regarding the treatment of farmed animals.

The Montreal SPCA has already moved in the latter, more ambitious direction by using its advocacy and education to channel people's existing compassion for companion animals into concern for farmed animals. Unfortunately, members of the general public typically put companion and farmed animals into completely different boxes, attributing different capacities and purposes to them and applying different standards to them, treating companion animals with compassion and farmed animals instrumentally. Few if any ethical theories hold that these categorical distinctions are defensible, but breaking down these moral silos is not easy.

There may be disagreement among staff and among supporters and donors about whether or how the Montreal SPCA's ethical commitments should be extended to farmed animals. Some SPCA policies could be interpreted as endorsing a "humane use" conception of ethics regarding farmed animals, which condones the instrumental use of animals so long as it is done "humanely." For example, the Montreal SPCA's official policies state that "[w]e believe that farm-animal welfare can be improved through humane farming, transport and slaughter methods and, most importantly, through reduced animal-product consumption."[5] In addition, not all of the SPCA's commitments regarding companion animals are applied to farmed animals. For example, the SPCA expresses opposition to all permanent confinement of companion animals but only singles out *intensive* confinement when it comes to farmed animals. Some SPCA members and supporters may believe that it is right to maintain this distinction between an ethic of respect for companion animals and an ethic of humane use for farmed animals. However, we suggest that these distinctions in SPCA policies should be seen as strategic and transitional, as temporary way stations on a long road to a society that rejects the instrumentalization of all sentient animals.

Explicitly opposing animal exploitation and animal agriculture comes with strategic risks for an organization such as the Montreal SPCA. For example, taking an explicit stance on animal agriculture might alienate staff, donors, and government agencies with whom the Montreal SPCA interacts. The risks that the adoption of a more ambitious position poses with respect to these different relationships are addressed in this document (see Sections 6.A and 4).

If the Montreal SPCA decides that the risks of taking such an explicit stance are too great, it will be crucial to develop a position and a way of talking about animals that do not implicitly accept that the interests of farmed animals are less important than those of companion animals.

Recommendation: The Montreal SPCA should be informed by an opposition to all animal exploitation, to any hierarchy between companion and farmed animals, and to any categorization of animals that instrumentalizes them. The long-term goal should be that the Montreal SPCA not only advocates for the welfare of farmed animals, but also works toward ending animal agriculture altogether. This need not mean that the Montreal SPCA publicly calls for an end to animal agriculture immediately, if this is perceived as too risky a strategy in the current climate. Informal strategies to challenge people's assumptions about the moral status of farmed animals, such as featuring farmed animals on social media channels, may be more appropriate strategies for now.

One risk associated with a strategy that does not involve public opposition to animal agriculture is that it is difficult to formulate the Montreal SPCA's formal policies in a way that does not implicitly assume and thus reinforce the view that farmed animals have a lower moral status than companion animals. Even if the Montreal SPCA does not publicly oppose animal agriculture, the formal policies should be formulated to rely as little as possible on an implicit categorization of different kinds of animals.

The opposition to animal exploitation should also inform how the SPCA operates internally. An important step in this direction concerns food served on SPCA premises. We recommend that the organization maintain its policy of serving only plant-based food at its events and staff meetings and that only plant-based meals be reimbursed through SPCA funds. The SPCA should also transition toward a plant-based diet for the resident animals in its shelter, starting with dogs (see Section 6.A). Such policies can make an important contribution to challenging perceptions about the moral status of farmed animals without risking a public backlash.

2.D Property Status

The Montreal SPCA operates in a legal context that relegates animals to the status of property, which sanctions the purchasing, selling, exchanging, renting, using, discarding, and destroying of animals as we would physical objects. The property status of animals is incompatible with the ethical framework outlined above (Section 1): if animals have non-instrumental value, then the law should not treat them as inanimate objects. Justice requires that animals enjoy legal personhood.

Of course, animals benefit from some legal protections, and the Montreal SPCA continues to play an important role in strengthening and enforcing these protections. The Civil Code of Québec now recognizes that animals are sentient beings with biological needs. Nevertheless, as long as animals are viewed as property, the legal protections they can have will remain extremely limited. In Western societies, property rights are of paramount importance and legislators are reluctant to restrict them. Effective advocacy in favor of animal interests seems largely incompatible with their status as property.

Recommendation: We recommend that the Montreal SPCA take the position that animals should not be property and that their legal status must change to accurately reflect their moral status.

2.E The Value of Animal Life

Public discourse around animals often recognizes that we have reason to reduce their suffering; there is often significant public support, for example, for legislation that restricts the pain that animal industries can inflict on animals. However, people's intuitions are much less clear when it comes to the *killing* of animals: some see it as not inherently problematic (if achieved painlessly) whereas for others, even the painless death of an animal—except for genuine cases of euthanasia (see Section 6.D)—is always intrinsically bad.

While animal ethicists debate what *precisely* makes death bad for animals, they typically agree that death is bad for sentient animals because, and to the extent that, it deprives them of things in which they have an interest, such as opportunities for well-being, pleasant experiences, satisfaction of desires, etc. Animals can have pleasurable experiences, complex desires, social relationships and attachments, and psychological connections over time. Death deprives them of important goods and of the opportunities that life makes possible. This gives us strong moral reasons not to end the lives of animals.[6]

At the same time, of course, SPCA staff frequently deal with animals for whom it is unclear whether continued existence would be in their best interest or whether it would involve so much pain that it is not in their interest to continue living. This includes animals with painful, fatal diseases. In such cases, it is crucial to assess the options available for the animal and the possible quality of life they can have. This must include not only general considerations (e.g., life expectancy, level of pain they are experiencing) but also considerations specific to the individual animal and their preferences. For example, cats vary in their desire for feline companions or their interest in accessing the outdoors. In addition, because SPCA staff work in highly non-ideal circumstances and under significant resource constraints, they are likely to face situations where preventing the death of one animal would require substantial resources—resources which would then not be available to save a potentially much larger number of animals. (We discuss this problem and possible responses in Section 6.D.)

These situations create difficult moral dilemmas for SPCA staff and are emotionally taxing for staff members who make decisions about these cases. Grief, mourning, frustration, and moral conflicts are bound to afflict SPCA staff (we return to this issue in Section 8).

Recommendations:

- The SPCA's work should be guided by the recognition that both suffering and death are bad for sentient animals with a strong interest in continued existence.
- Assessments of individual animals' well-being should make reference not only to their physical health (including levels of pain or pleasure) but also to considerations that affect their psychological well-being, such as boredom, loneliness, and the extent to which they can exercise control over their lives and satisfy important interests and desires, such as playing and socializing with others.
- Well-being assessments should allow for differences between individual animals rather than making assessments purely on the basis of species membership. In the context of a shelter, where there is often little time to get to know individual animals, it may be difficult to make such assessments. In a context where staff interact with specific animals over extended periods of time (e.g., in the context of Site B described in Section 3.A), there will be greater scope for making such assessments.
- The organization should recognize that staff are likely to have different intuitions about animal death and that life-or-death decisions can be extremely distressing for them. A transparent discussion of the ethics of killing and different views on the badness of death could allow for a finer-grained understanding of the moral conflicts staff experience and indirectly ease the

emotional labor of having to make tragic decisions. (See Section 8 For further suggestions on this issue.)

3 Internal Structure and Decision-Making

The mission of the Montreal SPCA is broad and complex. It covers objectives ranging from raising public awareness of and compassion for all sentient beings including farmed animals (see Section 4.A), the improvement of the welfare of the animals in various industries (see Section 4.B), the improvement of animals' legal situation (see Section 4.C), the enforcement of the legislation protecting animals and the care of seized animals (see Section 4.C and Section 5), caring for animals within the shelter (see Section 6), and responding to the needs of animals at risk in the community outside of the shelter (see Section 7).

With such a wide range of responsibilities assumed by different departments, disagreements among employees about policies and priorities are likely to arise, and this could in turn lead to frustration and conflict. For example, the efforts and means put into the rescue of one abused animal by the members of the investigations division might seem excessive to the staff working in the shelter division who could help a greater number of abandoned animals with those resources. Similarly, some of the animals seized in the Montreal SPCA's inspections work are farmed animals, exotic species, or animals with trauma-induced behavior problems—none of whom can be easily accommodated at the current SPCA site, and many of whom raise distinctive challenges concerning care and habitat needs.

3.A Relationship Between Departments and Respective Budgets

Problem: With such a large mission, it is to be expected that divergent views about several program and treatment priorities will emerge in the Montreal SPCA's work, including:

- Whether to prioritize the number of animals helped (e.g., reducing unwanted animals through spay and neuter clinics and other high-volume/low-cost strategies for reducing suffering) or prioritize the value of every life and individual rights (e.g., going to great lengths to avoid having to kill or euthanize an animal with chronic health conditions, complicated treatment or palliative care needs, or traits making them less "adoptable");
- Whether to try to do a few things very well or many things well enough (e.g., treat more animals but at the expense of more crowded conditions);
- Whether to prioritize crisis response or more preventative medicine (e.g., housing more surrendered animals or developing a low-income vet care clinic so fewer families would neglect or need to surrender animals);
- Whether to prioritize grassroots programs that serve the more immediate community and the animals living there (e.g., domesticated and liminal animals of Montreal) or general campaigns and programs on behalf of all animals in Québec (including wildlife, animals in factory farms, etc.);
- Whether to prioritize advocacy within current legislative limits (e.g., public education, community support and prevention programs) or longer-term advocacy aimed at legal and regulatory change and a fundamental shift in public attitudes toward animals.

These are all issues over which people might reasonably disagree, and it may be unrealistic to think that disagreement can be resolved through deliberation and rational analysis. An alternative approach would consider whether the SPCA can find ways to tolerate a diverse range of values and approaches among staff while mitigating daily friction caused by these differences. Friction may be exacerbated by certain features of the SPCA's current organizational structure, which could be mitigated through structural changes that would separate the different divisions/subunits and their budget streams, thereby allowing individual subunits to adopt different approaches to prioritization.

This section considers two related, but independent, proposals. The first, more ambitious, proposal is for physical separation of the SPCA into two locations better adapted to serving different groups of animals, therefore reducing the risk of friction among staff with different priorities and focus. The second proposal is for dedicated budgets for different subunits to reduce daily competition over resources and among different approaches to prioritization and decision-making.

Recommendation 1: Separate the SPCA into two physical locations to more effectively serve widely divergent dimensions of its mandate.

One division would be housed in the existing building in Montreal. Its work would focus on animal companions destined for adoption; feral cat programs; liminal animal rehab (e.g., pigeons, squirrels, and other nondomesticated animals who live in urban environments); community education; support and advocacy around prevention, care, and wildlife coexistence strategies (e.g., building designs that don't harm animals, strategies for minimizing conflicts); and working animals in the city. This division would shelter animals who are on a "faster turnover track," expected to return to the community through free release or in foster and adoption homes. Staff at this site would have considerable interaction with the general public. Call this Site A.

A separate, more rural, Site B would have adequate space to house large animals (from farm seizures and surrenders), dogs who require longer-term training for behavioral issues, indefinite accommodation for exotic and injured animals who cannot (or should not) be released or adopted, and animals held in limbo during criminal proceedings. Site B animals would be those on a much slower "turnover track," with some residents finding a permanent home at the site. Site B would house the inspections team, and its advocacy work would focus on long-term issues concerning farming, wildlife, and criminal/cruelty legislation. This site would not be set up for regular contact with the general public.

Reasoning: Two locations would help the SPCA better meet the needs of animals (e.g., larger and more appropriate spaces for large animals and long-term residents; greater physical separation between agitated animals). Creating a better environment for these animals would reduce stress on staff by enabling them to provide better care. This seems particularly important if, as is envisaged for Site B, the SPCA is effectively home for many animals, not just a short-term environment in which a certain level of stress might be more tolerable. The provision of a more spacious and peaceful environment might make it easier for investigators to deal with heartbreaking cases of animals in legal limbo or who cannot be released. Even if the ultimate decision about the fate of an animal goes the wrong way, it might help to know that at least for a significant interval of time the animal has lived in a positive environment and not a temporary shelter.

Moreover, by creating a physical separation between programs addressing fast turnover/high-volume cases and those involving more complex or long-term treatment, conflict between staff oriented toward these very different programs could be significantly reduced. Separate sites wouldn't change the fact that the SPCA has to make fundamental decisions about how to prioritize various dimensions of its mandate, priorities which staff would need to comply with. But it would create a clearer division of labor and reduce the extent to which these existential decisions have to be renegotiated across numerous individuals on a daily basis, allowing staff to focus on programs they are best oriented to, helping them to feel better supported, and facilitating the making of day-to-day decisions without them flaring up into debates about fundamental values and priorities.

It could even be that certain fundamental principles and decision-making procedures would look somewhat different in the Site A and B contexts. For example, at Site B, investigators might believe that they have a heightened duty to animals whom they have put into limbo or jeopardy through legal proceedings or animals who are being "instrumentalized" to some degree as good cases for advancing legal advocacy. They may believe that this justifies going to greater lengths to treat or rehabilitate an animal than would be the case in some other context.

Site B could play an important role for the organization and its goals. First, the site would offer residents much more opportunity for agency than is possible in the current shelter (and at Site A, in this proposal): it would offer a home in which residents have some control over the kinds of lives they want to lead, for example, when it comes to their day-to-day activities and the relationships, if any, they form with staff or other residents. More broadly, Site B also makes it possible to provide a space that prefigures the kinds of relationships that would exist in a more just world: it demonstrates what would be possible if we took animals' moral status and their capacity for agency seriously and how that would structure the relationships in which they stand with others.

Recommendation 2: Separate the Montreal SPCA into subunits that have discretion over their own set budgets rather than being in ongoing competition for limited resources with several other units.

Reasoning: Currently, it seems that the allocation of resources is subject to ongoing negotiation among multiple staff who may feel they are choosing, on a daily basis, between competing options that are like "apples and oranges." For example, they might face choices such as whether to (a) treat a complicated gingivitis case, (b) manage a complicated pregnancy, or (c) perform four sterilizations, each of which is seen as calling upon the same limited pool of money and staff.

An alternative approach is to set up separate budget lines for separate units (e.g., a dental clinic, a maternity clinic, a spay-neuter clinic, an infectious disease unit) each with its own dedicated staff and internal decisions about budget allocations. (The same staff might work in more than one subunit, but the decision-making processes would be separate.)

There would of course still be a need to decide on budget priorities among these subunits, but these larger priorities would be negotiated and fixed over longer time periods, allowing day-to-day decision-making to focus on narrower questions rather than clashing over fundamental ethical approaches and program priorities. This could significantly reduce frustration and risk of friction among staff. It might also encourage a clearer establishment of priorities within subunits. For example, a spay-neuter clinic might decide to prioritize treatment, but a dental unit might decide to divide its budget between treatment on the one hand and development of a public education campaign on the other. Within the limits of their budget lines, staff within each unit will be free to decide on their own priorities, without having to constantly defend each decision against all the competing claims of other programs.

An organizational approach that reduces conflict between values and facilitates decision-making can help separate immediate and day-to-day ethical decisions about the treatment of an individual animal from longer-term ethical commitments, priorities, and policies of the SPCA. The latter can be semi-institutionalized through budgets, decentralized decision-making, location, and staffing decisions. These longer-term ethical decisions are subject to review and revision but not on a day-to-day basis. This approach helps to limit the extent to which staff with different priorities and ethical orientations feel they are in daily competition for resources and narrows the scope and stress of daily decision-making. It also allows staff to focus their energies on dimensions of the SPCA mandate that best suit their ethical orientation and for the SPCA to benefit from this specialization.

3.B Decisions About Controversial Issues

Problem: In its day-to-day operations, the SPCA must make decisions about a host of ethically challenging and often contentious issues, for example in relation to euthanasia, abortion, and how best to deal with overpopulation in the shelter. While discussions about difficult ethical, organizational, and financial issues are necessary and important, all too frequent discussions about day-to-day decisions can easily become exhausting for everyone involved.

Recommendations: The Montreal SPCA should add an Ethics Board to its structure. The Ethics Board should be comprised of SPCA staff members as well as persons from outside the SPCA, such as lawyers or ethicists. This Board will be available to offer advice in relation to particularly complex ethical decisions to be made by the organization. As part of this process, such a Board could also review available evidence and empirical research relevant for specific questions and assess how reliable those findings are and to what extent they are applicable to the specific circumstances of the Montreal SPCA and the context in which it operates. The Board could also be tasked with developing decision aids to help with ethically charged decisions that must be made on a day-to-day basis (e.g., decisions trees about euthanasia and non-euthanasia killing).

Reasoning: An Ethics Board—perhaps modeled on ethics committees in hospitals—could facilitate difficult decisions and ease some of the mental burden and strain that such decisions impose on SPCA staff. While an Ethics Board may not be able to help with all of the time-sensitive decisions the SPCA faces, it can offer helpful advice in cases where there is time for external consultation.

One important role that an Ethics Board may serve is to review current SPCA policies in light of emerging empirical literature. Changes to SPCA policy and everyday shelter operations that may have a direct impact on animal well-being must always be informed by robust scientific evidence and empirical research. An Ethics Board would be able to assist the SPCA in assessing available research and in determining whether new evidence is sufficient to warrant changes to SPCA policy or operations.

In addition, it makes sense for the development of decision trees and other kinds of decision aids to be delegated to a separate body rather than for the Montreal SPCA to develop such instruments internally. Decision trees in particular can provide a welcome aid for the many complex and controversial ethical decisions the SPCA makes on a day-to-day basis (e.g., when it comes to ending animals' lives). The Ethics Board could develop decision trees in consultation with relevant SPCA staff and the SPCA Board to delineate how such decision trees could be used and which limitations must be borne in mind.

3.C Ethical Commitments of Staff

Recommendation: We recommend that the Montreal SPCA be explicit about its values in its Mission Statement (perhaps using the suggestions made in Section 1 and Section 2 of this document as a guide) and that it consider making a commitment to these values a consideration in hiring and appointment procedures for staff at the Montreal SPCA as well as for its Board.

Reasoning: For the SPCA to be effective, it is crucial that SPCA staff agree among themselves on the basic principles and commitments that should underpin their work. Agreement between the SPCA staff and the Board is also important, not least because the Board has the authority to dismiss the Executive Director (and other senior staff members). Making explicit its own values and ensuring that both staff and Board members are committed to these values facilitates the organization's smooth operation. Taking into consideration a commitment to these values in hiring and appointment procedures helps ensure continuity in the organization over time.

This is not to say, of course, that there couldn't be disagreement among staff or between staff and the Board about specific values or about how they should be interpreted in the context of the Montreal SPCA's work. However, a clear ethical framework can help clarify potential disagreements and allow for clearer discussion on how they might be resolved.

4 Relationship with the Public, Donors, Industry, and Government

4.A Public Perception

Considering the Montreal SPCA's mission to protect *all* sentient beings and raise public awareness and compassion, and considering the large scale of exploitation to which farmed animals are subject, it seems appropriate and important for the Montreal SPCA to take a clear and public stance against animal agriculture (see also Section 2.B).

Problem: If campaigns for the protection of farmed animals are perceived negatively, they could lead to the loss of donors, volunteers, and public support, all of which are crucial for the Montreal SPCA's everyday functioning.

Recommendation: The Montreal SPCA should clearly defend the interests of farmed animals and increasingly advocate for an end to animal exploitation.

Reasoning: If donors, volunteers, the media, or the general public withdraw their sympathy and support from the Montreal SPCA, this could quickly undermine its capacity to effectively pursue its goals. However, there are reasons to be hopeful that the public would be supportive of campaigns targeting animal agriculture. First, experience with previous campaigns suggests that donors do not respond negatively when the Montreal adopts ambitious positions. Indeed, two recent campaigns that initially seemed to run against public opinion—the SPCA's public denunciation of the way farmed animals are treated (the campaign "Animals" launched in 2018) as well as a public stance to defend "pit-bull type dogs framed as dangerous" (in 2016–2017)—didn't seem to have any effect on donations (in the first case) and even increased donations (in the second case). These anecdotal examples suggest that a more proactive defense of farmed animals might have a neutral or even positive effect on public support and donations. Public attitudes are in flux, and for every donor or volunteer who opposes such campaigns, there might be another potential donor or volunteer who is excited about an organization that is committed to a broader rethinking of human–animal relations, beyond companion animals.

Second, veganism doesn't seem to raise as much hostility in Quebec as it does in other parts of the world. The numerous vegan restaurants in Montreal, for instance, are full of customers who otherwise have an omnivorous diet. The annual Montreal Vegan Festival now attracts almost 20,000 people, only a very small minority of whom are actually vegan. It is reasonable to think that a stance that is more consistent with the mission of protecting all sentient animals from exploitation would be accepted by the public.

4.B Relationship with Industry
Problem: While the SPCA does not currently collaborate with animal industries, it does offer its perspective on industry standards, guidelines, and codes of practice. The Montreal SPCA might

consider developing collaborations with the industry if this allows them to push for the adoption of more demanding animal welfare commitments and, once these are adopted, to hold companies accountable for respecting these standards. It could also use such collaborations to push for better training programs for workers, which in turn would make it harder for companies to shift blame to employees when cruel treatment of animals is exposed. Such collaborations with the industry might also give the SPCA access to otherwise confidential information about the industry's future plans, enabling them to plan future campaigns more strategically (e.g., not focus on improvements that the industry has already decided to adopt). At the same time, it is crucial to keep in mind that such collaborations are in tension with the SPCA's mission and commitment to "raising public awareness and helping develop compassion for all sentient beings." In particular, the industry can use its association with an animal protection organization to improve its public image and ultimately sell more animal products.

Recommendation: We recommend that the SPCA seek dialogue or collaboration with the animal industry only when there is a high likelihood of achieving concrete and significant benefits for animals. Such discussions and collaborations should not be maintained unless they are used to maximize pressure on the industry to improve their treatment of animals. We recommend that the SPCA prioritize collaborations with distributors and restaurant chains (especially those that are large enough to have a significant influence on the producers) over those with producers.

Reasoning: In situations where concrete gains for animals can reasonably be expected from a collaboration with industry, these gains could in principle be worth the risk of improving the public image of the companies concerned. This risk, however, must not be underestimated. There are good reasons to believe that the industry will only improve animal welfare standards if this promises to increase its profits: for example, because it has financial reasons to adopt changes that happen to improve animal welfare or because collaboration with animal advocates is good publicity and increases business. Consequently, any collaborations with the industry should not extend beyond what is strictly necessary to achieve improvements that could not have been obtained otherwise and that will not end up improving the industry's image and thereby contribute to animal exploitation.

Negotiations with distributors or restaurant chains (e.g., encouraging supermarket chains not to sell eggs from factory farms) are more promising (and likely to demand less compromise of the Montreal SPCA) than those with producers, since—unlike producers—distributors have less to lose by replacing animal products with plant-based ones.

4.C Relationship with Government

The Montreal SPCA seeks to improve the legal situation of animals from two main angles: first, by lobbying and campaigning for stricter animal welfare legislation and, second, by building legal cases in an effort to obtain strict sentences for those who violate existing animal welfare laws and to underscore that the violation of such laws is a serious crime.

Problem 1: On the one hand, the Montreal SPCA ought to be committed to the long-term goal of eliminating animal agriculture (see Section 2.B). On the other hand, it seems reasonable for the organization to moderate its demands to policymakers to increase the likelihood that bills that can improve the legal protections of animals' interests are actually adopted. How ambitious should the Montreal SPCA be in its interactions with policymakers?

Recommendation: We recommend that the SPCA not refrain from presenting ambitious demands with regard to how the law should be improved and not hesitate to criticize relevant governmental agencies when they fail to implement stronger animal protection legislation or enforce existing legislation. Given growing public support for the protection of farmed animals, the SPCA could also work with politicians to include efforts to protect animals in their election campaigns.

Reasoning: When deciding what legal changes should be promoted, the SPCA should align its demands to the long-term objective of changing animals' legal status as property (see Section 2.C).

When advocating for improvements in the conditions in which animals are kept, it is important not to create obstacles for subsequent, more demanding steps. In order to be considered an improvement, a legal change should not only improve the situation of currently exploited animals but also represent a step toward the eventual establishment of their legal personhood and rights protecting them from exploitation.

Recent studies show that although only a minority of the population are willing to adopt a vegan lifestyle, a substantial number are opposed to the exploitation of animals for food and would even be in favor of closing slaughterhouses. In the United States, for instance, up to 34% of the population indicate that they are in favor of banning slaughterhouses;[7] a study estimates that 17% of the population of Switzerland are in favor of closing slaughterhouses; the number goes up to 35% if we look at the French-speaking part of the country only.[8] It is not unreasonable to suppose that the situation is similar in Quebec and Canada more broadly.

Assuming that what is true in the United States and in Francophone Switzerland is also true in Quebec and Canada, this knowledge should be used to motivate politicians to include animal protection in their platforms. Politicians have strong incentives to align themselves with animal industries, which often put considerable effort (and funds) into lobbying politicians. However, the data suggest that the populations these politicians represent are more critical of animal agriculture than politicians seem to assume, and a commitment to democracy requires that they give greater weight to the views of their voters and less to industry demands.

Problem 2: Part of the Montreal SPCA's work toward the improvement of the legal protections of animals consists in negotiating with the ministère de l'Agriculture, des Pêcheries et de l'Alimentation du Québec (MAPAQ). A possible advantage of collaborating with the MAPAQ is that it could give the Montreal SPCA useful information and allow it to influence the ministry from the inside. Additionally, since the MAPAQ delegates to the Montreal SPCA inspection powers related to the enforcement of provincial animal welfare legislation, it might seem important to maintain a courteous relationship and avoid confrontation (see Section 5).

At the same time, the MAPAQ is closely aligned with animal industries.[9] This creates a fraught situation for SPCA staff who feel that they can only make very moderate demands of the MAPAQ and must refrain from publicly criticizing it for failing to protect animals so as not to undermine the Montreal SPCA's relationship with the ministry.

Recommendation: We recommend that the SPCA not constrain its activities in opposition to animal agriculture, even if that risks undermining its relationship with governmental agencies. This extends to campaigns that publicly denounce governmental agencies that fail to protect animals. Public criticism should especially be favored over collaboration when evidence of the MAPAQ's failure to prevent animal abuse can be used in media campaigns.

Reasoning: Working closely with the MAPAQ is risky because it could legitimize animal agriculture since it allows industry to claim that "animal advocates" are involved in industry oversight (even though the Montreal SPCA's powers do not in fact extend to animals used in commercial farming). In addition, having to maintain this relationship may lead the SPCA to refrain from more ambitious projects that are critical of animal agriculture. It is therefore important to assess what the Montreal SPCA can concretely achieve through its relationship with the ministry. What is more, past experience suggests that publicly opposing the MAPAQ can lead the ministry to make concessions, for example by strengthening the Montreal SPCA's inspection powers (as it did in response to a previous campaign).

5 Law Enforcement

Problem: The Montreal SPCA enforces provincial animal welfare legislation as well as the animal cruelty provisions of the Canadian Criminal Code. These enforcement powers are granted to the Montreal SPCA by the MAPAQ and the ministère de la Sécurité publique du Québec, respectively. These relationships create a difficult situation for the Montreal SPCA. Being perceived as "too radical" could create the impression that the Montreal SPCA has a conflict of interest when using these powers: it is in charge of policing industries to which it is fundamentally opposed. The perception of a conflict of interest could lead the SPCA to lose its enforcement powers. If the Montreal SPCA were to lose these powers, they would revert to the MAPAQ (in the case of provincial legislation) or to the police (in the case of the Criminal Code).

If the Montreal SPCA were to lose its investigation powers related to the Criminal Code, then enforcement would be left to the police, and complaints about animal abuse and neglect might not be nearly as well monitored as they are currently. First, the cost of sending police officers would be much higher than the cost of sending SPCA inspectors, whose salaries are lower and who are paid not by the government but by a nongovernmental agency financed by donations. Second, the police are already overworked with enforcing legal offences against human beings, which are generally considered more serious than those against animals. If the Montreal SPCA's powers with respect to provincial law reverted back to the MAPAQ, this would likely leave animals much less protected than they currently are, given the close alignment of the MAPAQ with industry interests.

At the same time, in an ideal world, the law would be properly enforced by a public agency rather than a private organization. Some animal advocates think that animal defense organizations should not engage in enforcement work as it encourages the government to shirk its responsibilities.

Recommendation: The issue of whether the SPCA should seek to retain or relinquish its law enforcement powers is one over which there can be reasonable disagreement, and ultimately SPCA staff need to reach a democratically informed conclusion over which path they pursue. However, if the SPCA chooses to seek to retain their law enforcement powers, their efforts should not lead to a weakening of the core commitments specified in their mission statement. Moreover, irrespective of whether the SPCA seeks to retain or relinquish its law enforcement powers, it should continue to advocate for animal welfare legislation to be enforced by a body other than MAPAQ. This could be an already existing ministry whose mandate is not potentially in conflict with animal protection, such as the ministère de la Justice or, alternatively, a yet-to-be created ministry exclusively dedicated to animal protection.

We recommend the following approach:

1. If the Montreal SPCA concludes that it is important to maintain enforcement powers, it should ensure that necessary transparency, oversight, and accountability mechanisms are in place to guarantee procedural fairness in applying the law but not compromise on core commitments in order to retain law enforcement powers;

2. Lobby for a transfer of the responsibility for the application of provincial legislation protecting animals (as well as promulgation of by-laws, administration of permits, etc.) from the MAPAQ to the ministère de la Justice or to a new ministry especially endowed with the mission of protecting animals;

3. Develop a training program for police officers to increase awareness of crimes against animals and develop expertise in investigating these.

Reasoning:

Regarding 1: Animal protection organizations are susceptible to having their law enforcement powers challenged when they do not meet the strict standards of transparency, oversight, and accountability that apply to law enforcement agencies.[10] By ensuring that it complies with such standards, the Montreal SPCA can make itself less vulnerable to calls for a removal of enforcement powers. However, the organization needs to remain vigilant about the tradeoffs involved and not seek to retain its law enforcement powers if it has to compromise on its core activities and commitments in order to do so.

Regarding 2: The MAPAQ's mandate creates a close alignment with the animal agriculture sector, which in turn means that the ministry is not well placed to enforce animal welfare legislation when this impacts industry interests. A ministry such as the ministère de la Justice or a new ministry specially created for animal protection would not have a similar conflict of interest when it comes to enforcing animal welfare legislation. Hence, we recommend that the SPCA request that the Prime Minister's cabinet move the responsibility for the application of provincial animal protection laws from the MAPAQ to the ministère de la Justice.

Regarding 3: The Montreal SPCA cannot completely eliminate the risk of losing its law enforcement powers, and there may in fact be reasons to welcome the decision to let the police enforce the law. The Montreal SPCA should seek ways to mitigate any negative effects such a change would have on animals. By developing a training program for police officers, the SPCA could impart its knowledge and experience on a future generation of animal welfare law enforcers. Its role in developing such a program could be crucial in ensuring that law enforcement remains efficient and driven by the interests of animals, even when no longer under the auspices of the Montreal SPCA. By working with the police, the Montreal SPCA could also help maintain efficient enforcement of the law and responsiveness to any complaints of animal abuse.

6 Shelter Operations

6.A Plant-Based Food for Shelter Animals

Problem: Because the best interpretation of the SPCA mandate and of animal ethics leads to the long-term goal of ending all forms of animal exploitation (see Section 2.B) it seems clear that the SPCA should eventually serve only plant-based food to animal residents of the shelter. However, this could trigger a backlash from donors, employees, or volunteers who might have doubts that plant-based diets are appropriate for companion animals. If this backlash is strong enough, it could undermine the SPCA's capacity to actively advocate for animals, companion or farmed.

Recommendation: We recommend that, as a first step toward this goal, the Montreal SPCA transition the dogs at the shelter to plant-based food. The Montreal SPCA should communicate to the public that this is consistent with its mandate to protect both farmed and companion animals, with scientific knowledge that dogs can thrive on a plant-based diet as well as with Montreal's communal norms on responsible dog guardianship.

Reasoning: This may seem symbolic, but there is an important question of consistency and principle at stake: taking a public stance in defense of farmed animals may seem insincere when the Montreal SPCA chooses to feed factory-farmed animals to shelter residents. To continue feeding animal flesh to dogs, therefore, could be seen as implicitly reinforcing society's double standards about companion versus farmed animals. It implicitly says that it is appropriate to raise and kill farmed animals in order to feed our companion animals. It implicitly condones the instrumentalization of farmed animals in order to express our compassion for companion animals. It would surely be preferable if the SPCA could find a way not to reinforce that double standard in its own internal practices. And switching to plant-based food for dogs can be a way for the SPCA to proactively challenge the instrumentalization of farmed animals.

Why target dogs? To transition toward a consistent vegan stance, it might be useful to begin on a smaller scale, with a relatively self-contained issue. Plant-based food for dogs at the shelter seems a good test case. It relates in the first instance to the internal practices of the SPCA and so does not require negotiating with industry or government. Additionally, while the SPCA is inevitably involved in making tragic choices about which animals to save or kill, feeding farmed animals to dogs does not seem to fit into the category of a "tragic choice." Except for dogs who, for medical reasons, must be on a special diet that cannot be plant-based, there is no tragic necessity to feed meat to dogs. It may be inconvenient or expensive but shifting to a plant-based diet would not jeopardize the lives of other animals or humans. When social norms regarding what good dog guardians feed their dogs have changed, then options should be explored for moving residents of other species toward a plant-based diet when it is safe for their health.

How can this transition be made without losing public support? The risk of endangering public support is real, especially if the shift to a vegan diet is perceived as the SPCA imposing their own moral values on animals at the expense of animal welfare or as expressing moral disapproval of the practice of many benevolent "pet-lovers"[11] (and of many other animal shelters) who simply want to do what is best for their companions (and residents). If people are not already on board with the moral ideal that farmed animals have the same moral status as companion animals, a vegan shift is likely to put them on the defensive. Plenty of empirical evidence suggests that the more cherished a practice or an identity is, the more resistant it is to change. Indeed, the evidence shows that people tend to discount any information that contradicts their cherished practice or identity— for example, people may continue to believe that a vegan diet is nutritionally deficient, practically difficult, or financially infeasible no matter what the evidence shows. This seems to be what happened in the case of the Los Angeles Animal Services Commission's attempt to shift to plant-based food for its shelter dogs (see Chapter 5). We believe it crucial that the SPCA advocate change not as an outsider but as a trustworthy and loyal member of the Montreal community, one who demonstrates understanding and commitment to the communal norms. This requires the SPCA to go beyond giving principled moral arguments and hard scientific facts and to offer a reinterpretation of the norms of responsible "pet ownership" and love in ways that fit, rather than threaten, the collective self-understanding of the community of animal lovers.[12]

6.B Overpopulation and Living Environment in the Shelter

Problem: A general challenge for animal shelters is the restricted space for animals within their buildings, as well as the restricted budget on which they operate. These two factors determine how many animals the SPCA can take in, appropriately feed, and provide care for. On the one hand, the contracts the Montreal SPCA has with the city districts mean that animals cannot be turned away, and it is good to rescue as many animals as possible. On the other hand, the more crowded the shelter, the lower the quality of life of each resident, as living space for each animal is reduced and SPCA workers have less time for individual animals. If they are not adopted quickly or transferred to another organization, some animals may spend a very long time under these non-ideal conditions. This puts pressure on the Montreal SPCA not to take in stray animals who are not sterilized or who are at-risk. It might also lead the organization to release relinquished or found animals who are adoptable back into the streets after providing medical care and sterilization, following what is sometimes called a *stray cats return program* (SCRP) practice (i.e., a return to field [RTF] program) applied to socialized cats, or even kill them to avoid overcrowding in the shelter.

How should the Montreal SPCA balance these competing considerations: providing space and care for as many animals as possible while ensuring that each resident has a reasonable quality of life while at the shelter?

Recommendations: We recommend that all adoptable animals who are brought to the Montreal SPCA should be medically assisted, checked for microchips, spayed or neutered, kept in the shelter or placed with a foster family, and then put up for adoption. This includes companion animals who are surrendered to the society by their guardians, stray animals who are brought in by concerned community members, and animals picked up by shelter staff after having been reported as at risk by community members (all animals reported by community members, unless they are tagged and show no signs of being unsterilized or at-risk, should be examined by shelter staff).[13] Unchipped animals should be listed on a well-publicized website to improve their chances of being reunited with their guardians (see Section 7.A), and animals who are not claimed within a few days of being at the shelter should be sterilized, medically evaluated, and put up for adoption.

The SPCA should continue to pursue strategies that reduce the number of animals who need to be admitted and kept at the shelter, such as advocating for neutering of companion animals and organizing low-cost and accessible sterilization clinics for guardians with limited financial means. Other strategies proposed in this document (e.g., offering subsidized medical care to animals adopted from the SPCA; offering educational classes, animal training courses, or behavioral therapies to render adoption easier) could also help ease the overpopulation problem. The SPCA should also lobby for the prohibition of producing and selling companion animals by breeders and pet stores.

In addition, we recommend that the SPCA ask their Ethics Board to determine two numbers:

1. The number of animals housed at the SPCA at which *optimal* care can be provided for individual animals;
2. The maximum number of animals who can be housed at the SPCA while maintaining a *decent* quality of life for each resident.

These two numbers depend on the space available and the number of employees and volunteers who take care of the animals, as well as the budget (which covers food, veterinary costs, etc.). The Montreal SPCA should attempt to operate at, or below, the first number as much as possible.

During peak times (e.g., summer) or crises (e.g., confiscated animals), it may be necessary to go up to the maximum number; this may affect the residents' well-being but keeps it an acceptable level. If there is an emergency situation and the upper limit is reached, other options for the animals concerned should be explored (such as residency in other animal shelters) to secure the well-being of the animals as well as of SPCA employees. Schemes such as an "emergency fostering program" may also help ease this strain.

When it is not possible to find alternatives for these animals, it is appropriate to temporarily go beyond the maximum number of residents. Once operating above the maximum number, certain criteria that normally apply in other parts of the organization may need to be relaxed. Once the number of residents has again been reduced, the organization can revert back to its "regular" operating principles.

Reasoning: Ideally, there would be enough space at the Montreal SPCA for all animals in need. However, while a range of strategies may help reduce the number of animals in need, overpopulation is likely to remain a significant problem for the foreseeable future. Specifying the upper limit of animals who can be housed at the shelter while ensuring a decent quality of life does not do away with the problem of overpopulation: as an open-admission shelter, the Montreal SPCA cannot and should not turn away any animals brought to its doors or in need of rescue. However, the approach we suggest here allows for more systematic decision-making in response to this situation.

First, having these concrete numbers coupled with knowledge about anticipated spikes in numbers of animals brought to the shelter (e.g., during Montreal's moving season in July, when many companion animals are abandoned or lost) facilitates planning for these emergency situations, for example by having a list of emergency fosterers and maintaining good relationships with other responsible sheltering organizations and fostering networks in the province that can be called on to assist with these situations.

Second, certain rules that apply when the shelter is operating in its "ideal" range might be relaxed when the maximum number of animals has been exceeded. For example, it may be appropriate to adopt less strict rules for adoption than apply when the shelter is operating within its "ideal" range of residents. As we emphasize in Section 6.G, the Montreal SPCA should have in place certain screening procedures for prospective adopters to signal that animals have moral standing and that their well-being matters: the adoption process is an important opportunity for challenging people's views about the moral status of animals. At the same time, this goal must be weighed against the objective of ensuring that animals quickly find adoptive families; this is in the interest of the adopted animal but also frees up space and resources that the Montreal SPCA can use to help other animals. While during "regular" operation these tradeoffs may speak against certain adoption schemes (e.g., ones that use marketing language, such as "Adopt a cat and get a second one for free") the tradeoff may work out differently once the shelter reaches a point where overpopulation affect animals' well-being. Once the number of residents returns to the "ideal" range, the Montreal SPCA can revert back to its regular approach to adoption.

While this approach does not do away with the basic problem of overpopulation that characterizes the work of open-admission shelters, relying on specific numbers can facilitate strategic planning and more systematic decision-making. Allowing for the temporary relaxation of certain rules makes the Montreal SPCA more flexible in its approach but tying these temporary relaxations to specific numbers prevents arbitrariness and unfairness.

6.C Abortions

Problem: Many SPCAs face the problem of overpopulation: there are too many animals in need and not enough space, resources, and foster families to take care of all of them. Unneutered stray cats (but also other animals such as stray dogs) who frequently get pregnant are a notorious problem in many regions. If these animals are transferred to the Montreal SPCA, the SPCA must find housing and foster families for them and spend additional resources on the offspring. The SPCA is not an ideal place for animals to give birth as it is a stressful environment. Moreover, leaving pregnant animals on the street is not an acceptable option since newborns' chances of survival are rather low given the range of challenges they face, including parasites, deformations because of inbreeding, cold temperatures, lack of food and water, and car accidents. For the Montreal SPCA, this raises a difficult question: Is it ethical to end these animals' pregnancies and abort the fetuses?

Recommendations:
- The Montreal SPCA should continue to pursue strategies that reduce the need for abortions, such as the TNRM program (see Section 7.A) and public education. In cases of budget restraints, it seems advisable to focus on neutering female animals for reasons of efficiency.
- For pregnancies that aren't prevented through these efforts, aborting embryos and fetuses can be morally justified under

current circumstances (insufficient resources, not enough foster and adoptive families, etc.).

Reasoning: We must distinguish (1) the effect of the abortion on the embryos and fetus and (2) the effect of the abortion on the pregnant animal.

1. With respect to the fetus, early abortions pose less of an ethical issue than late abortions: early in pregnancy, embryos and fetuses are likely not yet sentient, not conscious, and do not have an interest in continued existence. While some research stipulates that animals do not become sentient and therefore cannot feel pain until after birth, these assessments are notoriously difficult to make. It is possible that the fetus becomes sentient during the pregnancy and therefore has an interest in continued existence. Note, however, that the interest that a fetus has in continuing to live is significantly weaker than the interest of an adult animal. This is simply because the fetus is not as invested in or psychologically connected with their future. A weaker interest in continued existence can be outweighed by other factors, notably the fact that, if not aborted, the life of the animal would be miserable if no foster family can be found or if the animal has to live on the street under deplorable conditions. If the fetuses are sentient, the abortion must be as quick and painless as possible for them. Lethal injections in the embryos before they are aborted may be used to reduce any suffering and distress to a minimum.

2. How does abortion affect the pregnant animal? Answering this question needs to be sensitive to both empirical and ethical questions. The empirical questions primarily relate to the effect of abortion on the pregnant animal's well-being. Most abortions are conducted by removing the uterus entirely. This certainly involves stress for the animal in question: anesthesia, surgery, recovery time for wound healing, etc. Furthermore, it is an open question whether pregnant animals are aware of

their pregnancy and their offspring. If they are not aware, then they are not harmed by being deprived from raising their offspring, making the abortion less of an issue. If, however, they are aware of losing their offspring and this causes psychological stress, this must be taken into consideration and weighed against other relevant considerations. The ethical question we must ask is whether sentient animals have procreative rights, especially when abortions involve removing the animal's uterus, thus depriving them of the option to procreate in the future. Prima facie, there are grounds for respecting animals' reproductive freedoms. However, pregnancy and raising babies can put considerable stress on animals, and not all animals may have an interest in reproducing. Furthermore, we currently live under non-ideal circumstances where many animals face deplorable circumstances. The physical and psychological effects of the abortion on the mother animal certainly matter ethically, but, given the restricted resources and lack of foster families, even late-term abortions seem ethically justified in the present circumstances.

6.D Ending Animal Lives

Employees of the SPCA frequently have to make decisions about whether to end the lives of animals in their care. Often, all such killing is simply referred to as "euthanasia," to indicate that the animal was killed painlessly, irrespective of *why* the animal was killed. This, however, obfuscates important distinctions that are crucial for making reasoned decisions about when it is morally appropriate to end an animal's life. We suggest here that the shelter adopt a narrow definition of "euthanasia" to distinguish it from other kinds of killing that are likely to occur in the shelter. More specifically, two kinds of cases must be kept separate.

The first kind of case involves animals who have a serious, terminal illness and/or are enduring unbearable suffering with little prospect of alleviation or recovery. The justification for ending an animal's life in this kind of case is that it will bring their immediate pain and suffering to an end. Ending the life of an animal for these reasons constitutes an act of *euthanasia*.

The second kind of case is more complex. The justification for ending an animal's life is not the animal's immediate well-being. Rather, shelter workers may decide to kill an animal in order to avoid some future or greater harm to the animal themselves or other animals. For example, it might be decided that an animal should be killed because the resources required to make them suitable for adoption would prevent the shelter from rescuing and rehoming many more animals. Ending the life of an animal for such reasons constitutes an act of *non-euthanasia killing*.

This section discusses each kind of case in turn and makes recommendations about how SPCA employees should think about the ending of animal life and what they should do, practically speaking, with regard to these two different kinds of circumstances.

Decisions About Euthanasia

Problem: Euthanasia involves ending the life of an animal who has a serious, terminal illness and/or is enduring unbearable suffering with little prospect of alleviation or recovery. While some cases of euthanasia will be clearly justified and, indeed, required (see Section 2.D), other cases may be more difficult to judge. The difficulty arises because it is not always easy to tell when an animal's interest in continued life is cancelled out by the presence of prolonged and acute pain and suffering. That is, it can be difficult to judge when an animal's quality of life has decreased to the point where killing them is the morally right thing to do.

Recommendation: When an animal's quality of life is so low that, on balance, it no longer has an interest in continued life, it is morally permissible to euthanize them. We recommend that, for decisions about such cases, the Ethics Board (see Section 3.B) devise a decision tree that can be employed to help with such choices. The decision tree should only refer to cases of genuine euthanasia (i.e., cases where the animal's quality of life has been severely and permanently diminished). Moreover, items included in the decision tree should be empirically verifiable as indicators of good or diminished quality of life, and sensitive to species as well as individual differences (along the lines we suggest in Section 2.E).

In its internal discussions as well as public documents, the SPCA should clearly distinguish between genuine cases of euthanasia and cases where an animal is killed for other reasons.

Reasoning: The interest that animals have in continued life depends on their health and opportunities for a minimally good life. In cases where animal well-being is severely and permanently compromised and where there is little opportunity for a minimally good life, it would be better for those animals to have their lives ended.

Transparency about which animals are killed by the SPCA is crucial for good public relations and for ensuring that the SPCA is accountable. For example, many animal shelters have been subject to scrutiny and criticism for "euthanizing" animals for the wrong kinds of reasons, which has resulted in a public backlash in the form of unfavorable media coverage, decreased donations, and reduced volunteering.

Decisions About Morally Permitted Non-Euthanasia Killing

Problem: Given the non-ideal conditions in which the SPCA is working, the number of animals in need of care is often far greater than the time and resources available to provide that care adequately. While the SPCA is committed to only killing animals in cases of genuine euthanasia, as defined above, in non-ideal conditions there may be circumstances in which killing for non-euthanasia reasons is the only morally appropriate course of action for shelter workers. In these other cases, factors are present that make the animal either unsuitable for adoption, significantly reduce the likelihood of them being adopted, or mean that they would require significant resources (e.g., expensive medical treatment, behavioral therapy) in order to become suitable for adoption. Animals who are difficult to rehome are a significant drain on SPCA resources, and they are likely to experience diminished quality of life the longer that they reside in the shelter. Several kinds of case present themselves.

- Animals who are difficult to rehome due to species characteristics (e.g., exotic species who require very specific care and environment which are difficult to find in adoptive homes).
- Animals who are difficult to rehome due to severe problems in behavior and temperament (e.g., animals who have exhibited aggressive behavior, which suggests that they may be a danger to other animals, humans, or themselves). Similarly, animals who suffer from severe separation anxiety or phobias.
- Animals who are difficult to rehome due to a chronic medical condition(s) that potential adopters will find difficult and/or costly to treat and/or manage (e.g., type 1 diabetes, arthritis, and kidney disease).
- Animals who would be easy to rehome but have a temporary or curable medical condition(s) that is difficult and/or costly for the shelter to treat and/or manage, such as ringworm.

The problem facing the SPCA is what to do with animals of these kinds who have medical, behavioral, and species-specific needs that make the prospect of them being rehomed very unlikely or their care very costly.

Recommendations: In the first instance, the SPCA should seek to introduce practical measures that would reduce the need for killing. This would include (but is by no means limited to):

- Adopting programs that reduce the number of animals that come into existence (e.g., the TNRM program, as discussed in Section 7.A).
- Moving animals who are unlikely to be adopted from Site A to Site B (as mentioned in Recommendation 1, Section 3.A above), where they can have a long-term or even permanent home.
- Continuing to fund rehabilitation and socialization programs for animals with behavioral and psychological problems.
- Devising ways of keeping animals and their guardians together to reduce the number of animals surrendered to the shelter. One such way would be to help guardians meet the medical needs of their animals; see Section 7.B.

- Initiating a public campaign to increase the number of voluntary foster carers and offer training on how to respond to common medical or behavioral problems.
- Considering campaigns that lower obstacles to adoption, such as the SPCA's petition to encourage landlords to permit renters to have companion animals in their homes.

Aside from these practical measures, the SPCA should also actively investigate other long-term solutions that can help achieve this goal, including advocacy work.

Insofar as the SPCA continues to admit all animals who need assistance it should not adopt a no-kill policy. Instead, the SPCA should set its ideal "live release rate" and make its goal—and its strategy for achieving that goal—public.

We also recommend that the Montreal SPCA ask the Ethics Board to devise a decision tree for cases of non-euthanasia killing to help staff make decisions about individual cases. This decision tree would ultimately help to distinguish between cases of impermissible and permissible killings. Moreover, a decision tree could help staff to determine when non-euthanasia killing is not only morally permissible but also morally required. The importance of clear and systematic decision-making procedures should not be underestimated. Given that killing animals with an interest in continued life is a grave wrong, SPCA staff must ensure that they have adequate justification for the act of killing, and a decision tree would help to ensure that they do.

It is important to stress that this recommendation is only necessary under the very non-ideal conditions that the SPCA often operates in. Outside of these conditions—when time and resources are available and demand low—non-euthanasia killing is morally wrong and therefore not permitted. Hence, killing animals for non-euthanasia reasons is a serious moral matter and although very challenging circumstances may permit, and sometimes require, SPCA staff to end animal lives for non-euthanasia reasons, staff must not become complacent about killing animals who have a significant interest in continued life. Indeed, the Montreal SPCA must always act with a view to realizing the ideal goal of never killing an animal who could have a minimally decent life if time and resources were no issue.

Reasoning: There is a crucial difference between euthanasia, which is always morally permissible (or even required), and other instances of killing that are only rendered permissible because of the non-ideal setting in which the SPCA works. Ultimately, animals killed in these circumstances often have a strong interest in continued life because they may have, or at least have the capacity for, a minimally decent standard of well-being. While killing in these cases may, in specific circumstances, be morally permitted, the animals in question are nonetheless wronged because their interest in continuing to live is set back. Ideally, the SPCA would never kill an animal that has an interest in continued life.

The interest that animals have in continued life means that the SPCA should do all that it can to ensure that animal lives are not ended unless there is a genuine case for euthanasia. Many of the recommendations suggested here are ways of increasing the number of animals who leave the shelter alive and decreasing the number of animals who need rescue in the first place. When taken in conjunction with the SPCA's core values, the discussion of ending animal lives indicates that the SPCA must be committed to making the task of lifesaving a priority of its operations.

Nonetheless, given the challenges faced by the SPCA, killing may, for the time being, remain a necessary part of standard operational procedures. Insofar as the SPCA maintains an open admission policy there may be times when it struggles to care for and assist all the animals in need with the limited resources that it has. We suggest that killing in some cases is, in these non-ideal conditions, morally justified because the lack of time, resources, staff (particularly those with specific specializations, e.g., dog trainers), and appropriate adoptive homes makes some individuals regrettably burdensome in a way that justifies killing them. Indeed, in some cases the costs involved in saving one animal (including harms that accrue to other animals because fewer resources are available to help them) may mean that, on some occasions, non-euthanasia killing is not merely morally permissible but also morally required—it may, in deeply regrettable circumstances, be the morally right thing to do.

This does not mean that an animal who is killed for non-euthanasia reasons is not wronged. Rather, the animal is wronged, but shelter workers have reasons that justify or require killing. The two main reasons that might justify killing are (a) when the prospect of the animal having a good life in the long-term is very unlikely (e.g., if they are very unlikely to be rehomed or are too unsafe to be rehomed and an adequate alternative arrangement cannot be found) and/or (b) when the animal requires a large amount of time and resources which could be used for other animals who stand a better chance of leading a good life and being adopted.

When faced with no other option, these reasons may permit shelter staff to end the life of an animal for whom death was not in their best interest. However, since the animal has a significant interest in continued life, they have a right not to be killed and killing violates that right. Importantly, the perpetrator of this wrong is not the SPCA or the individual who carries out the act of killing—those agents only do what is best in an otherwise tragic situation. Rather, the state and, more broadly, all members of the political community are responsible for the wrong done to animals killed in this kind of case.[14] This is because non-euthanasia killings occur as a direct consequence of the distributive injustice allowed by the current political and economic institutional order. If the SPCA had appropriate state funding, then shelter staff would not have to make difficult decisions about who to save. Since shelter staff have very little influence over the institutions and policies that create the moral tragedy they face, they will often bear little to no responsibility for the wrong done to the animals killed. This explains how some instances of non-euthanasia killing are morally permitted, which means the shelter workers are permitted to perform the killing, and yet the animal is still wronged—a wrong perpetrated by the state and the wider political community.

All that said, it is important that the SPCA is transparent about which animals have their lives ended and why. As mentioned above, being transparent about this is crucial to good public relations since it leaves little opportunity for accusations of deception. Moreover, setting a public goal might have the additional benefit of garnering public support. By making it clear what the SPCA wants to achieve and how it can achieve it, they can make their agenda a community project. In this way, members of the public may be more willing to support the SPCA through donations, volunteering their time, or by offering to care for foster animals.

This final point is not just a matter of prudence. The unjust social circumstances that have led to more animals needing rescue than the SPCA has resources to care for is a burden that the entire community is responsible for. By working with members of the public, the SPCA can raise awareness about how animals are being failed by the current institutional system and cultivate an ethos of responsibility. In this way, the SPCA can work to promote a better society in which domesticated animals are regarded as full members of the community who are deserving of care and respect.

6.E Palliative Care

Problem: Some animals are terminally ill but have not yet reached a state where their quality of life is so low that euthanasia is appropriate. Currently, the SPCA has a palliative care program for these animals. This program provides medical care at the end of the life of these animals to alleviate their suffering before death. Many animals are placed in foster families for this, and the SPCA pays for the medical care involved. The SPCA thereby keeps the right to make medical decisions about the animal (except if the family adopts the animal, in which case they become responsible for the costs of the animal's medical care). As this program is cost- and time-intensive (foster families have to be found, etc.), there is disagreement about its use: Would it be better to kill these animals rather than expending time and resources on their palliative care?

Recommendation: We recommend that the SPCA keep its palliative care program in place for animals for whom palliative care is in their best interest (i.e., animals who can have a reasonably good life if placed in a foster family). Animals whose quality of life is so low that euthanasia is appropriate (see Section 6.D) are not suitable for the palliative care program.

Reasoning: While palliative care programs are resource-intensive, they provide proper care for those animals who are terminally ill but who have not yet reached a point where their quality of life has become so low that euthanasia is appropriate. By giving these animals the opportunity to benefit from the goods that life has to offer, the palliative care program protects animals' interest in continued life. The palliative care program also creates positive relationships between an animal and specific human beings at a crucial stage of the animal's life. This is precisely the kind of relationship that would exist in a more just world so this program also plays the important role of prefiguring more just circumstances. Finally, the palliative care program signals to the general public that animals matter— even when they are old, have chronic health issues, or are terminally ill. In this way, the palliative care program contributes to the objective of changing norms and attitudes regarding animals.

6.F Exotic Animals

Problem: Among the animals sheltered by the SPCA, some are exotic (e.g., turtles, guinea pigs, snakes, iguanas, and parrots). There are currently no specific guidelines for these animals. One issue is that neither the shelter nor prospective adopters can provide a good environment for them: a parrot should ideally live in a flock, a snake shouldn't be longer than its vivarium, and many lights are needed to keep iguanas warm from nose to tail. SPCA staff estimate that only 1% or 2% of "adopters" can provide a suitable environment for these animals. The fact that many exotic animals have long life expectancies (e.g., turtles live for 30–40 years) heightens this problem. Prospective adopters often take in such animals even though they do not have a plan for the animal's whole life.

Recommendation: Ideally, exotic animals would be placed with families or sanctuaries that can meet their needs. For many exotic animals, this will not be a viable option, given the difficulty of meeting their needs. Site B (discussed in Section 3.A) could also be an appropriate home for these animals. However, given exotic animals' often highly specific needs and requirements, realistic options for these animals will likely compromise their well-being in certain ways. When this is the case, staff must assess the quality of life these animals can have in such non-ideal conditions; if no option can be found that ensures that the animal has a life worth living, it may be required to end their life.

Reasoning: Though exotic animals are difficult to care for, they have an interest in continued life as well as an interest in the necessities that make a minimally decent level of well-being possible. Ideally, exotic animals would be placed in appropriate adoptive homes to protect these interests, either in private homes or in sanctuaries. This, however, is a realistic possibility only for a small fraction of them, given the often very specific needs of exotic animals that can be difficult to meet in a private household. Given the difficulty of finding appropriate homes, a permanent home with the SPCA may be the only option for some of these animals. Of course, this solution is less than ideal and will only be possible if there are resources available to support the care of these animals at Site B.

When exotic animals cannot be adopted or permanently housed at the SPCA or with other organizations, there are three further options: placing them in homes that aren't ideal for them, releasing them into the wild, or considering ending their lives as an instance of morally permissible killing (see Section 6.D). At this point, much depends on the quality of life of these animals in non-ideal conditions: if they can have a life worth living either in non-ideal foster homes or in the wild, these options should be preferred; otherwise, it would be better to end their lives (see Section 6.D, non-euthanasia killing). It is therefore crucial to assess these animals' quality of life in non-ideal conditions—that is, in the non-ideal environment that we can expect them to have both in foster homes and in the wild.

6.G Adoption Process
Problem: Finding adoptive families for its residents is a central aspect of the Montreal SPCA's activities. On the one hand, a smooth

and straightforward adoption process can place animals quickly in their new homes, ease overpopulation within the shelter, and prevent prospective adopters from turning to breeders or pet shops. On the other hand, a more demanding adoption process, in which prospective adopters are asked to make various commitments with respect to the treatment of the adopted animal, can ensure that animals are matched with families that can meet their specific needs and reduce the number of animals who do not have an adequate quality of life in their new homes, are returned to the shelter, or even abandoned. This is particularly important because not all adoptive families are equally able or willing to provide good homes for the animals they adopt, and there are good reasons for SPCA staff to investigate each prospective adopter's motives for adopting as well as their capacity to offer a good home to the animal.

Recommendations: We must find an appropriate balance between, on the one hand, wanting to make the adoption process as quick and easy as possible to reduce the number of animals in the shelter and, on the other, making the process more thorough to ensure that adopters are aware of what it means to adopt an animal and the responsibilities they are taking on and that the adopted animals' welfare is secured.

We recommend that the adoption process include:

1. A conversation between the prospective adopter and a member of staff to discuss the needs of the animal to be adopted, provide information on how to respond to problems that may arise (e.g., what to do when cats scratch furniture), and dispel false beliefs that prospective adopters might have (e.g., explain what declawing involves). Staff should be trained so that they can engage in a friendly and nonconfrontational way with prospective adopters while also gaining relevant information about their intentions and the kind of environment they will be able to provide for the animal, etc. Staff should ensure that would-be adopters are committed to:

    a. meeting the needs of the adopted animal and seeking assistance (from the SPCA or a vet) if there are concerns about the animal's well-being or behavior;

    b. meeting general requirements, such as not to physically punish the animal for bad behavior, not to leave the animal alone for extended periods of time, not to abandon the animal when family circumstances change, etc.;

    c. meeting species-specific requirements (e.g., that cats not be declawed);

    d. meeting any requirements specific to the animal who is to be adopted (e.g., to provide a certain amount of exercise per day in the case of a dog known to require a lot of physical activity).

2. An adoption form, to be signed by the adopter, that formalizes these commitments.

3. A phone call by the SPCA to the adoptive family after the adoption to ask how the animal is settling into their new home and to answer any questions that may have arisen.

Staff should encourage adopters to contact the SPCA in case of any problems with the animal and highlight the possibility of returning the animal if problems cannot be resolved (e.g., if the adopted animal does not get along with already existing companion animals in the household).

If, at any stage of the adoption process, the staff member suspects that the prospective adopter is unable or unwilling to provide appropriate care for the animal they are hoping to adopt, the staff member should refuse the adoption.

We caution against an "open adoption" approach that includes special events, such as "Adoption Days" where adoption fees are waived or reduced to encourage adoption, because the way such events are often publicized ("Adopt an animal and get a second for free!") could undermine the important message that animals and their well-being matters and that the decision to adopt comes with responsibilities and should be taken seriously. During times of overpopulation, it may be necessary and appropriate to consider such events to reduce the number of animals in the shelter (see Section 6.B). However, the tone of such events must always reflect the seriousness of adoption and that the relaxation of adoption procedures is only a temporary measure in response to a crisis situation.

We recommend that the Montreal SPCA offer as much information as possible to the adoptive families, as well as educational classes, animal training courses, or online advice on how to solve behavioral problems.

Reasoning: The SPCA must strike an appropriate balance between competing goals. On the one hand, they must not make the process so burdensome that it requires too many SPCA resources or becomes an obstacle for prospective adopters, thereby reducing the numbers of animals that are adopted. On the other hand, it is important to ensure that adoptive families can provide good homes for the animals they seek to adopt and also that the adoption process communicates to members of the public that animals and their well-being matter.

Our recommendations are based on the understanding that it is important to assess whether or not adopters can provide appropriate homes for the animal they hope to adopt and to use the interaction to raise awareness of animals' interests and the seriousness of adoption. Asking prospective adopters to sign commitments (e.g., not to declaw their cats, to provide physical activity) encourages adopters to treat their adopted animals well and signals to the adopter the importance of the animal's needs but is not so intrusive or burdensome that would-be adopters would be discouraged from adopting.

Special adoption "events," on the other hand, especially those that are almost "party"-like or holiday-themed, are problematic because there is a risk that they attract adopters whose decision to adopt is not well considered. In addition, such events can undermine the message that adoption decisions require careful consideration and should not be made on a whim and thus be inconsistent with the norms the SPCA should communicate to the public (see Section 2.A). While special adoption events may be necessary in cases of overpopulation, their tone must be consistent with the seriousness of the animals' well-being.

A considerable proportion of failed adoptions (when an adopted animal is brought back to the shelter, given away, sold, or killed) are caused by unrealistic expectations and lack of resources or knowledge to overcome the behavioral problems of the animal (like not using the litter box or barking at everyone, for instance). Therefore, staff should make sure to give as much information as possible to the adoptive families and offer training classes or advice on how to solve the behavioral issues the adopted animals might have.

6.H Information About "Breeds"

Problem: The breeding of companion animals reflects the problematic assumption that animals can be altered to meet to humans' aesthetic preferences, for example by making their noses flatter or their legs shorter. Many breeding practices leave animals with significant health problems in addition to reinforcing the problematic belief that animals exist to meet our needs and satisfy our aesthetic preferences.

Recommendations:

- The SPCA should not seek to determine or keep on record the "breeds" of specific animals, such as "Siamese" for cats or "Golden Retriever" for dogs.
- SPCA staff should decline requests from adopters for specific breeds unless there is an appropriate reason for the adopter to be concerned about breed (e.g., when adopters have allergies that respond better to some breeds than others). When "breed" is used as shorthand for specific characteristics (e.g., adopters request a specific dog breed because their home cannot accommodate a large dog), SPCA staff should ascertain the required characteristics with the adopter to match them with a shelter animal.
- SPCA staff should consider educating adopters looking for specific breeds about problematic breeding practices and resulting health problems for animals.

Reasoning: In light of the problems that breeding has caused for animals, it is important that organizations such as the SPCA not support breeding practices and oppose them whenever possible. By refusing to identify individual animals' breeds or respond to adopters' requests for specific breeds, and by seeking conversations about these issues with members of the public, the SPCA can signal its opposition to breeding practices.

6.1 Dangerous Animals and Behavioral Issues

Problem: Animals who arrive at the SPCA can have behavioral issues that make them dangerous for other animals or humans, for example because they have been abused, traumatized, or simply not socialized. This is especially problematic in the case of large dogs. Many such animals can overcome these problems with appropriate medical care and behavioral training, often to the point where they could be adopted into a home. However, this training is typically very time-consuming and usually cannot be provided on SPCA premises. In addition, making exact assessments of whether or not an animal still presents a risk to others is difficult. If an animal adopted from the SPCA subsequently turns out to be aggressive toward others, this could lead to negative responses to the Montreal SPCA, especially because animals who attack humans often receive significant media attention. Recent debates about "dangerous breeds" of dogs have heightened public attention to this issue.

Recommendations:

- In its interactions with the media and the public, the Montreal SPCA should resist the idea that certain breeds of dogs are inherently dangerous and emphasize that behavioral issues affect individual animals—often as a result of abuse and mistreatment.
- The Montreal SPCA should continue to emphasize that rehabilitation and behavioral therapy should be provided for dangerous or aggressive animals and that it is unethical for courts to order that aggressive or dangerous dogs be killed without serious efforts at rehabilitation having been made.

- The Montreal SPCA should continue to partner with therapists and vets who can help dogs with behavioral problems to maximize the number of animals who can be successfully treated and rehabilitated.
- The Montreal SPCA should not put up for adoption animals for whom there is a risk that they could be a danger to other animals or to humans. Exceptions could be made in cases where the adopter has expertise in dealing with dogs with behavioral problems (e.g., people with veterinary training) and/or can provide a particularly suitable environment (e.g., people with large properties, allowing the dog to be isolated from "triggers").
- Site B, discussed in Section 3.A, could be a long-term home for dogs who are no longer dangerous if given appropriate care.
- Animals who remain a danger to others despite behavioral therapy might be candidates for permissible killing (as discussed in Section 6.D).

Reasoning: Our recommendations seek to address the problem from different angles. First, educating the public about the behavioral problems animals may develop as a result of abuse and mistreatment could help increase compassion toward individual animals. Since the idea that particular dog breeds are aggressive and inherently dangerous contributes to misperceptions, this also needs to be addressed in communications with the public. Second, care and therapy can address behavioral problems to the point where animals become adoptable or can live out their lives on SPCA premises.

7 Animals in the Community

7.A Community Cats and the TNRM Program

Montreal has a large population of community cats—cats who have no "owner." Some of them are socialized cats who have gotten lost or have been abandoned by their guardians, whereas others are feral cats, some of whom are better equipped to survive outside. Many of these cats are not sterilized and procreate rapidly. As a result, a large number of cats are condemned to wander the city's alleys and many suffer from cold, thirst, hunger, diseases, accidents, fights with other animals, or random acts of cruelty from humans.

In this section we outline how the SPCA should deal with sociable community cats, feral colony cats, and feral non-colony cats.

Adoptable Community Cats

Problem: There are many free-roaming cats who have been abandoned by humans, kittens seemingly without mothers, cats who are lost, and community cats who spend their time with humans but are not "owned" by anyone in particular. These cats are usually brought to the shelter by a concerned member of the public or picked up by the Montreal SPCA after having been reported as at risk by a community member. At-risk cats include those who, whatever their state of health, have no clear identification (e.g., a collar with ID tag) and so potentially no human guardian. Given the limited resources of the Montreal SPCA, it may be difficult to house all these animals for adoption. Consequently, stray cats who are brought to the shelter may be vulnerable to non-euthanasia killing discussed in Section 6.D of these guidelines.

One increasingly popular practice among progressive shelters is *return to field* (RTF), applied to non-feral cats.[15] When a member of the public brings a healthy, at-risk cat to the shelter or reports such a cat to be picked up by animal control services, shelters with an RTF program will endeavor to leave or return the cat to where they were originally found as part of what is sometimes called a *stray cats return program* (SCRP) or *shelter, neuter, and release* (SNR) program. There are several reasons why RTF programs have gained popularity. First, they have reduced the need for non-euthanasia killing at shelters. Second, there is some evidence that unchipped lost cats are more likely to be reunited with their owners if they remain where they are. Third, kittens who may seem abandoned are often not; the mother may simply be absent because she is looking for food. Thus, bringing the kittens into a shelter may result in a worse outcome for them than if they are returned to the place where their mother expects to find them.

While it has been argued that RTF has made a significant contribution to the reduction of non-euthanasia killing at some shelters, the practice of leaving at-risk, non-feral cats outdoors or returning them to where they were found raises two main concerns. First, not all cats are equal. While RTF may be appropriate for cats who are sterilized and have experience of living on the streets, not all community cats who are brought to the shelter have the skills necessary to survive outdoors. Many free-roaming, at-risk cats are lost or abandoned, and, since they are used to having humans satisfy their basic needs for food, water, and shelter, they may find it difficult to meet these needs themselves and may experience considerable distress having no guardian to seek out. Moreover, if they are ill-equipped to navigate the dangers of the local environment, they will be vulnerable to injury or death caused by road traffic accidents or wild animals, for instance. Even cats who are well adapted to living outside are likely to experience suffering and die prematurely. Second, not all environments are equal. The ability of a cat to survive outside of human domiciles very much depends on the conditions that they are being left in or returned to. While in some settings the conditions may be quite favorable, other locations are far more hostile. So, while RTF may be a promising strategy in places that have a temperate climate and quiet roads, cats in less favorable conditions may face premature death or injury.

Recommendations: Each cat who is brought to the shelter should be evaluated (the criteria used for this evaluation should be adopted in consultation with the Ethics Board; see Section 3.B). All animals who are reported by a member of the public, if they are suspected to be at-risk, should be brought to the shelter for an assessment of their general condition. All healthy, at-risk animals who are friendly and able to live with humans should be checked for a microchip, medically assisted, sterilized, and put up for adoption. For those animals who might have been lost, we recommend that the Montreal SPCA develop effective practices to reunite them with their human caregivers before putting the unclaimed animals up for adoption. Feral cats should be directed to a TNRM program.

Reasoning: Many stray cats are taken or reported to the Montreal SPCA by concerned community members because they are either lost, abandoned by humans, or, in the case of some kittens, orphaned or abandoned by their mothers. These animals have very little chance of living a minimally decent life because they are vulnerable to injury, attacks, starvation, dehydration, or being involved in road traffic accidents. Failing to rescue these animals when they are reported as at risk or returning these animals to where they were found may significantly compromise their well-being before ultimately leading to their premature death. Given the threats, hazards, and challenges that face community cats who do not have human guardians, all those who can live happily with humans have an interest in having their basic needs met by adoptive humans. This means that such animals should be brought to and kept at the shelter or placed in foster families until adoption. Not to bring these animals to the shelter or to subsequently return them to where they were found would be to expose them to a dangerous and uncertain future. Applying the practice of RTF to animals who are particularly vulnerable and who could benefit from being adopted (a practice also known as SCRP or SNR) standardly involves the withdrawal of assistance by the shelter and is equal to abandonment. Since the SPCA has a responsibility to secure decent life prospects for animals in need whenever it can, it should always take in community cats who are sociable or who could be socialized and try its best to find good adoptive families for them. It is not morally acceptable to apply RTF to sociable community cats as a way of resolving the shelter overpopulation problem.

It is also important to acknowledge that policies that have worked for shelters elsewhere may not be right for the Montreal SPCA. A handful of formal studies have been undertaken at specific shelters or in specific regions that speak in favor of RTF applied to sociable community cats. However, both the small sample sizes and variability in context make it difficult to be confident that RTF is always effective to reduce the number of animals dying prematurely. RTF is often run alongside other programs (like TNR-type programs), which can make it difficult to ascertain how much RTF is responsible for decreases in non-euthanasia killing and admissions. Finally, much of the existing research focuses on the impact that RTF has on shelter admissions and non-euthanasia killing and less on the wellbeing of those cats returned to their original location. Though there is some limited evidence that suggests that RTF does not lead to an increase in the number of cats dying on the streets, we need to know that returned cats are not enduring lives of misery and suffering before we can be confident that RTF without a designated guardian is morally acceptable.

The Montreal SPCA should develop more effective practices to reunite lost animals and their human caregivers. As long as citizens are not aware that lost animals are often brought to the SPCA's shelter, they won't think to look there to find their lost companion. To remedy this problem, different strategies might be employed including a regularly updated page for lost animals on the SPCA website and making sure that municipalities widely advertise this service to their citizens. The SPCA might also make use of Facebook groups and other social media neighborhood groups such as Nextdoor to raise awareness of the SPCA's website and its announcements on animals who are lost and found.

Feral Colony Cats

Problems: In response to the large population of community cats, the Montreal SPCA has initiated a TNRM program. This program covers cats who are not socialized, do not have the temperament to live with humans, and live in colonies with other cats. When a local resident takes care of community cats in their neighborhood by providing them with shelter, water, and food, they can be recognized by the City of Montreal as responsible for a cat colony and benefit from the TNRM program at the Montreal SPCA. This means that they, as colony caretakers, can trap cats and bring them to the SPCA for free medical treatment, sterilization, and ear tipping. The cats will then be returned to the colony caretaker to be released near shelters, food, and water sources. The goal of this program is to reduce the community cat population and provide non-adoptable cats with what they need to have at least a minimally decent life in the usually difficult circumstances they face.

Though this program has largely been a success, it has raised several concerns. First, those who take responsibility for community cats don't always have the means to trap the cats, bring them to the SPCA for sterilization, and offer a space for the sterilized cats to recuperate. Second, the sterilization procedure violates cats' interest in bodily integrity and is highly stressful for them. Finally, local residents are often critical of TNRM program because they perceive free-roaming cats as a public health problem and a nuisance (because of odors, noise, etc.). Some of them would prefer for the cats to be killed than fed and sheltered by their neighbors.

Recommendations: The TNRM program should be maintained, supported, and expanded along the following lines:

- The Montreal SPCA should continue to convince municipalities of the virtues of the program and encourage them to provide more support to citizens who are willing to take care of community cats.
- New and less invasive methods of contraception should be employed if/when available.
- The Montreal SPCA should seek to educate citizens about the benefits of the program for both residents and feral cats.
- The possibility of expanding this program to other liminal animals (raccoons, squirrels, rats, etc.) should be explored.

Reasoning: An efficient TNRM program for all feral cats combined with a mechanism for placing socialized cats in adoptive families is likely to be the most efficient way to reduce the number of free-roaming cats, which in turn would reduce inconvenience to residents.

Indeed, the TNRM program is much more effective than either ignoring the apparently healthy feral colony cats (who will rapidly reproduce) or killing them (which violates the animals' interests in being provided with assistance). Moreover, killing the cats instead of neutering and releasing them might create what is called the "vacuum effect," whereby cats who are removed from their environment are soon replaced by other cats who are drawn in by the available resources. This means that the problem of overpopulation remains. By contrast, when sterilized and released under the supervision of a designated colony caretaker, community cats use the resources that nonsterilized cats would otherwise have had at their disposal, which over time leads to a decrease in the overall population. Informing local residents and councils about the vacuum effect could strengthen their support for TNRM program. The Montreal SPCA should continue in its efforts to convince municipalities to participate in the TNRM program.

If available, contraceptive methods that are less invasive than traditional, surgical sterilization, could enhance the efficacy of the TNRM program. For example, oral contraceptives that could be added to the cats' food could reach a much larger number of cats than if they had to be brought to the SPCA for surgery. They would also reduce the need for cats to go through capture, surgery, and recovery and thus make the program much less stressful. A reduction in surgical sterilization would also free up SPCA resources.

Feral Non-Colony Community Cats

Problem: The TNRM program applies to feral cats who are brought to the SPCA by colony caretakers for medical assistance, sterilization, and ear tipping. The TNRM program was put in place as a way of assuming the responsibility to rescue community cats who, because they are not good candidates for adoption and still have an interest in staying alive, should be allowed to live outside, in the neighborhood they are used to, while benefiting from necessary help to survive or better deal with the difficult conditions of a semi-wild life. The TNRM program not only helps to limit the community cat population but also to meet feral cats' basic needs without impeding their agency. The "maintain" part of the program strengthens their ability to thrive even in the harsh conditions of homelessness. However, because this program is currently limited to cats who live as part of colonies, it leaves non-colony cats in a situation where they face either non-euthanasia killing at the shelter or the high risks of suffering from cold, thirst, hunger, accidents, attacks, etc. if left to fend for themselves.

Recommendation: We recommend the extension of the TNRM program to non-colony feral cats. Those community cats who are not good candidates for adoption and who will likely (with human assistance) thrive living a semi-wild life where they were found should be returned to that location and be placed under the responsibility of a designated citizen who will provide them with shelter, food, water, and basic medical assistance. The Montreal SPCA, with the collaboration of the city of Montreal, should support the caregivers of those individual community cats through the TNRM program.

Reasoning: Non-colony community cats, even if they were born in the streets and are used to its dangers, face a high risk of suffering and death. Still, they have an interest in continued life. The RTF practice is presented as an effective means to avoid killing these healthy animals. But it is misleading to think that we must make a choice between leaving these cats to fend for themselves or killing them. A third, more morally appropriate, option is available: extending the TNRM program to those feral cats who do not live in colonies.

This policy would see feral non-colony cats treated similarly to those who live in colonies. An individual cat who is trapped either by a community member or by an SPCA officer and brought to the shelter must be evaluated to determine their temperament and fitness for "extended TNRM" (i.e., TNRM applied to feral, non-colony cats). The precise criteria for assessing suitability for RTF should be determined in collaboration with the Ethics Board but, as noted above, any cat who is socialized or has a temperament suited to living with humans will not be suitable for extended TNRM. Feral non-colony cats are not socialized and/or do not have a temperament suited to living with humans, so they may be eligible for TNRM provided they are not seriously unhealthy, disabled, declawed, very young, or inexperienced. Once the cat has been deemed suitable for the extended TNRM program, they should be medically examined and treated, sterilized, ear-tipped, and assigned to a designated citizen living near their home area. The designated citizen will be responsible for ensuring that the cat is able to meet their basic needs by providing food, water and shelter as appropriate. As part of the extended TNRM program, the Montreal SPCA should support citizens who care for feral non-colony cats by offering assistance with trapping and transportation when a cat needs to be brought to the SPCA shelter for medical treatment, as well as professional advice regarding how to take care of those non-socialized cats.

For all feral cats, irrespective of whether they live in colonies or not, the Montreal SPCA should aim to encourage citizens to get involved in helping them so as to develop a network of residents ready to take on responsibility for these cats. It should also negotiate with the city of Montreal so that it allows the maintenance of temporary shelters, encourages the donation of food that designated citizens can feed the community cats, and prohibits the removal of food and water stations. This is important for a number of reasons. First, it improves the lives of community cats, who often suffer immensely, particularly during the harsh Montreal winters. Second, supporting feral cats in their own communities and environments is a way of recognizing and facilitating their agency. Third, acknowledging and accepting the presence of community cats in our cities is a step toward more just relationships: in a more just world, we would accept that these animals have a right to our shared territory and carve out a space in which these communities can flourish. This involves caring for these animals in ways that facilitate their agency (e.g., by providing additional food sources or responding to medical emergencies).

Some of these efforts could be extended to other urban animals who—like squirrels, racoons, pigeons, or rats—are often considered nuisances and stigmatized in public discourse. For example, certain aspects of the TNRM program could also be adapted to other kinds of animals that live in the city. Non-domesticated animals are of course much better equipped to deal with life outside than is the case for socialized cats, and they are not suitable for adoption. However, there might be reasons to consider ways to reduce their numbers through non-surgical contraception measures.

Additionally, the SPCA could encourage citizens to rely on nonfatal methods for preventing rodents or raccoons from entering their houses rather than using traps or poison. By emphasizing that we share our cities with urban wildlife and by identifying how we can coexist with them, organizations such as the SPCA can help change people's attitudes toward these animals, which is a crucial step toward the creation of more just relationships.

7.B Veterinary Care for Companion Animals Outside the Shelter

Problem: Private veterinary care can be expensive, and guardians can find themselves unable to afford important medical care for their animals. This can lead to situations where guardians forego treatment or even abandon their animal.

Recommendation: We recommend that the SPCA investigate the possibility of providing low-cost veterinary care for animals who have been adopted from the SPCA, for families on low incomes. Free services of capture, transportation, and veterinary care should also be offered to community cat caregivers under the TNRM program.

Reasoning: It is highly problematic when animals don't receive veterinary treatment or are abandoned because their guardians cannot afford their medical care. The lack of affordable veterinary care also increases the likelihood of animals being abandoned at the SPCA. If the SPCA were to offer low-cost veterinary care for animals who have been adopted from the SPCA, this could help ensure that animals receive appropriate medical care and that the financial burden is no longer a factor in decisions about the medical care that animals receive. A low-cost veterinary care program would also encourage adoption from the SPCA rather than "purchasing" animals from breeders.

In order to encourage the participation of citizens in the caring for feral community cats as part of the Montreal SPCA's TNRM and *shelter, neuter, release, and maintain* programs, help with capture, transportation, and free veterinary treatment of returned-to-field animals should be provided.

8 Issues for Staff

Problem: SPCA staff work in highly non-ideal circumstances, with limited resources. They are in effect caught in a moral tragedy that is not of their making and about which they can do little. Are there ways to ease the strain?

Recommendation: We recommend that the SPCA directly incorporate staff's psychological well-being into its goals and projects. This could include:

- Recognizing and acknowledging that staff will have emotional responses to certain cases, such as attachments to particular animals, and that it is unrealistic and undesirable to suppress these.
- Adopting programs or policies directly aimed at handling the difficult emotions and emotional labor involved in this work environment. These might include support groups or rituals to facilitate and support expressions of grief and other emotions, deliberate efforts to highlight and celebrate successes, and other strategies.
- Articulating goals interpersonally (e.g., "prioritizing projects and actions which will be most effective in helping animals *while meeting our own needs for attachment, accomplishment, and joy in a supportive and sustainable work environment*") instead of using impersonal formulations (e.g., "prioritizing projects and actions which will be most effective in helping animals").
- Allowing for exceptions and special cases, when doing so enables staff to cope and continue in their work.

Reasoning: Grief, sadness, and frustration are unavoidably part of the reality of working for an animal shelter. It is important that when people express these emotions they are not seen (by themselves or others) as unprofessional or failing to cope. The capacity to feel deeply about the animals in their care is crucial to staff motivation, judgement, and effectiveness—a strength that needs to be valued and nurtured. Good outcomes for the animals are inseparable from a supportive environment for staff.

Therapeutic interventions, such as coping strategies and relaxation techniques, could help staff in dealing with the emotional burden their work involves.[16] Rituals around particularly stressful events, such as deaths of animals who have lived in the shelter for a long time or a long, arduous court case that is eventually dismissed, can facilitate and support expressions of grief, anger, and other emotions.

It is natural for us to become more attached to particular individuals in the course of working with them (or to feel more responsibility or more pain in witnessing their suffering). If we deny this reality, then we might consider it a problem if, for example, a staff member engages in special pleading for a particular "hard case" animal rather than treating all cases with scrupulous even-handedness. Part of caring for the psychological health of SPCA staff might entail willingness to entertain exceptions and special cases, especially when doing so enables staff to cope and continue in their work. This needn't undermine general compliance with agreed upon norms and guidelines but could provide a safety valve releasing pressure on staff coping with ongoing triage circumstances.

Notes

1. Any cat without a collar or chipped ear confirming that they are part of a TNRM program should be considered at risk, even if they appear healthy.
2. https://www.spca.com/app/uploads/2018/06/SPCA_By_Laws_2015.pdf.
3. https://www.spca.com/en/mission-and-policies/ (accessed November 8, 2018). In this document, when we speak of "animals," we mean "sentient animals." Sentient animals are those animals who have the capacity for negative or positive sensations or emotions. This implies that sentient animals have the capacity to experience the world from a subjective point of view.
4. Throughout this document, "animals" refers to "nonhuman animals"; see Section 2.B for further clarification on terminology.
5. https://www.spca.com/en/mission-and-policies/
6. For a detailed discussion of these issues, see Chapter 1, this volume.
7. See Bailey Norwood's survey for *Food Demand Survey* (FooDS), vol. 5 issue 9, January 2018. http://agecon.okstate.edu/files/January%202018.pdf

8. https://20min.ch/ro/news/suisse/story/ils-aiment-la-viande-mais-sont-con
tre-les-abattoirs-20019692

9. The mandate of the MAPAQ is to "promote the prosperity of the bio-food
sector and ensure the quality of food products within a sustainable development perspective." http://www.thesaurus.gouv.qc.ca/tag/terme.do?id=15641

10. See   https://www.animaljustice.ca/media-releases/animal-justice-will-interv
ene-in-lawsuit-challenging-ontario-animal-protection-laws

11. As noted earlier (Section 2.B), the SPCA should in its own communications
use the language of "companion animals" rather than "pets" with the goal of
shaping public attitudes. But our focus in this section is on the importance of
understanding how the general public currently thinks about norms of care,
and existing social norms are typically expressed in the language of "pet care" or
"pet ownership." We need to understand these prevailing social norms of "pet
care" in order to know how best to change them.

12. For further discussion of this general issue as well as the case of the Los Angeles
Animal Services Commission, see Chapter 5, this volume.

13. Cats at risk may show obvious signs of poor health, such as malnutrition, injury, disease, or psychological distress. However, any cat who does not have an
identification tag or a chipped ear confirming that they are part of a TNRM program should be considered at risk, even if the cat appears healthy. If a cat has no
clear human guardian, they are vulnerable to the many dangers that come with
having no support network (see Section 7.A).

14. For a fuller discussion of this account of the ethics of killing in animal shelters
see Chapter 2, this volume.

15. See, for example, *The Return-To-Field Handbook* (Bays et al.) published by the
Humane Society of the United States; https://humanepro.org/sites/default/
files/documents/return-to-field-handbook.pdf, accessed July 22, 2021. A similar practice that is becoming more popular is to avoid bringing to the shelter
animals who do not seem to have a guardian, leaving them where they were
found unless they are obviously injured or incapable of surviving. The worries
we express about the RTF practices apply to this as well.

16. There is a nascent literature concerning effectiveness of therapeutic
interventions (e.g., mindfulness, coping strategies, relaxation techniques, expressive writing, fostering positive relationships between caregivers and animals in their care) in order to support staff in animal care environments. See
Alexis Levitt and Lindsay Gezinski (2018) "Compassion fatigue and resiliency
factors in animal shelter workers," *Society & Animals* (in publication); Vanessa
Rohlf (2018) "Interventions for occupational stress and compassion fatigue in
animal care professionals: A systematic review," *Traumatology*, 24/3, 186–192;
Kerrie Unsworth, Steven Rogelberg, and Daniel Bonilla (2010), "Emotional
expressive writing to alleviate euthanasia-related stress," *Canadian Veterinary
Journal*, 51/7, 775–777.

PART II

1
The Value of Death for Animals

An Overview

Nicolas Delon

1.1 Introduction

This chapter reviews issues concerning the value of death for non-human animals, specifically those in shelters. Prominent views in animal ethics argue that, for many sentient animals at least, killing is morally wrong either because they have an inherent right not to be killed (Regan 1983) or, to some extent, because they have some future-directed desires (Singer 2011).[1] Utilitarians also argue that whatever has intrinsic value—pleasure, preference-satisfaction, the mere existence of consciousness—death is bad and killing wrong to the extent that it makes the world a worse place (Jamieson 1984; Norcross 2013; Lazari-Radek and Singer 2014). While this chapter will deal with the ethics of euthanasia in its last section, other chapters in this volume address the ethics of *killing*. Our focus here is on the *value* and *harm* of death.[2]

Throughout the 1980s and 1990s, an estimated 12–20 million dogs and cats were killed every year in the United States. The rate has only recently gone down to 3–4 million according to the Humane Society of the United States in 2014 (Kasperbauer and Sandøe 2016, 28). Some of these animals are killed because they are ill or injured, many others because they are "unwanted." Concurrently, so-called *no-kill shelters*, where 90% or more of animals are not killed, have

Nicolas Delon, *The Value of Death for Animals* In: *The Ethics of Animal Shelters*. Edited by: Valéry Giroux, Angie Pepper, and Kristin Voigt, Oxford University Press. © Oxford University Press 2023. DOI: 10.1093/oso/9780197678633.003.0003 been on the rise (the 10 remaining percent are either too unhealthy to survive or too aggressive to safely adopt out) (Abrell 2021, 36).

What makes an animal's life worth or no longer worth living? What, if anything, makes death bad for them? Answering the first question turns on more than an animal's current health. Sociologists Arluke and Sanders write of shelter workers' seeing "death as the alleviation of suffering":

> This was easy to do with animals that were very sick or old—known as "automatic kills"—but it was much harder to see suffering in "healthy and happy" animals. They, too, had to be seen as having lives not worth living. Workers were aware that the breadth of their definition of suffering made euthanasia easier for them. One worker acknowledged, "Sometimes you want to find any reason [to euthanize], like it has a runny nose," because killing was harder to do without a reason. . . . [I]t was thought better to euthanize healthy strays than to let them "suffer" on the streets. . . . Once in the shelter, healthy strays, along with abandoned and surrendered animals, were also thought better dead than "fostered out." (Arluke and Sanders 1996, 91–92)[3]

Many "open-admission" shelters kill animals due to resource or space limitations and because they know that many animals who cannot be rehomed would live miserable lives on the street. Underpinning the divide between shelters is a disagreement on the above two questions and how they inform the ethics of killing. Most animals who die in North American shelters are in relatively good health. Yet we usually define *euthanasia* as the act of painlessly killing an animal to put them out of their misery. As Kasperbauer and Sandøe (2016, 21) note, the fact that professional guidelines usually abide by this definition suggests that euthanasia is seen as a welfare issue, even though killing is often allowed on convenience grounds (Yeates and Main 2011). The American Veterinary Medical Association's guidelines state that it should be pursued "when death is a welcome event and continued existence is not an attractive option for the animal as perceived by the owner and veterinarians" (AVMA 2013, 7; Kasperbauer and Sandøe 2016, 21). In other words, euthanasia is to be done *in the interests of the animal.* In such guidelines, welfare is usually defined by reference to experiences, following the hedonistic conception of welfare found in the Brambell Report (1965). When future life would involve too much (i.e., "prolonged and unrelenting") suffering, euthanasia is seen as compassionate (AVMA 2013, 9). It is also the position that the organization People for the Ethical Treatment of Animals (PETA) takes on euthanasia (Abrell 2021, 88). Typically, an animal's life is no longer worth living, according to such guidelines, when they are experiencing severe pain or other states that have no easy remedy or suffering from illness or injury that guarantees future suffering not offset by other aspects of well-being (Kasperbauer and Sandøe 2016, 22). This chapter does not assume any specific conception of welfare. In contrast to the Brambell Report's narrow focus on negative mental states, animal well-being will hereafter refer to the full range of animal interests, including positive well-being.

Here's a simple thought. Death is bad.[4] In fact, it's often thought to be the worst thing that can happen to anybody—with exceptions: we sometimes hear about "fates worse than death." But in what sense is it bad? Under what circumstances? There are many questions that concern human beings as well as other animals, such as the "timing problem" (if death harms, when does the harm occur?); the Lucretian "late-birth" asymmetry (if premature death is bad, why isn't being born later than one could have been equally bad; if it isn't, then why think death is bad for us?); and Epicurus's well-known puzzle (no one ever experiences the harm of death while they exist).[5] More relevant to our purposes are questions that receive *different* answers when applied to humans and other animals. In this chapter, we ask whether death is bad for shelter animals and, if it is, how bad it can be. Sections 1.2–1.4 introduce three possible kinds of answer to these questions: death as a deprivation, death as thwarting desires, and death as interrupting a narrative. As we'll see, the Deprivation view comes out best against competing views. The Deprivation view retains its appeal despite objections and has many virtues. One is that it nicely accounts for the judgment that death is bad for animals, too. Another is that it makes sense of whether and when it is better for some animals in shelters to be killed than allowed to suffer (in shelters, on the street, or in the wild). Section 1.5 thus turns to the idea that death can be good for some shelter animals and asks how the decisions about killing individual animals should be made.

1.2   Deprivation

1.2.1   Life Comparative Account

A standard response to the Epicurean puzzle, that death is nothing to us, argues that death is bad for a person insofar as it deprives them of what would have been good for them had they continued to live. This response does not presuppose that the subject experiences the harm.[6] According to deprivationism, death is bad because of what it takes from the one who dies or prevents them from having (Feldman 1991; Bradley 2009, 2016; Broome 2013; Kagan 2012; Nagel 1979; Marquis 1989). This view has been applied to animals by several authors (e.g., Bradley 2009, 2016; Cholbi 2017; DeGrazia 1996, 2016; Harman 2011; Nussbaum 2006; Overall 2017; Regan 1983).[7] The basic argument is summed up by Ben Bradley (2016, 51–52) as follows:

1. Death is bad for an individual if and only if it makes that individual's lifetime well-being level lower than it would otherwise have been.
2. Death sometimes makes an animal's lifetime well-being level lower than it would have been.
3. Death, therefore, is sometimes bad for an animal.

Lifetime well-being accounts for the value for you of your whole life.

Deprivationism, sometimes called the *life comparative account*, is stated in premise 1. Those who oppose this argument reject premise 1 in favor of a different criterion or premise 2 by denying that animals have lifetime well-being. We'll address the former strategy in Section 1.3; the latter in Section 1.4.

Deprivationism is *comparative*: "the overall value of an event for a person is equal to the difference between the value of her actual life and the value of the life she would have had if the event had not happened" (Bradley 2009, 113). Death is bad if and insofar as it deprives one of a valuable future, so, assuming a future worth living, death is worse the earlier it comes. Bradley's view is hedonist—pleasant experiences are what makes life good—but other theories of value and well-being are compatible with deprivationism. Desires and psychological sophistication, meaning and narrativity, if they contribute to well-being, also contribute to the badness of death, as we'll see. Deprivationism as such is neutral with respect to what determines well-being.

Deprivationism explains why it can be permissible to cause animals pain to save them from life-threatening injuries or illnesses, as with "a young cat that could lead a long happy life if it is given serious surgery that would give it quite a bit of pain (even with painkillers) for a few days, followed by months of serious discomfort" (Harman 2011, 732).

Deprivationism explains why death can be bad for cats and dogs, but it doesn't straightforwardly explain why death is worse for *persons*—the technical philosophical term for a being who is self-aware, rational, and autonomous. In this instance, persons are normally capable of forward-looking thoughts, desires, and preferences; they have a conception of their own existence over time.[8] Some authors, such as DeGrazia (2016), accept deprivationism for the general badness of premature death for sentient creatures, but appeal to further theoretical principles to explain why death is typically worse for persons, provided by the following account.

1.2.2 Time-Relative Interests

According to Jeff McMahan's (2002, 2016) *time-relative interest account* (TRIA),[9] the badness of death depends on two factors:

1. the value of the life that the individual would have had, had they not died when they did;
2. the extent to which they are psychologically related to their possible future life at that time.

The TRIA discounts the harm of death, at the time of death, for weaker degrees of psychological connections to one's future self. Assuming the badness of deprivation, "how great a misfortune an individual suffers in dying varies with the quality and quantity of the life he would otherwise have had. Because animals lose less, their deaths are usually less bad" (McMahan 2016, 70). Unmodified deprivationism implies "that the worst death that an individual can suffer is immediately after beginning to exist." But this is implausible. According to the TRIA, a one-month-old human has a weaker interest in continuing to live than a five-year-old, who in turn has a weaker interest than a twenty-year-old. Even though the younger human has more to lose in quantity and maybe quality of life, what they lose must be discounted for weaker prudential relations across their different "selves" or life-stages.[10] The badness of death thus changes over time:

[A]s we mature psychologically, we gradually become both more substantial as possible subjects of misfortune and more closely psychologically connected to ourselves as we will later be, if death does not intervene . . . even though the amount of good life we have in prospect is steadily diminishing. (McMahan 2016, 71)

Analogous reasoning applies to differences *between* species:

Like ourselves in the earliest moments of our lives, most animals are, throughout their lives, largely psychologically unconnected to themselves in the future. They live mostly in the present. So not only is the life they lose through death inferior in quality and quantity, but they are also only weakly related to their possible future life in the ways that matter. (McMahan 2016, 71)

Because the badness of *suffering* is not relative to such connections, it may be worse for an animal, at a time, to suffer than die. This implies that sometimes it may not be in an animal's best interest to undergo painful surgery to prevent future suffering or death. But mildly painful surgeries for the sake of near-term well-being are permissible (compare *suffering now* and *suffering later*, McMahan 2016, 71–72). Section 1.5 returns to these questions.

These implications may seem counterintuitive. One may think that, whether living longer would be good for a cat should not depend on how strongly connected they are to their far future but simply how good their future life can be. Imagine animals whose current interests involve only things and events within the next five years; nothing that happens beyond that is "in their interest" because it is too far removed from them, psychologically speaking. Elizabeth Harman (2011) argues that the TRIA implies that we should not perform painful life-saving surgery on an animal to prevent harm that would occur more than five years later even if it enabled them to experience many more pleasant years. That's because, according to the TRIA, such animals lack a *present* interest in being alive in six years. The TRIA cannot accommodate our intuition that it would be better for them to go on living.[11] The TRIA thus refines deprivationism to take into account psychology, not just the amount of good in a future life, but it has its own troublesome implications. As we'll see, all theories come at a cost, especially deprivationism's main rival, desire-based views.

1.3 Desires

According to desire-based views, death is bad if and only if it frustrates certain *current* interests, whereas deprivationism also counts the satisfaction of *future* (as-yet unformed) interests as relevant to the loss of good. Some desire-based views have trouble accounting for the badness of death for animals who lack future-directed desires or are not self-conscious (Jamieson 1984; Singer

2011). Accordingly, they are more permissive with respect to killing animals, whether they are healthy or not, but even more so for animals whose future life involves significant suffering.

1.3.1 Categorical Desires

The view that some *sophisticated* form of desire explains the badness of death has been defended by Christopher Belshaw (2013, 2015, 2016).[12] The value of death, he argues, is not just a function of the value of the life lost and how early it occurs. A desire to continue to live is necessary for death's badness.

Belshaw draws on a distinction between *categorical* and *conditional* desires, made by Bernard Williams (1973) in his classic article on immortality. Both are future-directed desires. Conditional desires are those we want satisfied *on the condition that we will be alive*; categorical desires are those we have regardless and which *give us a reason to go on living* (Williams 1973, 85). For example, one typically will not want to undergo painful live-saving surgery just to get another cup of coffee tomorrow—I'd be happy to get another cup of coffee tomorrow, if I'm still alive, but it's not what gives me a reason to live. On the other hand, one may want to undergo surgery to fulfill the project of completing a novel or seeing one's children grow up—these give me a reason to live. The "salient difference" between such desires, writes Belshaw, "lies not in the objects themselves, but in our attitudes toward them" (2013, 275). We can imagine a conditional desire to complete a novel or, perhaps less plausibly, a categorical desire for the best cup of coffee. What matters is that we have a categorical desire for something if that thing gives us reason to go on living. These attitudes depend on cognitive capacities that most animals presumably lack; for example, an understanding of the difference between life and death (Cigman 1981, 58–59) or a sense of time and biography-relevant concepts (Varner 2012). As a result, most animals cannot take something that is valuable to them and see that value as giving them a reason to keep on living. They lack categorical desires, according to Belshaw.

In fact, Belshaw's view states two necessary conditions for death's badness: a desire to live and realistic expectations of a future life worth living. Quality of life per se doesn't ground an interest in living; desiring to live on might be unrealistic or delusional (2013, 292). Belshaw's view entails that, even though they'll have categorical desires in the future, death is not bad for babies, although it may be wrong to kill them because the wrongness of killing depends on further factors (2013, 293) (it's not bad either for fetuses, patients in permanent vegetative states, and late-stage Alzheimer's patients; 278–279). Another implication seems to be that, for a depressed person lacking categorical desires—desires that give reasons to go on living—death need not be so bad. Here Belshaw is more ambivalent. For instance, a teenager with only conditional desires still has an interest in living if she will likely develop categorical desires someday and her future life will be good (2013, 280–281).

Such implications are unacceptable to many critics (DeGrazia 1996, 237; McMahan 2002, 182; Bradley 2016, 57). Anyone who accepts them will not be troubled by the claim that death isn't bad for animals. But even if one rejects them, this might be for reasons that don't apply to other animals who, unlike children and teenagers, will never develop categorical desires.

So, why are categorical desires important? A simple thought is that they persist. Death does not frustrate conditional desires. When a desire is conditional on something that fails to obtain, it is neither satisfied nor frustrated: it is *cancelled* (McDaniel and Bradley 2008). Say I'm on the road and want to get a cup of coffee *if* there's a good coffeeshop in the next town. As it happens, there are only grubby convenience stores. My desire for that cup of coffee is not frustrated but cancelled. On to the next town! If I die tomorrow, likewise my desire will only have been cancelled. A categorical desire, by contrast, is one that death does not cancel. My early death would frustrate, not cancel, my desire to see my daughters grow up. When such desires are combined with the potential good future, their frustration makes death bad. This is, it seems, why it would be bad for me to die now: I have reasons to go on living grounded in persisting desires that are not conditional. Thus, even if categorical desires are not sufficient for death's badness[13] (*pace* Williams 1973), they are necessary, according to Belshaw.

If Belshaw's view is correct, and only persons can want to live, death is not bad for "lower animals" such as "cows, rabbits, frogs, worms." Their deaths "can be bad for owners, viewers, bystanders, friends, relatives, and dependents. . . . Maybe it can be bad, in some sense, for the universe," but not *for the one who dies* (2013, 279). It is not bad in a way that we should, morally, care about for those beings' sake. We should not "be exercised about [it], regret its occurrence, or make any sacrifices to prevent it" (290). This has radical implications. Consider the following cases:

> My cat will live for another three years, and good years, if I subject it to an extremely painful operation, with six months of bad side effects, right now. Many people think that future pleasure cannot straightforwardly compensate for present pain in an animal [*sic*] life. (Belshaw 2013, 288)

> We're in a car crash together, both now unconscious. A doctor might well, and reasonably, decide it is worth giving me some painful operation to save my life, because, as he believes, I would want this. Ought he to do the same for Baby? I think we should look upon a baby here much as we'd look upon a cat, and be most concerned with its present pain. (Belshaw 2013, 289)

In both cases, Belshaw suggests, the relevant interests are present interests in enjoying a positive balance of experiential welfare. If pain is bad for them and they lack a desire to live, then it is better for them to die (which doesn't entail that it is right to kill them or let them die). Death not being bad and being often good for these animals implies that we may often (sometimes should) kill our companion animals as soon as their pain cannot be managed (or wild animals whenever we get a chance) since the alternatives for them are worse (Belshaw 2016, 41–42). It also implies that we may kill happy animals for their meat (Belshaw 2015).

Let us now consider some potential objections to desire-based views.

1.3.2 The Relevance of Desires

Is a desire for *life itself* relevant to the badness of death? Many children or teenagers, because they haven't thought much about death or lack a robust conception of the difference between life and death, do not have desires for more life but still have many desires that *presuppose* that they go on living (Bower and Fischer 2018, 100). We may, with Bower and Fischer, decide to also call these "categorical desires" if, when "situated in appropriately complex mental lives" they give one reason to continue to live. The terminology isn't crucial, as long as we admit that some desires can give us reason to live even though they are not, strictly speaking, categorical (for Belshaw, the latter presuppose that one *wants to live* not just has desires that imply continuing to live). Do any animals possess future-directed desires in Bower and Fischer's sense?

Belshaw claims that we often misinterpret the meaning of animal behavior, as in claims such as: "horses do have desires, and it is apparent that they often act in order to continue living" (Bradley and McDaniel 2013, 128). However, Bradley writes, "Those who are suspicious of the mental lives of cows should, if anything, be more suspicious that they have *conditional* desires than that they have *categorical* ones" (2016, 54–55). For conditional desires do not appear to require less mental machinery. Granted, cows' future-directed desires may not extend very far, nor do they concern their life-as-a-whole. Even if their death was "typically *less* bad" than a human death, it would still be bad in frustrating current future-directed desires and preventing the formation and satisfaction of future preferences (Bradley 2016, 56–57). Belshaw contends that when animals like cows and foxes move to eat grass or escape a trap, they just want to eat the grass or to end the pain *now*. But, as Bower and Fischer argue, this hardly is a parsimonious theory:

> If it strikes you as *prima facie* implausible that these animals have a concept of the future and their continued survival, it should similarly strike you as implausible that they have a concept of the present. It seems, rather, like we should say that the content of the desire just doesn't

specify any time or range of time for its satisfaction—it's the tenseless desire for grass, not the tensed desire for grass *now*. (2018, 103)

Nothing bars such desires from "propelling" animals into the future. Moreover, we can look at which animals are capable of planning and anticipation. Bower and Fischer (2018, 104–105) cite reviews of evidence on fish (Brown 2015), chicken (Marino 2017), and pig cognition (Mendl et al. 2010). We can add some recent evidence on bovines (Comstock 2020; Marino and Allen 2017; for broader reviews of "mental time travel," see Mendl and Paul 2008; Roberts 2012). While studies on cats and dogs are harder to come by, it would be surprising if they lived strictly in the present. For instance, researchers emphasize the role of smell in dogs' perception of time (Horowitz 2016) and have found evidence of deception-like behavior in dogs (Heberlein et al. 2017), which plausibly requires forward-thinking. The evidence that cats possess more than a rudimentary concept of time is anecdotal. However, their desires for companionship, comfort, play, hunting, and exploration all require the persistence of elements of their environment, which fix the content and satisfaction conditions of some of their desires (see Bower and Fischer 2018, 106–107). We may thus accept that psychology matters yet reject the thesis that *categorical* desires are necessary.

Consider again Jeff McMahan's TRIA. McMahan objects to the categorical desires view that it can't account for the badness of death for infants and animals (2002, 182), yet he also notes that "desires do figure in several ways in the full explanation" of the badness of death by providing psychological connections across time, constituting "long-range ambitions, plans, goals, and projects" and thereby making one's life more "richly unified." Categorical desires, in particular, can express "an individual's personal values" and contribute to narrative unity (McMahan 2002, 182). But note that even this admission rests on the premise that desires matter because of their *contribution to goods* of which death deprives the dead. Desires just affect the discounting rate we should apply to the loss of future goods at the time of death. Simply put, things we care about are things we can have a stronger interest in having, which doesn't mean that things we do not care about are not things we have an interest in having.

Psychology matters, which is why McMahan introduces further factors determining death's badness. The disvalue of deprivation (factor 1) must be discounted for the absence of subsequent factors (184, 197–198):

1. The amount of good that is lost.
2. The strength of the prudential unity relations between the individual at the time of death and their future self when the future goods would have occurred.
3. How well the individual has fared before death in relation to the norm for individuals with psychological capacities comparable to their own.
4. Narrative structure—how unified the individual's life is and how the future life they lost would have shaped the narrative.
5. Invested efforts in one's own future and whether death renders them retroactively futile or pointless.
6. Whether the individual's character or actions made them "deserving" of the goods they lost (i.e., it's worse to lose goods you've rightly earned than ones you got through a stroke of luck).
7. Whether the individual desired or valued the goods they lost at the time of death.

In all these possible ways, animals who are not persons have less to lose. For example, "most animals lack the capacity for many of the forms of experience and action that give the lives of persons their special richness and meaning" (195). Their relationship to time also affects the quality of their experience: "Each day is merely more of the same. . . . There is no scope for tragedy—for hopes passing unrealized, projects unwillingly aborted, mistakes or misunderstandings left uncorrected, or apologies left unmade" (197). Accordingly, premature death is less of a harm for cats and dogs than it is for persons losing a proportionally comparable amount of future goods (i.e., whose death is similarly premature relative to the relevant life expectancy benchmark). The TRIA, unlike Belshaw's view, accounts for the badness of animal death, but, like Belshaw's view, it purports to explain the special badness of persons' death. Even so, deprivation remains decisive.

In sum, desire-based views make controversial theoretical and empirical assumptions. They also presuppose a desire-based theory of value and well-being, unlike deprivationism, which is neutral. Even if some future-directed desires are relevant to the badness of death, death can still be bad for animals. Deprivationism thus comes out ahead. Its initial appeal in solving Epicurean puzzles persists after closer examination of its main rival. However, even granting deprivationism, we might object that death isn't very bad for animals because there is something that death can ruin for us but not for animals: a story.

1.4 Narratives

Diachronic unity, or integration within a life, can affect the badness of death. Typically, a person's life can form a meaningful whole, exhibiting some structure and direction. For infants and fetuses, "[d]eath does not spoil a good story for the simple reason that the story has hardly begun" (McMahan 2002, 176). The importance of narratives to identity and well-being has been emphasized by many authors (DeGrazia 2005; Lindemann 2013; Schechtman 1996; Varner 2012).

In an influential paper, David Velleman (1991) rejects the premise that animals can have lifetime well-being, without rejecting deprivationism. Animals cannot accumulate well-being or care about their life story because they have no conception of themselves over time. Hence, he argues, nothing can detract from their lifetime well-being. If death is bad because it detracts from lifetime well-being, then it cannot be bad for animals.

Velleman distinguishes between *momentary* well-being (at a time) and *diachronic* well-being (over time). Diachronic well-being is determined at least partly by facts about narrative structure—the fate of projects and whether early efforts paid off—over and above facts about momentary well-being at particular times. A life can even be better with less of the latter if a successful or redeeming narrative contributes to lifetime well-being. Furthermore, for something to be intrinsically good for one, one must be capable of caring about it. Call it, following Bradley, the "capacity to care condition" (2016, 61). Cows have only momentary well-being. Since they lack the capacity to care about how their lives as a whole go, they cannot have lifetime well-being or even better life sequences than others. They can only care about how things go for them *at any given time*: "For a lower animal, then, momentary well-being fails not only of additivity but of cumulability by any algorithm at all. Consequently, the totality of this subject's life simply has no value for him" (Velleman 1991, 77).

However, the capacity to care condition has bizarre implications: a future of agony cannot be worse for the cow, overall, than a future of pleasure, and so it can never be better for them to die than face miserable prospects (see Bradley 2016; McMahan 2002, 488–489). Velleman's narrative view implies that there never is a reason to justifiably kill an animal for their own sake; that death or a future life of suffering are, from the animal's perspective, equivalent prospects, although *at any given moment* it is worse for them to suffer than not.

As noted, McMahan argues that narratives might give greater value to one's life as a whole, and perhaps a narrative psychology helps to confer coherence upon it. Bradley concedes as much (2016, 62). However, it does not follow that, for life to be intrinsically valuable for someone, they must be able to care about it. We can aggregate well-being across an individual's moments even if that "individual cannot care about the aggregate well-being in its life" (Bradley 2016, 62). Even if narratives matter, they are not necessary for life to have value.

A final way in which narratives might matter is if they are required for one's life to be meaningful, and meaning is a key ingredient of death's badness. John Martin Fischer argues, drawing on Williams (1973) and Susan Wolf (1997, 2010), that categorical desires also determine meaningfulness in life by grounding projects, which determines the special badness of death for meaning-seeking creatures (Fischer 2020, 81). Fischer also contends that nonhuman animals lack the capacities to live meaningful lives, which pre-suppose categorical desires: "Only a being who can act freely, and is in contact with reality (in a suitable way), can live a meaningful life. Such a being writes his or her story through free will" (Fischer 2020, 23).

But this account of the special badness of death of persons does not exhaust the grounds on which death can be bad. It is just worse, "possibly a tragedy," for a being with the capacity to lead a mean-ingful life. But "none of this implies that the cat's life is not important to the cat, or that *nothing* of value is lost when a cat dies" (Fischer 2020, 23). Fischer thus lays out a two-fold account of the badness of death (83): it is a deprivation of what would be, on balance, a good continuation of life, and it thwarts categorical preferences about the future. The death of a nonperson, who lacks categorical desires, merely robs them of future pleasant experiences.

But even if we accept Fischer's view about the special badness of death for meaning-seeking creatures, there are questions about what specifically it implies for the deaths of animals. First, we could dis-pute the view that animals are incapable of living meaningful lives (Purves and Delon 2018; Thomas 2018).

Furthermore, if some animals can have meaningful lives without categorical desires, then deprivationism entails that it is worse for them to die than for beings who are incapable of meaning.

Finally, we may note that narratives matter but not necessarily from the *first-person* point of view. James Rachels (1983) argued that death is an evil when it ends a life in the biographical, not merely bi-ological, sense, and that having such a life is sufficient for a right to life that extends to at least most mammals. Lori Gruen writes,

> Being the story-tellers we are . . . allows us to make meaning of the deaths of humans as well as nonhumans in our families and communities. Whether or not other animals are able to imagine the foreclosed possibilities of the deceased, humans do have the capacity to dwell on the harms that come not simply from missing the dead, but from mourning the loss of what could have been. (2014, 61)

This and the fact that other animals appear to grieve or understand death (King 2013; Monsó and Osuna-Mascaró 2020) suggest that death is at least a "social harm" (Gruen 2014). Accordingly, the attitudes of people working and living with animals should inform our judgments about the overall value of their death (Abrell 2021; Arluke and Sanders 1996; jones and Gruen 2016). We turn to this question in the final section.

1.5 The Goodness of Death

> The distressing fact is that the point of optimum life span for shelter animals is likely to be much earlier in its life than for companion animals who have morally decent human guardians. . . . As a form of shelter population control, euthanasia has a role in ensuring that a larger portion of shelter animals do not live long enough that they would have been better off dead. (Cholbi 2017, 277)

Shelters have to make innumerable hard decisions. They host animals who are terminally ill, are in great pain, and will likely die in a matter of weeks; animals who are terminally ill but whose pain is manageable and who may have a year of active life ahead of them; animals with chronic illnesses whose treatment is painful but whose pain can be managed; animals who cannot be rehomed because of aggressive behavior and for whom shelter life is miserable; and animals whose species-specific needs are difficult to meet in captivity, such as pythons and parrots.[14] One general question regarding the killing of animals is whether its justification turns on the same considerations as human euthanasia. A more specific question is what information we need, if it is permissible, to make such decisions in shelters.

1.5.1 Asymmetries

We already came across the idea that for animals "suffering matters more," that death need not be "a terribly tragic misfortune for an animal" even though their suffering counts (nearly) as much as that of a person (McMahan 2002, 199). That view is presumably widely shared. Yet, at the same time, "[m]any people are reluctant to accept that euthanasia can be legitimate in the case of persons. . . . they believe that the life of a person has such great value that it should generally be preserved even if continued life will involve the endurance of great suffering" (McMahan 2002, 199). How can we explain the intuition that many people who care about animals also approve of the painless killing of shelter animals who cannot be rehomed or cured?

The "more extreme variants" of *Suffering matters more* imply that, for animals whose suffering matters a great deal, "it would usually be best, other things being equal, to kill any such animal painlessly" (McMahan 2002, 201). If killing an animal can prevent protracted suffering, and suffering always matters more than death, then killing them appears to be morally unobjectionable except when it would harm human beings. In fact, on the strong version of *Suffering matters more*, almost "any painless killing of an animal would count as euthanasia" (McMahan 2002, 201). Belshaw (2016) comes close to such a view. But if we accept that many animals' lives contain suffering, and death matters very little to them, then the cases of justified killing will proliferate.

McMahan rejects this extreme view (2002, 201), but he finds the weaker versions defensible. Death being normally less bad for animals, killing them is also less seriously wrong. For instance, it can be better for a young stray animal to die than face near-term prospects of significant suffering (202). According to the TRIA, their present time-relative interests in avoiding *future* suffering are weak (because their mental lives are weakly connected), but their interest in avoiding *immediate* suffering is strong. It all depends on the distribution of the balance of good and bad experiences over time. But, McMahan notes, similar reasoning applies to persons. Bracketing "additional constraints on *killing*," such as respect for autonomy, McMahan thus puts pressure on the initial asymmetry (McMahan 2002, 201). *Suffering matters more* presupposes "an asymmetry between an animal's capacity for happiness and its capacity for suffering" (203). The idea is that "animals are incapable of many of the higher dimensions of [positive] well-being accessible to persons: for example, deep personal relations, aesthetic experience, achievement through the exercise of complex skills, and so on" (McMahan 2002, 203). It is very hard to justify prospects of suffering, especially for stray animals, if few goods of significance are likely to compensate for it. According to McMahan, then, it is easier, in many cases, to justify the killing of animals with poor prospects than human euthanasia.[15]

Likewise, Michael Cholbi (2017) has recently argued that the euthanasia of companion animals and the assisted killing (or suicide) of humans only share "a superficial similarity" (264). Many considerations pertaining to both voluntary and involuntary euthanasia fail to apply to animals. Considerations of autonomy are unlikely to be of much help. Animal euthanasia is thus "better classified as *non-voluntary* euthanasia, the beneficent killing of a being neither in concert with, nor contrary to, its consent" (266). Moreover, because of cognitive differences, animals' fear of death is "far less mediated by their beliefs and attitudes than our fear of death is" (267). Our focus should therefore be on animal *well-being*. This does not automatically make the question easier to resolve.

1.5.2 When and Who

Cholbi appeals to a comparative account of the value of death (see Section 1.1). It estimates the value of death by comparing the actual life of a being, at the time of their death, to the life they probably would have had if they had continued to live—the nearest counterfactual life, to be precise. This may be a life as long as the average life expectancy or, less plausibly, the maximum life span for their species, or the life they would have had if, say, they had received treatment for the cancer that killed them. Whatever the benchmark, if they would have been better off had they survived, death harmed them; if they would have been worse off, death benefitted them. If both lives are equally good, then the individual is neither harmed nor benefitted (Cholbi 2017, 268).

Take twelve-year-old dog Ridge, who has cancer. In contrast to Cholbi's example, let's assume Ridge currently lives in a shelter. According to the comparative account, whether to euthanize Ridge at a given time depends on whether, at that time, "Ridge does not stand to gain by living longer, but also loses nothing by dying at that point" (269). This would be the right time to die—at the point of "*optimum life span*." The crucial question is whether, on balance, they stand to lose or gain. We can never determine with precision the right time. But when, with reasonable approximation, more life would be neither a benefit nor a harm, euthanasia is *permissible*; when more life would be harmful, it is *required*. A surprising implication is that euthanasia is never *merely* permissible (i.e., optional). It is either forbidden (too soon) or obligatory (at, near, or after the optimum cutoff point) (270–271).

Euthanizing *near* the optimum point involves "conscientiousness and awareness of the possible sources of distortion in [one's] decision-making," such as financial considerations ("too soon" cases) or strong emotional attachment ("too late" cases) (270). Cholbi's argument does not concern shelter animals. Typically, the decision to euthanize belongs to the guardian, while the procedure is performed by a veterinarian. However, the question of who counts as a guardian or the authorized spokespeople in shelters is ambiguous.

Let us bracket the issue of authority, which guardians have with respect to their companion animal, to focus on the person who is best situated to know what's best for the animal. Shelter animals have often gone through several households, spent time on the street, and their personal histories may be obscure. This leaves many gaps in the knowledge required to make informed decisions. We can nonetheless assume that some designated staff possess the appropriate moral authority to decide whether and when to euthanize, if the question is an open one. Unlike guardians, shelter workers are not in an asymmetric position of authority with respect to animals. They have less discretion, and their decision is more likely to be directly informed by veterinarians. However, an Ethics Board can also inform decisions and clarify responsibilities under a "decision tree."[16] Assuming that properly informed staff have the right to euthanize, how can we ensure that their (and the board's) judgments will best reflect the foregoing considerations?

First, note that the relationship of guardianship partly captures the relationship between shelter workers and animals insofar as the former are supposed to be acting *for the sake of the animals* rather than out of sheer efficiency or convenience. Granted, shelter workers lack valuable information that comes from long-standing relationships (Cholbi 2017, 277), but their authority regarding this particular animal is still grounded in the animal's interests.[17]

Now consider the epistemic issue. Since the relevant moral facts are intrinsic facts about well-being rather than facts about the animal–guardian relationship, the decisive criterion is the optimum life span of the animal given reasonable expectations concerning their future quality of life. The discretion that befalls on guardians or workers does not hinge on their special relationship as such but on their privileged epistemic position—their "intimate knowledge" in the case of guardians (274). Given that they are typically less attached to animals than a guardian would be, shelter workers' decisions are less likely to be biased. There is no reason to suspect that they are less capable to act in the animals' best interest or to assume that guardians' decisions cannot be distorted by their familiarity, despite their enjoying a "depth and continuity" of knowledge, including of personality, sensitivity to pain, disabilities, and so on (Milligan 2009, 404).

In any case, decisions will have to be sensitive to species, personality, and other factors determining the profile of the animal, including age and health, and whether they're the kind of animal likely to be adopted soon, would fit well in an apartment, be safe around children, or fare well under shelter conditions. While such considerations may not pertain to intrinsic facts about well-being, they are nonetheless relevant to expected quality of life. Furthermore, when workers can reconstruct a narrative about an animal—say, who was abused or already endured a lot of pain—different decisions can be made based on equivalent medical prognoses and levels of suffering. For instance, future suffering may be worse while future pleasures would have more significance for an abused dog—two considerations that can point in opposite direction, since one might want to redeem past suffering by at last giving the dog a good life. This is something both guardians and shelter staff factor into their decision. Here, telling a story (albeit not from the animal's standpoint) could help.[18] A dog who suffered with abusive guardians or who was seized from a puppy mill should, perhaps, get priority in the attribution of resources over another dog who did not endure such suffering, even given equivalent prospects. These are, again, complex ethical questions on which an Ethics Board can help make progress.

Guardians and workers can draw on knowledge that the animal lacks, such as their medical record, their history of abuse, their needs and personality. Whoever occupies the privileged epistemic position will have discretion in deciding whether and when to euthanize. Their decision, however, should primarily (albeit not exclusively) be done considering the animals' interests. In some way, this makes the notion that shelters euthanize due to resource constraints overly simple. Because of their limitations, many shelters cannot afford to offer a good life to many animals, so the killing is done in their best interest considering material constraints. Killing can prevent future harms, such as the harm of being kept in a shelter for a very long period or the harm of being returned to the streets or wild. Of course, shelter staff would need to have a reasonable belief that it is better for an animal to be killed now rather than suffer terribly in a year or so because of the effects of shelter life. Or, they would need to have a reasonable belief that, if their shelter can and will release some animals, these animals would fare well in the wild or that it is better to let them take their chances. Whether death, now, would be good hangs on several factors as well as the most plausible interpretation of "the best interest" of the animal. Such an interpretation itself depends on how one weighs competing values such as welfare and freedom. Because this chapter is neutral about the best theory of well-being, it cannot answer these questions. But we have laid a blueprint that can help in the decision-making process.

1.6 Conclusion

Despite theoretical disagreements, we can cautiously conclude that death is of significance for many animals found in shelters. Desires may be relevant, but it would be reckless to conclude that their lives are not worth living or death never bad for them just because they lack sophisticated desires. Death is bad because it deprives animals of a valuable future. But, by the same token, death can be good when it prevents a future life of misery. Given our uncertainties, both theoretical and moral, deprivationism recommends that one treat animals as if a premature death would normally be bad for them. Yet there are circumstances that can justify killing in the shelter context without having to claim that death, for these animals, does not matter. The value of death depends on an animal's interests, their psychology, and their life prospects. The justifications for killing them turn on further factors, including the interests of other stakeholders and what one knows about the animal.

Acknowledgments

Many thanks to Bob Fischer, Valéry Giroux, Angie Pepper, Duncan Purves, and Kristin Voigt for their input.

Notes

1. In the first (1979) and second (1993) editions of *Practical Ethics*, Singer endorsed different explanations of the wrongness of killing within a preference-based axiology. In subsequent work with Katarzyna Lazari-Radek, they endorse hedonism, where the disvalue of death is reducible to the net amount of pleasant experiences it subtracts from the world (Lazari-Radek and Singer 2014).
2. See Jaquet's and Pepper's contributions in this volume.
3. Based on Arluke's ethnographic research in a "kill-shelter" in a large metropolitan area in the United States.
4. Epicurus famously wrote, "So death, the most terrifying of ills, is nothing to us, since so long as we exist, death is not with us; but when death comes, then we

do not exist. It does not then concern either the living or the dead, since for the former it is not, and the latter are no more" (Epicurus 1940, 30–31). Because Epicurean challenges are about our attitudes toward death (fear and anxiety), which other animals probably lack, we will set them aside.

5. See Fischer (2020) for an excellent review and critical discussion.

6. Accepting deprivationism leads into another challenge, set forth by the Epicurean philosopher Lucretius in his poem, *De Rerum Natura*, according to which prenatal existence and posthumous existence are "mirror images" of each other and call for symmetric attitudes. For the same reasons as above, we can set it aside. See Fischer (2020) for critical discussion.

7. On some versions of the view, it can be bad *that* a conscious animal dies (impersonally or "for the world"), yet bad *to* self-conscious animals only (Norcross 2013).

8. Deprivationism combined with an objective-list or perfectionist theory of well-being can account for this judgment, if greater well-being involves goods such as knowledge, aesthetic appreciation, and virtue and persons' lives contain more of such goods than do animals' lives.

9. McMahan also defends a TRIA of the *wrongness of killing*, which depends on but is not equivalent to the TRIA of the *badness of death*.

10. By "prudential" philosophers mean, roughly, what is in a being's own interest, or what it is rational to care about for the being's own sake.

11. McMahan (2016) argues that such animals' time-relative interests, at the time of surgery, are only comparatively weak, not nonexistent. If surgery involves significant suffering, it may not be good for them to receive treatment. But we may still consider an animal's *future* interests in determining what is best for them, such as whether a shelter animal will benefit in a few years from undergoing surgery now. By the same token, if an animal is healthy now but will suffer greatly in the future (say, because they cannot be rehomed), we may best prevent future suffering now by ending their life (see Section 1.5).

12. Also see Cigman (1981) (categorical desires underpin the right to life) and Wolf (1997) (categorical desires are necessary for meaning in life). Others deny that (many or most) animals have an interest in or right to life because they lack concepts or self-consciousness (Frey 1980; Tooley 1984; Singer 2011; Varner 2012).

13. Either because people may be wrong about death being bad for them even if they have categorical desires or because their reason to avoid death may not be overriding or fully coherent (Belshaw 2013, 276).

14. Thanks to Angie Pepper for helping me frame the introduction of this section.

15. After reviewing many more technical complications (2002, 487–492), McMahan concludes that formulating a fully coherent view is difficult: "The positive justification for animal euthanasia therefore remains elusive" (493).

16. See Section 3.B of *The Ethics of Animal Shelters: Guidelines and Recommendations*, this volume.
17. This is simplifying a bit. Shelter workers have duties to animals who are not currently in the shelter, too. They must consider, when deciding whether to prolong the life of some animal, how this may affect another animal's chances of being rescued.
18. See Gruen's (2014) quote in Section 1.4.

References

Abrell, E. (2021) *Saving Animals: Multispecies Ecologies of Rescue and Care.* Minneapolis: University of Minnesota Press.

Arluke, A., and C. R. Sanders (1996) *Regarding Animals.* Philadelphia, PA: Temple University Press.

AVMA (2013) *AVMA Guidelines for the Euthanasia of Animals.* Schaumburg, IL: AVMA. Https://www.avma.org/KB/Policies/Documents/euthanasia.pdf.

Belshaw, C. (2013) "Death, value and desire." In F. Feldman, B. Bradley, and J. Johannsen (eds.), *The Oxford Handbook of Philosophy of Death.* New York: Oxford University Press, 274–296.

Belshaw, C. (2015) "Meat." In B. Bramble and B. Fischer (eds.), *The Moral Complexities of Eating Meat.* New York: Oxford University Press, 9–29.

Belshaw, C. J. (2016) "Death, pain, and animal life." In T. Višak and R. Garner (eds.), *The Ethics of Killing Animals.* New York: Oxford University Press, 32–50.

Bower, M., and B. Fischer. (2018) "Categorical desires and the badness of animal death." *Journal of Value Inquiry* 52(1), 97–111.

Bradley, B. (2009) *Well-Being and Death.* Oxford: Oxford University Press.

Bradley, B. (2016) "Is death bad for a cow?" In T. Višak and R. Garner (eds.), *The Ethics of Killing Animals.* New York: Oxford University Press, 51–64.

Bradley, B., and K. McDaniel. (2013) "Death and desires." In J. S. Taylor (ed.), *The Metaphysics and Ethics of Death.* Oxford: Oxford University Press, 118–133.

Brambell, F. W. R. (1965) *Report of the Technical Committee to Inquire into the Welfare of Animals Kept under Intensive Livestock Husbandry Systems.* London: H.M.S.O.

Broome, J. (2013) "The badness of death and the goodness of life." In B. Bradley, F. Feldman, and J. Johansson (eds.), *The Oxford Handbook of Philosophy of Death.* Oxford: Oxford University Press, 218–233.

Brown, C. (2015) "Fish intelligence, sentience and ethics." *Animal Cognition* 18(1), 1–17.

Cholbi, M. (2017) "The euthanasia of companion animals." In C. Overall (ed.), *Pets and People: The Ethics of Our Relationships with Companion Animals.* New York: Oxford University Press, 264–278.

Cigman, R. (1981) "Death, misfortune and species inequality." *Philosophy and Public Affairs* 10(1), 47–64.

Comstock, G. (2020) "Bovine prospection, the mesocorticolimbic pathways, and neuroethics: Is a cow's future like ours?" In L. S. M. Johnson, A. Fenton, and A. Shriver (eds.), *Neuroethics and Nonhuman Animals.* Cham: Springer, 73–97.

DeGrazia, D. (1996) *Taking Animals Seriously: Mental Life and Moral Status.* Cambridge: Cambridge University Press.

DeGrazia, D. (2005) *Human Identity and Bioethics.* Cambridge: Cambridge University Press.

DeGrazia, D. (2016) "Sentient nonpersons and the disvalue of death." *Bioethics* 30(7), 511–519.

Epicurus (1940) "Letter to Menoeceus." In W. J. Oates. (ed.), C. Bailey (tran.), *The Stoic and Epicurean Philosophers: The Complete Extant Writings of Epicurus, Epictetus, Lucretius, Marcus Aurelius.* New York: Random House.

Feldman, F. (1991) "Some puzzles about the evil of death." *Philosophical Review* 100(2), 205–227.

Fischer, J. M. (2020) *Death, Immortality, and Meaning in Life.* New York: Oxford University Press.

Frey, R. G. (1980) *Interests and Rights: The Case Against Animals.* Oxford: Oxford University Press.

Gruen, L. (2014) "Death as a social harm." *Southern Journal of Philosophy* 52(S1), 53–65.

Harman, E. (2011) "The moral significance of animal pain and animal death." In T. L. Beauchamp and R. G. Frey (eds.), *The Oxford Handbook of Animal Ethics.* Oxford: Oxford University Press, 726–737.

Heberlein, M. T. E., M. B. Manser, and D. C. Turner (2017) "Deceptive-like behaviour in dogs (Canis familiaris)." *Animal Cognition* 20(3), 511–520.

Horowitz, A. (2016) *Being a Dog: Following the Dog into a World of Smell.* New York: Scribner.

Jamieson, D. (1984) "Utilitarianism and the morality of killing." *Philosophical Studies* 45(2), 209–221.

jones, pattrice, and L. Gruen (2016) "Keeping ghosts close: Care and grief at sanctuaries." In M. DeMello (ed.), *Mourning Animals: Rituals and Practices Surrounding Animal Death.* East Lansing: Michigan State University Press, 187–192.

Kagan, S. (2012) *Death.* New Haven, CT: Yale University Press.

Kasperbauer, T. J., and P. Sandøe (2016) "Killing as a welfare issue." In T. Višak and R. Garner (eds.), *The Ethics of Killing Animals.* New York: Oxford University Press, 17–31.

King, B. J. (2013) *How Animals Grieve.* Chicago: Chicago University Press.

Lazari-Radek, K. (de), and P. Singer (2014) *The Point of View of the Universe: Sidgwick and Contemporary Ethics.* Oxford: Oxford University Press.

Lindemann, H. (2014) *Holding and Letting Go: The Social Practice of Personal Identities.* New York: Oxford University Press.

Marino, L. (2017) "Thinking chickens: A review of cognition, emotion, and behavior in the domestic chicken." *Animal Cognition* 20(2), 127–147.

Marino, L., and K. Allen (2017) "The psychology of cows." *Animal Behavior and Cognition* 4(4), 474–498.

Marquis, D. (1989) "Why abortion is immoral." *Journal of Philosophy* 86(4), 183–203.

McDaniel, K., and B. Bradley (2008) "Desires." *Mind* 117(466), 267–302.

McMahan, J. (2002) *The Ethics of Killing: Problems at the Margins of Life*. Oxford & New York: Oxford University Press.

McMahan, J. (2016) "The comparative badness for animals of suffering and death." In T. Višak and R. Garner (eds.), *The Ethics of Killing Animals*. New York: Oxford University Press, 65–85.

Mendl, M., S. Held, and R. W. Byrne (2010) "Pig cognition." *Current Biology* 20(18), R796–R798. doi:10.1016/j.cub.2010.07.018

Mendl, M., and E. S. Paul (2008) "Do animals live in the present?: Current evidence and implications for welfare." *Applied Animal Behaviour Science* 113(4), 357–382. doi:10.1016/j.applanim.2008.01.013

Milligan, T. (2009) "Dependent companions." *Journal of Applied Philosophy* 26(4), 402–413.

Monsó, S., and A. J. Osuna-Mascaró (2020) "Death is common, so is understanding it: The concept of death in other species." *Synthese* 199(1), 2251–2275. doi:10.1007/s11229-020-02882-y

Nagel, T. (1979) *Mortal Questions*. Cambridge: Cambridge University Press.

Norcross, A. (2013) "The significance of death for animals." In B. Bradley, F. Feldman, and J. Johansson (eds.), *The Oxford Handbook of Philosophy of Death*. New York: Oxford University Press, 465–474.

Nussbaum, M. C. (2006) *Frontiers of Justice: Disability, Nationality, Species Membership*. Cambridge, MA: Belknap/Harvard University Press.

Overall, C. (2017) "Throw out the dog? Death, longevity, and companion animals." In C. Overall. (ed.), *Pets and People: The Ethics of Our Relationships with Companion Animals*. New York: Oxford University Press, 249–263.

Purves, D., and N. Delon (2018) "Meaning in the lives of humans and other animals." *Philosophical Studies* 175(2), 317–338.

Rachels, J. (1983) "Do animals have a right to life?" In H. B. Miller and W. H. Williams (eds.), *Ethics and Animals*. Totowa, NJ: Humana Press, 275–284.

Regan, T. (1983) *The Case for Animal Rights*. Berkeley: University of California Press.

Roberts, W. A. (2012) "Evidence for future cognition in animals." *Learning and Motivation* 43(4), 169–180. doi:10.1016/j.lmot.2012.05.005

Schechtman, M. (1996) *The Constitution of Selves*. Ithaca, NY: Cornell University Press.

Singer, P. (2011) *Practical Ethics*. 3rd ed. New York: Cambridge University Press.

Thomas, J. L. (2018) "Can only human lives be meaningful?" *Philosophical Papers* 47(2), 265–297.

Tooley, M. (1984) *Abortion and Infanticide*. Oxford: Oxford University Press.

Varner, G. (2012) *Personhood, Ethics, and Animal Cognition: Situating Animals in Hare's Two-Level Utilitarianism*. Oxford: Oxford University Press.

Velleman, D. J. (1991) "Well-being and time." *Pacific Philosophical Quarterly* 72, 48–77.

Williams, B. (1973) "The Makropoulos Case: Reflections on the tedium of immortality." In *Problems of the Self.* Cambridge: Cambridge University Press, 82–100.

Wolf, S. (1997) "Happiness and meaning: Two aspects of the good life." *Social Philosophy and Policy* 14(1), 207–225.

Wolf, S. (2010) *Meaning in Life and Why It Matters.* Princeton, NJ: Princeton University Press.

Yeates, J. W., and D. C. J. Main (2011) "Veterinary opinions on refusing euthanasia: Justifications and philosophical frameworks." *Veterinary Record* 168(10), 263. doi:10.1136/vr.c6352

2

Caring in Non-Ideal Conditions

Animal Rescue Organizations and Morally Justified Killing

Angie Pepper

2.1 Introduction

Questions about when to end the lives of animals are central to the operation of most animal rescue shelters. It is widely agreed that if an animal experiences severe pain or suffering for a prolonged period, and their condition is untreatable, then euthanasia may not only be permissible but morally required. Though killing in these circumstances is commonly held to be acceptable, the idea that one could morally justify killing shelter animals for reasons other than their own well-being is deeply disputed and widely condemned. In light of this, shelters increasingly face pressure from animal advocates, the media, and the public to implement a policy of never killing animals who are healthy and/or adoptable. However, no-kill policies are notoriously incompatible with another policy central to large rescue organizations, namely, that of open-admission, which pledges that no animal shall be turned away. Faced with limited space and resources, and animals who need a great deal of time and attention to make them suitable for adoption, it is often incredibly challenging for shelters with an open-admission policy to provide adequate care to all of the animals who require their protection. Thus, open-admission shelters regularly kill animals who could, but

Angie Pepper, *Caring in Non-Ideal Conditions* In: *The Ethics of Animal Shelters*. Edited by: Valéry Giroux, Angie Pepper, and Kristin Voigt, Oxford University Press. © Oxford University Press 2023.
DOI: 10.1093/oso/9780197678633.003.0004

for the want of more time, money, or a suitable home, have led reasonably good lives.

In this chapter, I set out a rights-based framework for thinking about the wrong done to shelter animals who are killed for non-euthanasia reasons. The chapter is structured as follows. The next section motivates two claims that must hold for it to be true that workers in open-admission shelters face a tragic choice predicament—a predicament where all possible answers to the question of what they should do seemingly involve serious moral wrongdoing (Nussbaum 2000, 1007). Specifically, I offer reasons to think that the nonhuman animals with whom shelter workers interact have (i) a right not to be killed by humans and (ii) a right to be rescued. In Section 2.3, I introduce a tripartite distinction in the ethics of killing that shows us when killing is morally permissible and when it is not. In Section 2.4, I map this tripartite distinction onto three kinds of killing that might occur in animal shelters: genuine euthanasia, injustice-dependent justified killing, and absolutely unjustified killing. Importantly, this discussion shows how sometimes shelter workers have a full moral justification to kill an animal for non-euthanasia reasons and yet the animal killed is nonetheless wronged. This wrong, I will argue, is perpetrated by the state, which is responsible for the distributive injustice that makes it impossible for shelter workers to care for all of the animals who are owed assistance. In Section 2.5, I maintain that when shelter workers are justified in killing animals for non-euthanasia reasons, all individuals within the political community are responsible for the wrong done to those animals. I conclude with Section 2.6, which summarizes the argument and underscores the explanatory power of the account.

2.2 Nonhuman Animals Rights to Not Be Killed and to Be Rescued

A central claim of this chapter is that many workers employed in open-admission shelters are locked into a tragedy that is not of their own making. This means that they are routinely and unavoidably confronted with the tragic choice of either killing animals who have a significant interest in continuing to live or failing to care for the animals they are tasked with protecting. The tragic nature of the situation depends on two claims about shelter animals: (i) that they have a right not to be killed by humans and (ii) that they have a right to be rescued by humans.

If the animals in question lack either one or both rights, then the tragedy, as I envisage it, does not arise. This is because killing healthy or adoptable animals would not directly wrong them if they had no right not to be killed, and returning animals to the streets would be a viable option if they had no right to rescue.[1] Thus, the tragic predicament facing shelter workers depends on the nonhuman animals with whom they interact having both a right not to be killed *and* a right to rescue. I now defend each right in turn.

There are many arguments available in defense of the idea that nonhuman animals have a general right not to be killed by us, but arguments that currently enjoy the most support are grounded in the idea that sentient animals have a basic interest in continued life. For example, one might argue that animals "have an interest in living to experience the goods that lie in prospect for them" (McMahan 2008, 67; see also Regan 2004, 117–118; DeGrazia 2016). This view holds that death is bad for animals because it deprives them of future goods. Alternatively, one might argue that animals have an interest in continued life because death would thwart the satisfaction of their current desires. Aaron Simmons defends this idea by arguing that dispositional desires—desires that endure over time and do not depend on us consciously attending to or experiencing them—are sufficient to ground an interest in continued life. On this view, some animals "have an interest in continued life insofar as they cannot continue to enjoy the things that they enjoy unless they are able to continue living. Life is necessary as a means to the satisfaction of their various enjoyments in life" (Simmons 2009, 389). Whichever position one adopts, the basic thought is that sentient animals have an interest in continued life because without life nothing else is possible.[2]

Establishing that many nonhuman animals have an interest in continued existence doesn't yet get us to the claim that they have a right not to be killed, but it is the first step in a common strategy for defending this right.

Step One: Show the animal has a significant interest in continued life.
Step Two: Show that their interest in continued life is sufficient to place us under a duty not to kill them.[3]

This strategy depends on us adopting the popular position that rights protect fundamental interests (Raz 1986). On this view, an individual has a right whenever they have an interest that is sufficient to ground duties in others. To claim that nonhuman animals have a right not to be killed by us is to claim that their interest in continued life is sufficient to ground duties in us not to kill them. Why should we think this? I believe that the answer lies in the value of an animal's life for the animal. To be clear, I do not mean the value that the animal consciously or reflectively attributes to their own life because many nonhuman animals are unable to do that kind of valuing. Rather, it is the value of the animal's life *for* the animal (Korsgaard 2018, 65). As I mentioned above, continued life is a necessary condition for everything else that an animal might have an interest in, and thus it is arguably the most important interest that they have. The idea that we are under a duty not to kill nonhuman animals comes easily once we acknowledge how fundamental continued life is for them.

Importantly, the duty not to kill and its correlative right are not absolute and there are circumstances in which killing is morally permissible or even required. (I'll consider euthanasia as one such exception in a moment.) Nonetheless, affording animals a right not to be killed means that we have, in general, very stringent reasons not to kill them; reasons that cannot merely be weighed against other reasons or cancelled out by competing considerations.

Now let us turn our attention to the right to rescue. Plausibly, the same interest that grounds the right not to be killed also grounds the right to rescue. If animals have a significant interest in continued life, this places us under a duty to rescue them from situations that imperil their lives. For example, companion animals who have been abandoned by their human guardians are often unfit for life without human care and will likely succumb to the harsh realities of life on the streets or in the wild. Thus, companion animals who are lost or abandoned have a right to be rescued in order to protect their lives.

In addition to the interest in continued life, sentient creatures also have a significant interest in not experiencing pain or suffering. Pain and suffering involve unpleasant sensations and/or emotional experiences that negatively impact the subject and have the potential to seriously undermine their well-being. Since pain and suffering threaten well-being, sentient animals have a fundamental interest in avoiding these negative experiences. Accordingly, all domesticated animals who are at risk of serious harm have a right to be rescued because they have a right to be protected against the pain and suffering associated with injury, illness, hunger, and other kinds of physical and psychological trauma.[4]

Now that we have both rights on the table, it might be thought that the tragic choice confronting shelter workers must always be settled by not saving new animals instead of killing ones already in care. This, one might argue, is because killing is always worse than letting die. Accordingly, if the open-admission policy requires the killing of some animals in order to make space or free up resources for some others, then the policy ought to be overridden and newcomers must be turned away.

I think this judgment is too quick for several reasons. First, it is far from clear that the option of turning animals away, releasing them from the shelter to fend for themselves, or simply not responding to reports of animals in need, is preferable to painless killing.[5] This is especially true of orphaned and abandoned animals who do not have the skills to survive; injured and sick animals who are disoriented, in pain, or debilitated in ways that make survival difficult; and the victims of human abuse. Without rescue, most of these animals will suffer terribly before dying. The idea that the most appropriate response to their suffering is abandonment is unconvincing.

Second, the nature of the tragic predicament facing shelter workers is that they cannot save all the animals in need and so they must make decisions about who to save. In this unique situation, the answer cannot straightforwardly be to save animals on a first come, first served basis. This is because not all animals in need have an equal prospect of a decent life or require the same level of resources to be rescued and rehomed. Sometimes shelters can save many more animals in need—including those who are yet to be admitted—by sacrificing existing shelter animals who have more costly health complaints or who are less easy to rehome. (I discuss this point in more detail in Section 2.3.)

Last, and crucially, insofar as the funding for many large shelters depends on their commitment to an open-admission policy, they exist only because they are prepared to make tragic choices regarding who can be saved. Demanding that such shelters abandon the open-admission policy would ultimately result in the dissolution of the organization and fewer animals being rescued overall. The current situation is, of course, far from ideal, but, in the non-ideal conditions in which some of these shelters are forced to work, saving some animals is better than saving none.

2.3 The Ethics of Killing: A Tripartite Distinction

I have suggested that it might sometimes be the case that killing a nonhuman animal is preferable to not saving some other(s), but such a conclusion might be thought to be at odds with our received views on the ethics of killing. Assuming the nonhuman animal right not to be killed is as demanding as the human right not to be killed, some might object that it is never permissible to kill an individual in order to save some other(s). Since competing claims cannot be weighed against an individual's right not to be killed, and the right excludes utility-maximizing considerations, trading one individual's life for that of some other(s) is never justified.

Though not without force, this position is one that few people subscribe to because it has the counterintuitive implication that no matter how many others are imperiled—fifty, a thousand, or even a million—we ought never to sacrifice one person in order to save them. The claim that innocent humans enjoy absolute immunity against being intentionally killed is hard to maintain when respecting the right condemns so many others to death.

If we grant that it might sometimes be permissible to kill innocent individuals to save others, or indeed, that sometimes morality might require such killing, we need to know why this is and what this means for the individuals involved. Given this, I set out a tripartite distinction in the ethics of killing humans that will later help us to distinguish between cases of permissible and impermissible killing in the context of animal shelters.[6] My central claim in this section is that an act of killing falls into one of three categories: it is either (i) morally justified and consistent with the killed individual's right not to be killed, (ii) morally justified yet infringes the killed individual's right not to be killed, or (iii) morally unjustified and in violation of the right not to be killed. Let's consider each category in turn.

2.3.1 Morally Justified Killing Consistent with the Right Not to Be Killed

Sometimes it is permissible to kill an individual because one has a moral justification that is consistent with the individual's rights. Suppose that terminal illness reduces your life to a state of unbearable suffering and further imagine that you live in a jurisdiction that permits physician-assisted suicide. If you seek a good death and consent to physician-assisted suicide, then your doctor has a moral justification to administer the drugs that will end your life.[7] Importantly, in this case, your doctor's action will be entirely consistent with your right not to be killed because you are in state of permanent and unbearable suffering and you *waive* your right when you consent to the administering of fatal drugs.[8] Similarly, if a villainous aggressor were intent on killing you, you would be morally justified in killing them in self-defense if there were no other way to prevent them (Thomson 1991; Quong 2009). In this case, the act of killing would be entirely consistent with the villainous aggressor's right not to be killed because they *forfeit* that right when they culpably threaten your life. In short, if an individual has waived or forfeited their right not to be killed, then killing will not transgress that right.

Unless it is waived or forfeited, an individual's right not to be killed obtains and places others under a duty to refrain from killing them. But what should we say of individuals who do not have the cognitive capacities to waive or forfeit their rights? That is, how should we think about the limits of the right not to be killed for individuals who are not moral agents? Given the view sketched in Section 2.2, I think it plausible that the interest in continued life delimits the scope of the right not to be killed in the case of agents who lack the capacity for moral agency. Consider a terminally ill human infant whose life is one of irreversible and unbearable suffering. In this case, agony and distress far outweigh the benefits of living and so it seems reasonable to assume that the infant no longer has a significant interest in continued life. Indeed, it might be judged that death is in the infant's best interests since continued life is harmful, and they have an interest in a swift and humane death. Thus, the infant no longer has any of the interests that the right not to be killed might plausibly be said to protect.

To summarize, sometimes there is a moral justification for killing, and that justification is compatible with the right not to be killed. In the case of moral agents, permissible killing occurs when the individual waives or forfeits their right not to be killed. In these instances, others are released from the duties grounded in the right. In the case of agents who lack the capacity for moral agency, when an individual no longer has an interest in continued life but instead has a weighty interest in having their suffering ended, killing them does not transgress their right not to be killed.

2.3.2 Morally Justified Infringement of the Right Not to Be Killed

Sometimes killing is morally justified yet *infringes* the right not to be killed. When you are morally justified in doing what another has a right that you do not do, you *infringe* her right. In this kind of case, killing is permissible (because it is morally justified) but nonetheless wrongs the individual killed (because their right is infringed). This is importantly different from cases where the right is transgressed without justification: where there is no justification for doing what another has a right that you do not do, then you *violate* her right. We will address the latter category in a moment, but, for now, let us concentrate on cases where the right not to be killed is justifiably infringed.

Though there is much disagreement over the details, many have argued that there are some instances in which the right not to be killed can be justifiably infringed. Standard examples of this kind of justified infringement include the killing of innocent threats in self-defense and lesser-evil killings. With regard to the first case, theorists writing on the ethics of defensive killing maintain that it is permissible for you to kill an individual who innocently threatens your life even though they bear no moral responsibility for the threat they pose (e.g., Quong 2009).[9] Though the innocent threat has a right not to be killed by you, you, too, have a right not to be killed by them, and most theorists find it incredibly counterintuitive to suppose that morality requires you to sacrifice yourself when you, too, are innocent. In these circumstances, you have a moral justification (not merely a moral *excuse*) to do what the innocent person has a right that you do not: namely, kill them.[10] Killing in this case would thus be justified, but, since the innocent individual's right not to be killed is still intact, it would also constitute an infringement of the right.

Similarly, many moral philosophers think that there are occasions where lesser-evil justifications make intentionally killing innocent individuals permissible (e.g., Frowe 2018; Rodin 2011). When one has a lesser-evil justification, one is justified in doing some harm to avert a greater harm. For example, if you can prevent fifty innocent people from being killed by sacrificing one innocent person, then you may have a lesser-evil justification to sacrifice the one. Though agents in cases like this may have a justification to kill morally innocent individuals, it is not the case that the innocent victim suffers no wrong. The right that innocents have not to be killed is neither waived nor forfeited, and so when their right is not respected, they *are* wronged. Importantly, rights infringements produce a moral remainder; something that calls for action of some kind, such as compensation, the introduction of measures to avoid similar situations arising in the future, and appropriate reactive attitudes such as regret.

2.3.3 Morally Unjustified Violation of the Right Not to Be Killed

Morally unjustified acts of killing are straightforwardly impermissible. Killings of this kind lack the reasons needed to make an act of killing consistent with the right not to be killed or reasons that would justify infringement of the right. Since killings of this kind lack moral justification, they violate the right to life and thus wrong the individuals killed. Moreover, the agent who kills is morally blameworthy unless they have a moral excuse.

2.4 Justified and Unjustified Killing in Animal Shelters

Having sketched a rights-based framework for thinking about the ethics of killing, let's now consider killing in the context of animal shelters. As I noted earlier, decisions about when to kill animals are central to the operations of most large animal rescue organizations. Moreover, for open-admission shelters, these decisions are complicated by the fact that they have limited resources and regularly cannot save all animals in need of their care.

This last point is central to thinking about the ethics of killing in animal shelters. The complexity of the moral situation means that when evaluating acts of killing, one must take into consideration not just the actions of the shelter workers who perform the killing but also the actions of the state, which is ultimately responsible for the tragic circumstances imposed on shelter workers. Though it is primarily individual humans who neglect, abuse, and abandon animals, the state has a duty to protect animals from such failures of care and step in when animals are failed by human citizens. Moreover, not all animals in need of shelter assistance are the victims of neglect or cruelty; some never had human companions and others have human companions who are no longer able to care for them as a result of death, illness, poverty, or homelessness. In all these cases, the buck stops with the state, which is responsible for ensuring that shelters have the resources needed to rescue and care for all animals in need. This means that when the state fails to provide adequate resources to shelters, it bears significant responsibility for the tragedy imposed on shelter workers.

In what follows, I look at the permissibility of killing in different scenarios, from both the perspective of the shelter worker and of the state. By proceeding in this way, we can see how, even if a shelter worker has full moral justification to kill an animal, that animal may nonetheless be the victim of a grave injustice perpetrated by the state. I discuss three kinds of killing: genuine euthanasia, injustice-dependent justified killing, and absolutely unjustified killing.

2.4.1 Genuine Euthanasia

Cases of genuine euthanasia fall into the first category discussed in Section 2.3: they are cases of justified killing that are consistent with the general right not to be killed. When an animal's life is reduced to a chronic state of untreatable acute pain and suffering, continued life is bad for the animal and death is now good for them. In such cases, shelter workers are justified in killing because the usual reason they have not to kill an animal is no longer present. To be precise, since the animal in question no longer has a significant interest in continuing to live and now has a significant interest in a swift and humane death, the shelter worker is no longer under a duty not to kill the animal. Moreover, the shelter worker may in fact be morally required to kill the animal to satisfy the animal's interest in not suffering.

On my view, genuine euthanasia occurs when the individual has had their just entitlements to healthcare satisfied and yet their lives continue to be blighted by permanent and unbearable suffering. It might be that in such circumstances there is no existing medical intervention available to treat the individual and reverse their fortune. Or it might be that the treatment required is not one that justice demands be provided; it might require doing direct harm to others or making use of very rare natural materials, for example. That death is now best for the animal in these kinds of cases is a result of cosmic bad luck and the limits of medical progress as opposed to distributive injustice.

Of course, determining precisely what each individual is entitled to as a matter of justice is a complicated business that cannot be worked out here. But the guiding thought, for our purposes, is that if an individual has a just claim to some treatment or medical intervention, then refusing to treat them or withdrawing treatment will not count as a case of genuine euthanasia. To make this more tangible, consider the following two cases. First, imagine a dog, Dani, who has an inoperable brain tumor and for whom there is no treatment available to slow or reverse the progress of the disease. If the shelter vet determines that death is now in Dani's best interest, then killing Dani would count as a case of genuine euthanasia. This is because Dani's just entitlements to healthcare have been met but sadly the disease exhausts the medical resources available. By contrast, imagine a cat, Felix, who requires urgent tooth removal needed to relieve the suffering caused by severe dental disease. If the shelter vet cannot afford to carry out this work and instead recommends killing Felix to alleviate his suffering, this is not a case of genuine euthanasia (rather it is a "better off dead" case discussed at length in the following section). It is not a case of genuine euthanasia because Felix plausibly did not receive his just entitlement to healthcare.

In cases of genuine euthanasia, the state does not wrong the animal. Since killing was consistent with the animal's interests, the state does no wrong by permitting such killing to take place. Importantly, in cases of genuine euthanasia, the state has satisfied its duty to the animal by ensuring that their just entitlement to healthcare has been met (given that they ensure that the shelter has the resources to provide a humane death). Moreover, insofar as the state permits the painless killing of animals whose interest in death now outweighs their interest in living, the state acts justly both with regard to those animals and those who care for them.[11]

2.4.2 Injustice-Dependent Justified Killing

On the view I am defending here, whenever an animal has a strong interest in continued life, killing them cannot be justified as a case of genuine euthanasia. This is significant because nearly all killings in animal shelters are described as euthanasia even though death is not in the immediate interest of many of the animals killed.[12] To be clear, animals who are killed because they have behavioral problems that make them difficult to rehome, or because the shelter already has too many of the same kind of animal (e.g., cats with black coats),[13] or because they require labor- and time-intensive medical treatments for minor health complaints (e.g., ringworm)[14] are not killed because death is good for them. The central reason for killing animals in these cases is that their care is costly and reduces the shelter's capacity to save other more "adoptable" or "rescuable" animals.

As I noted in the introduction, non-euthanasia shelter killings are widely condemned both outside and inside the sheltering community. There have been numerous exposés in Western societies that have brought non-euthanasia shelter killing to the public's attention. In the United Kingdom, for example, the Royal Society for the Prevention of Cruelty to Animals is routinely accused of *needlessly* killing healthy animals.[15] Similarly, shelters run by People for the Ethical Treatment of Animals (PETA) in the United States have been heavily criticized by the media and supporters of no-kill shelters for killing adoptable animals.[16] While I don't want to suggest that these criticisms are entirely baseless, I think we need to be cautious about claiming that shelter workers *always* act impermissibly when they perform non-euthanasia killings.

Shelters that have an open-admission policy and operate with insufficient resources are sometimes unable to give adequate care to all animals who need it. For some shelters, despite reasonable (and often unreasonably demanding) efforts, not all animals can be saved. In such circumstances, it is sadly inevitable that some animals will be unjustly killed. Particularly difficult cases involve

- Animals who have special species-specific needs which make rehoming them, and caring for them in shelters, very challenging.
- Animals who have severe problems in behavior and temperament, such as those who have displayed very aggressive behavior and pose a threat to humans and other animals.
- Animals who have a medical condition(s) that is difficult to treat and/or manage long term.
- Animals who require very expensive or time-intensive healthcare treatments to make them fit for adoption.

Under current conditions, shelter workers face difficult and emotional choices about what to do with these animals. Their decisions are further complicated by the fact that life in the shelter is suboptimal for most animals. Shelters are typically noisy, cramped, and stressful environments, which invariably impair the physical and psychological health of long-term residents. These adverse health effects compound the challenge of rehoming difficult cases because they make the animal increasingly less likely to be adopted and, in the long run, significantly diminish the animal's well-being.

Given all of this, shelter workers may sometimes have a lesser-evil justification—where killing is justified to prevent some greater evil—for killing animals who have a significant interest in continued life. Importantly, there are two different kinds of cases that must be evaluated separately. In the first kind of case, killing a particular animal is justified to prevent a greater evil from being done to *that* animal. Since killing in this kind of case is done in the animal's best interests, I'm going to refer to killings of this kind as "better off dead" cases.[17] In the second kind of case, killing a particular animal is justified to prevent a greater evil being done to *other* animals. I'm going to refer to killings of this kind as cases of "sacrificial killing." Let's examine each kind of case in turn.

2.4.2.1 Better Off Dead

In "better off dead" cases, the animal in question continues to have a significant interest in living but unjust features of their situation make the chances of a good life very unlikely. In this kind of circumstance, shelter workers may reason that it is better to kill an animal now rather than expose them to greater harm in the future. Consider the following example:

> Sandy, a golden retriever, was brought to the shelter by a concerned member of the public who found her wandering the streets, emaciated, dehydrated, and suffering from sarcoptic mange.[18] Though with time, effort, and other resources Sandy's state of health may be improved, the shelter is at capacity. Reasonable efforts have been made to find another local organization or individual who will care for Sandy but no alternative placement is available.

The shelter workers tasked with deciding what to do with Sandy may determine that although Sandy has a significant interest in staying alive, the current unjust circumstances mean that, regrettably, death is the *best option available* to Sandy. Given her current state of health, Sandy is evidently unable to care for herself on the streets and so releasing Sandy to take her chances and fend for herself is not a humane option.[19] Yet there is no space at the shelter and no alternative placement has been found. In this kind of case, killing is justified by appeal to the animal's interests—death is the best option (or least evil option) for the animal given the unjustly limited options. Moreover, the shelter worker acts in a way that is consistent with the animal's right not to be killed because death is, in these unjust circumstances, the best option for the animal.

Note, however, that when we look at things from the perspective of the state, the moral situation is very different. Although Sandy is in dire straits and needs a lot of care to make her suitable for adoption, her ailments are treatable and a good life is, in principle, possible. This means that Sandy has a significant interest in continuing to live. The fact that, in practice, a good life for Sandy is extremely unlikely is a direct result of the state's failure to ensure that open-admission shelters have the resources required to care for all those in need. Moreover, many animals in Sandy's circumstances do not get that way by accident. Shelters are frequently tasked with caring for animals who have been physically and psychologically harmed by humans through neglect, cruelty, and abuse. That the state permits such high levels of mistreatment and violence to animals is also a failing. In these cases, the state is doubly responsible for the wrong done to killed animals: it is responsible for failing to protect these animals against human abuse, and it is responsible for not ensuring that there are sufficient resources to satisfy these animals' right to rescue.

We are now able to see how shelter workers may have a full moral justification to kill animals in Sandy's position—animals for whom death is the best available option in the tragic circumstances—and yet the animal in question is nonetheless wronged. The source of the wrong is that the animal has their interest in continued life set back because there is an unjust constraint on the options available to them, and the agent who perpetrates the wrong is the state because it is responsible for the shortage of resources and unacceptably high levels of animal abuse. The state effectively violates the rights of animals in "better off dead" cases to rescue and to not be killed by creating, or failing to rectify, conditions in which neither rescue nor a good life is possible.

In sum, there may be some circumstances in which shelter workers are fully morally justified in killing an animal who has an interest in continued life. In these circumstances, death is regrettably the best option available because of background injustice. Though the shelter worker may have a full moral justification for the act of killing, the animal has a right not to be killed and thus they are wronged. However, the animal is not wronged by the shelter worker because the shelter worker does the best thing for the animal in tragic conditions. Rather, the animal is wronged by the state because the state has essentially imposed the tragedy on both the animal and those tasked with caring for them.

2.4.2.2 Sacrificial Killing

Let's now consider a slightly different kind of case. In cases of "better off dead," an animal is killed because it is the least evil option *for them*, whereas "sacrificial killing" occurs when the death of one animal is the least evil option *for others*. So, in cases of sacrificial killing an animal is sacrificed for the good of others. To see the contrast more starkly, imagine the following:

> Charlie is a friendly seven-year-old Staffordshire bull terrier who has been brought to the shelter because his elderly human guardian has gone into a care home. The local authorities have recently passed a by-law making it illegal to purchase or adopt pit bull-type dogs,[20] and they are actively and effectually pursuing lawbreakers. A potential adopter is visiting the shelter and, with full knowledge of the new law, is prepared to give Charlie a home. The shelter does not have the capacity to house Charlie indefinitely and they have been unable to secure a place for Charlie at a sanctuary for "dangerous" dogs.

Shelter workers in this case have two options: allow the potential adopter to give Charlie a home or kill Charlie. Unlike Sandy, a good life is available to Charlie with the potential adopter, so death is clearly not the best option for him. One might think, then, that killing Charlie is not morally justified.

However, that conclusion is too quick. Allowing the potential adopter to take Charlie home involves breaking the law, which may have serious repercussions for the shelter and its staff. If the shelter is found out, it may have its license to keep animals revoked, it may have its funding from local authorities stopped, it may become embroiled in lengthy legal battles, and individual members of staff may be liable to prosecution. These are all significant costs that, if incurred, would significantly diminish, and perhaps even end, the shelter's ability to save animals in need. Thus, shelter workers may justifiably determine that obeying the law and killing Charlie is necessary to preserve their ability to continue rescuing other animals. Importantly, the justification for killing Charlie is a lesser evil justification—it is less bad to kill Charlie and save countless others than to save Charlie and risk being closed down, which will undoubtedly result in the death and suffering of hundreds of other animals.

Of course, depending on the situation, the shelter may be permitted to save Charlie and perhaps even morally required to do so.[21] This is because the risks that shelters face in this kind of situation—where they are forced to obey an unjust law or policy—can vary greatly. If the law is not enforced, violations carry only minor penalties, the shelter has access to free and effective legal representation, or the shelter has significant social and political power, then the risks to the shelter may not be that great. In cases where risks to the shelter and its staff are morally tolerable, the shelter may be required to violate the unjust policy or law. There is no way of knowing in advance when a shelter is permitted or required to obey or violate an unjust law. When shelters find themselves in these situations, they will need to identify all of the likely negative implications associated with each available course of action, carry out a careful risk assessment, and seek legal counsel.

Let's return to Charlie. The fact that Charlie is killed to protect others makes a difference to how we should evaluate the act of killing. Though the shelter worker has a moral justification for the act of killing, the act of killing is not consistent with Charlie's right not to be killed. This is because allowing Charlie to be adopted is a better option for him than death. This would suggest, given the tripartite distinction in the ethics of killing detailed earlier, that the shelter worker who kills Charlie *infringes* Charlie's right not to be killed. Unlike "better off dead" cases, where the shelter worker does not transgress the animal's right not to be killed, "sacrificial killing" cases require shelter workers to act in a way that is justified but transgresses the animal's right not to be killed.

Given that the shelter worker has a full moral justification in both cases, what difference does this make? There are a few things worth noting. Whenever we are forced by circumstance to justifiably transgress a right, we become morally tainted by the infringement. Moreover, it's plausibly much harder, psychologically, to kill animals when death is not the best available option *for them*. So, the moral stress caused by "sacrificial killing" is likely to be much higher. Last, since infringements create a moral remainder, feelings of regret or remorse on the part of the shelter worker are not just understandable, but morally fitting.

Though shelter workers may have a moral justification for "sacrificial killing," the animal in question is nonetheless wronged. As with "better off dead" cases, the wrong is ultimately perpetrated by the state since it is the state who is responsible for the tragic circumstances imposed on both the animal and those tasked with caring for them.[22] In cases such as Charlie's, the state is responsible for both adopting and enforcing a law that makes Charlie vulnerable to being killed and for not providing alternative avenues of rescue such as state funded sanctuary. Thus, the state is responsible for creating and sustaining the unjust conditions that lead to animal rights infringements. Importantly, the state is not merely responsible for the infringement of the right not to be killed; rather it violates its duty to protect the rights detailed in Section 2.2.

In reality, most of the cases faced by shelter workers are likely to be a combination of "better off dead" and "sacrificial killing." Consider the following:

On Monday ten indoor cats were brought to the shelter following the death of their human companion. The cats are in reasonably good health, but all have ringworm. Ringworm is highly contagious, and treatment is very labor-intensive. The shelter had capacity, so workers began caring for those ten cats. On Thursday forty more indoor cats were brought to the shelter after being seized in a case of animal hoarding. However, the shelter is now at capacity. The forty incoming cats are young, in good health, and likely to be adopted relatively quickly. Reasonable efforts have been made to find another local organization or individuals who will take the cats but no alternative placement is available. The forty incoming cats could be saved and rehomed if the ten cats taken in on Monday are killed.

The shelter workers tasked with deciding what to do face a tragic predicament between saving ten and saving forty. The ten cats that were brought to the shelter on Monday are not street cats, and returning them to where they were found is not a humane option. The fact that ringworm requires a lot of labor and time to treat means that the ten cats take up space and resources that might be spent on saving many more animals. Furthermore, since ringworm is highly contagious, there is always the threat that the infection will spread to other animals in the shelter. In this kind of case, I argue that shelter workers would be morally justified in killing the ten cats in order to save the forty different cats received on Thursday.[23] But also note that killing is the least evil option for the ten cats themselves. It would be inhumane to either release the cats to fend for themselves or keep them for an indeterminate length of time in overcrowded and highly stressed conditions.

In cases that have a dual justification, the shelter worker may permissibly kill the animals that the shelter does not have the resources to care for. Moreover, unlike pure "sacrificial killing" cases, the shelter workers act in a way that is consistent with the animal's right not to be killed. This is because while the animal is killed to preserve the resources needed to save many others, it is also the case that death is the best available option for the animal(s) themselves.

This argument is likely to be met with much incredulity; especially by people committed to the claim that animals have a right not to be killed that is of comparable strength to our own. The right not to be killed is supposed to block the weighing of interests in continued life. For this reason, I cannot be killed just because five other people need my organs. It is very bad luck for those five other people that they are seriously ill, but I cannot be sacrificed to save them. Similarly, one might argue, it is very bad luck for the incoming animals in need, but resident shelter animals cannot be sacrificed to save them; their right not to be killed protects against this kind of tradeoff.

I think that this objection mischaracterizes the tragic predicament facing shelter workers. The situation in many open-admission shelters is akin to triage situations in the human medical context.[24] Healthcare systems usually have plans in place to deal with any "mass-care events" caused by natural or manmade disasters (O'Laughlin and Hick 2008).[25] Planning for disaster scenarios is important because healthcare professionals need decision-making procedures in place to ensure that limited healthcare resources will be distributed effectively and ethically. While not without critics, triage policies for mass-care events are usually designed to satisfy utilitarian considerations (Greenacre and Fleschner 2017, 36; Tolchin et al. 2020, 1). This means that disaster triage procedures are usually designed to either maximize the number of lives saved or maximize the number of quality-adjusted life years. Accordingly, resources should be dedicated to those patients who are most likely to survive or those who are not just likely to survive but have a good quality of life for some years to come.

No one (to my knowledge) writing on the ethics of disaster triage thinks that these utilitarian considerations should be altogether abandoned. Some authors suggest that other considerations (e.g., patient autonomy, egalitarianism, justice) ought, where appropriate, to feature in our thinking about how to distribute limited healthcare resources (O'Laughlin and Hick 2008). For instance, if healthcare professionals are confronted with many patients with the same chances of survival but not enough resources to save them all, then some unbiased principle of selection is required. Others suggest that there needs to be more transparency and public consensus on triage protocols: since some people are going to lose out, we need to agree as a community who will lose out and why in disaster scenarios (e.g., Greenacre and Fleschner 2017). However, consequentialist considerations will likely continue to be central to disaster protocols because unbiased principles, such as "first come, first served," have the perverse implication that valuable resources must sometimes be dedicated to those who are not likely to survive or have a good quality of life in subsequent years. Thus, while humans have an equal right to be rescued, there are some contexts in which some of us will inevitably (and rightly) be sacrificed in order to save others.[26]

Returning to open-admission shelters, many workers are operating in a constant state of triage. On my view, where resources are genuinely insufficient to save everyone, this renders some killing for non-euthanasia reasons permissible. Importantly, these killings are justified, not merely excused. Shelter workers can point to features *of their situation* that militate in favor of killing. For example, we can imagine someone saying "this animal is very unlikely to be adopted, and if we keep them alive, they will take up resources that could be used to save a number of animals who need our assistance and who are more likely to be adopted. While we would ideally kill none of the animals in our care, the non-ideal conditions that we face mean that it would be better for us to kill this one so that we can save these others." Note that this is a lesser-evil justification—shelter workers are permitted to do what's wrong because it is the least bad option of a set of all bad options. However, even though killing may be morally justified, this does not mean that no wrong has been committed. To recap, the animals killed are wronged, and the state is responsible for that wrong.

2.4.3 Absolutely Unjustified Killing

In cases of injustice-dependent justified killing, shelter workers have a moral justification for killing that depends on the unjust circumstances in which they find themselves. However, the state has no justification for imposing the unjust conditions that make the act of killing necessary. By contrast, in cases of absolutely unjustified killing, no agent—neither the shelter workers nor the state—has moral justification for the act of killing. Acts of absolutely unjustified killing are completely lacking in justification, and all agents implicated in such acts are morally responsible for the violation of the right not to be killed.

Shelter workers violate the rights of animals in their care if they kill those animals without adequate moral justification. For example, one cannot justify transgressing the right not to be killed by appealing to the protection of trivial interests. This means, for instance, that non-euthanasia killing could not be justified on the grounds that shelter staff want to go on holiday for two weeks or because enclosures need to be emptied for renovation work. Note, killing in these cases would not prevent some greater evil. Thus, killing for these kinds of reasons would be morally unjustified and would thus *violate* (not infringe) the killed animals' rights to life.

More complex, but nonetheless unjustifiable cases involve killing to prevent future harm. Life in the shelter will be far from ideal for many residents, but it will be, on balance, better than death. Undoubtedly, there will be cases where shelter workers can reliably predict that life in the shelter will ultimately impact an animal's life so negatively that their life will not be worth living. However, there is so much uncertainty involved in this kind of case—a suitable home may become available, or the shelter may receive more funding— that shelter workers cannot justifiably condemn an animal to death on the basis that prospective bads *may* outweigh prospective goods.

In these cases, the state, insofar as it ensures and promotes good welfare standards in shelters, carries out regular inspections of shelters, and supports struggling shelters, will not be responsible for absolutely unjustified killing in animal shelters. However, if the state does not support animal rescue organizations and does not monitor the provision of care in shelters, then it may be fully or at least partially liable for the wrong done to animals in those institutions.

2.5 Killing in Animal Shelters: Political Responsibility for Rights Violations and Infringements

Every night I had a recurring dream that I had died, and I was standing in line to go to heaven. And St Peter says to me, "I know you, you're the one that killed all those little animals." And I'd sit up in the bed in a cold sweat. Finally, when I realized it wasn't my fault, my dreams changed. After St Peter said, "I know you, you're the one that killed all those little animals," I turned to the 990,000 people behind me and said, "I know you, you made me kill all these animals." You grow into the fact that you are the executioner, but you weren't the judge and jury.

—Shelter worker (cited in Arluke 1994, 157)

We're never gonna beat this problem until everybody takes a small amount of responsibility.

—Shelter worker (cited in Frommer and Arluke 1999, 10)

In the preceding section, I argued that shelter workers sometimes have justification to kill the adoptable animals in their care and that in most cases of non-euthanasia killing the state bears responsibility for the violation of the right. But the issue of responsibility has not been fully resolved. Insofar as the state continues to fail in its duty to distribute resources fairly and secure the rights of animals to rescue and not to be killed, then shelter animals will continue to be killed. In what follows, I argue that all members of the political community share responsibility for the non-ideal conditions imposed on open-admissions shelters.

As we have seen, the challenges facing open-admission shelters are a direct consequence of distributive injustice. Shelters are unable to satisfy the interests of all the animals who need their assistance because they do not have the adequate resources to do so. This means that non-euthanasia killings occur as a direct consequence of the current political and economic institutional arrangements and the distribution of resources in society. If the state ensured that shelters received adequate resources to care for animals in need of rescue, then shelter workers would no longer have to make difficult decisions about who to save. Thus, it is the state's failure to satisfy *its duties* to animals that currently makes it impossible for animal shelters to fully protect animals, and shelter workers have very little influence over the institutions and policies that create the moral tragedy they face.

Importantly, this is not about charity. The problem is not that these animal welfare organizations have failed to amass sufficient charitable donations or that the problem could be solved if only people would give more. Though increased charitable donations would undoubtedly help to ameliorate the situation, it is not an appropriate response to the just claims of nonhuman animals. We have a duty to assist nonhuman animals, which is to say that they are *owed* our assistance. Satisfying these duties should not be contingent on charitable giving but guaranteed by appropriate institutional support.

In the absence of a just institutional arrangement, I want to suggest that all members of the political community in which the shelter operates bear shared responsibility for the wrong done to animals killed for non-euthanasia reasons. Some of my readers may balk at this claim. If you've never had a companion animal, never abandoned an animal, never sold an animal, never purchased an animal, never taken an animal to a shelter, then how can you be responsible for non-euthanasia killings that occur in animal shelters?[27] Unless your actions have somehow contributed to there being animals in need, one might argue, you should bear no responsibility for the moral costs associated with these rights infringements and violations.

However, this response does not fully appreciate the structure of the problem. Sure, the problem arises in part because some humans act irresponsibly with regard to animals, but the tragedy occurs because shelters have insufficient funding to do their job without killing animals for non-euthanasia reasons. Insofar as that is true, then all members of the political community bear responsibility for the tragic predicament facing shelter workers. Since dead animals cannot be compensated, and apologies won't matter to them either, the primary duty that issues from the infringed and violated rights not to be killed is to prevent similar infringements and violations.

Of course, few of us possess the political power and wherewithal to singlehandedly bring about the kind of institutional change needed, but that does not mean that there is nothing that we can do. At the very least we each have "an obligation to join with others who share that responsibility in order to transform the structural processes to make their outcomes less unjust" (Young 2011, 96). It is incumbent on us to mobilize with others to ensure that animal welfare organizations get the financial support required to rescue and rehome all animals in need.[28] We must also campaign for social and institutional change that will reduce the need for shelters. For example, if there were free healthcare for companion animals, free spay and neuter programs, stricter regulations on breeding, educational programs on caring for other animals, then fewer animals would need the assistance of animal protection organizations. And, should we find ourselves looking for a companion animal, then we should choose to adopt a shelter animal rather than purchase one from a private seller.

In addition to our responsibility to mobilize for social and institutional change, we also bear responsibility for the additional wrong which comes from the persistent imposition of a morally tragic choice scenario onto shelter workers. It is difficult for individuals who regularly confront these choices to escape without blemish, even when they do what rationality requires and pursue the morally best outcome they sometimes cannot avoid infringing a right. This is an unfair burden. But what is especially unfair is our—all other members' of the political community—refusal to acknowledge that this situation pollutes us all, morally speaking. It is not that shelter workers alone are tainted by the wronging that occurs, rather their causally proximate relationship to the wrong means they experience the tragedy of the situation more acutely. Irrespective of how we *feel* about the wrong that occurs in these cases, we are all responsible, and therefore all morally tainted by it.

This discussion brings into view quite how pernicious and misleading public condemnation of non-euthanasia shelter killings is. When animal shelters are accused of wrongful killing because the animals in question had the potential for a decent life if they had been rehomed, there is a failure to acknowledge the non-ideal conditions that open-admission shelters are forced to operate in and the moral tragedy that they routinely face. Moreover, there is a failure to acknowledge that the moral tragedy is one that animal shelters have very little control over and that the non-ideal circumstances that give rise to tragic choices are a result of *our* collective inertia.

Condemnation of this kind, therefore, attempts to apportion blame in a way that wrongfully exculpates the public.

2.6 Conclusion

In this chapter, I have distinguished between two kinds of morally justified killing in animal shelters. The first kind, genuine euthanasia, involves no wrong and is entirely consistent with the animal's rights. The second kind, injustice-dependent justified killing, though justified from the perspective of shelter workers, involves a wrong because it unjustly sets back animals' interest in continued life. Killings of this kind are often unavoidable in open-admission shelters operating in non-ideal conditions. In these cases, killing is justified because it is the best course of action in a tragic situation where all the options are bad.

While non-euthanasia killing can sometimes be justified, it is nonetheless a wrong against the animal killed. Importantly, I have argued that responsibility for this moral wrong lies not with those who perform the killing but with the state that permits and maintains the background distributive injustice that makes killing impossible to avoid. Moreover, when states fail in their duty to ensure that animal rescue organizations have the means necessary to care for all animals owed assistance, all members of the political community bear a responsibility to bring about a more just social and political order. The current organization of social and political institutions is not inevitable, and we have a responsibility to change them and eliminate injustice wherever it occurs.

I want to conclude by emphasizing the explanatory power of the framework developed in this chapter. By taking seriously the non-ideal conditions in which many rescue organizations currently operate, it explains why, when confronted with a tragic choice, shelter workers will sometimes have a moral justification for non-euthanasia killing. It also explains how the animals killed for non-euthanasia reasons are still wronged despite that justification. Moreover, the account explains why shelter workers experience agent-regret and moral stress as a result of routinely being required to kill unwanted animals in their care (Rollin 1986, 2011). Even though shelter workers may have a justification for non-euthanasia killing, which means that they are not responsible for the wrong done to those animals, a wrong nonetheless occurs, and being so intimately connected to that wrong unsurprisingly takes an emotional toll. And, last, the framework captures a sentiment widely shared among shelter workers that they alone are not responsible for the wrongful killing of animals (Frommer and Arluke 1999, 9).

Acknowledgments

I would like to thank Jess Begon, Carl Fox, Valéry Giroux, Rich Healey, Jan Kandiyali, Jonathan Parry, Liam Shields, and Kristin Voigt for helpful feedback on earlier drafts. I would also like to thank audiences at the Montreal SPCA, the Cambridge Centre for Animal Rights Law (Talking Animals, Law & Philosophy Series), and the MANCEPT Research Seminar Series for their many instructive questions and comments.

Notes

1. Most open-admission shelters admit all animals not because (or only because) they recognize that it is morally impermissible to turn animals away, but because their funding depends on them taking on all animals in need. I return to this point at the end of this section.
2. For a full discussion of the value and harm of death for nonhuman animals, see Nicolas Delon's contribution to this volume (Chapter 1).
3. To see this strategy in operation, see Cochrane 2012, chapter 2.
4. There is one obvious objection to the right to rescue. It has the counterintuitive implication that we have a duty to rescue prey animals from predators and, more generally, wilderness animals from the hazards of life in the wild. Whether nonhuman animals have such an extensive right to rescue is the subject of a lively and ongoing debate that I cannot address in any detail here. For a fuller discussion of these issues, see, e.g., Cormier and Rossi 2018; Johannesen 2020; Keulartz 2016; and Milburn 2015.

5. In recent years, return-to-field (RTF) policies have enjoyed increasing support within the sheltering community (Bays et al. 2019). These policies effectively involve returning animals who would be in danger of non-euthanasia shelter killing back to where they were found. The eligibility criteria for RTF can vary a lot depending on the shelter but most try to avoid returning especially vulnerable animals (e.g., animals who are injured, disabled, or diseased). This leaves open the possibility that lost, abandoned, and inexperienced animals will be returned to unfamiliar and hostile locations. Though there have been some studies on the benefits of RTF (e.g., Spehar and Wolff 2019, 2020) these are very small, shelter-specific studies that do not yet show that RTF could work for all shelters irrespective of the local climate and other local pressures. Moreover, these studies tend to focus on the outcomes for shelter intake and non-euthanasia shelter killings, and there is little follow-up on the well-being of returned animals. Insofar as animals have a right to rescue, far more research is needed to determine that RTF is compatible with animals' rights and, if it is, to develop morally appropriate eligibility criteria.

6. Two clarifications are in order. First, this discussion focuses on the right not to be killed, but the categories outlined are *mutatis mutandis* applicable to all rights. Second, this account applies to the rights of all sentient individuals irrespective of species-membership

7. This claim is not uncontroversial. However, many agree that if a person's life were reduced to permanent and unbearable suffering, then a doctor would have adequate moral justification—though not necessarily a legal permission—to assist in bringing about the person's death. Moreover, if we think that people have *a right* to a good death or to end a life of permanent and unbearable suffering, then perhaps healthcare services and professionals are under *a duty* to provide that.

8. There may be circumstances in which you can waive your right not to be killed that do not necessitate you being in a state of permanent and unbearable suffering. I will not explore such possibilities here.

9. There are a couple of notable exceptions, see Otsuka (1994) and McMahan (1994, 2018).

10. For more on the distinction between moral justification and moral excuse, see John Gardner 2007, 86.

11. It is arguably the case that states which prohibit euthanasia for humans wrong their citizens by denying them the right to a good death.

12. There are no definitive figures on the number of animals killed in rescue shelters for non-euthanasia reasons. One reason for this is that, in most states, many different rescue and protection organizations are working independently of one another, and no central body is responsible for collecting and collating data. There is also often a lack of transparency and honesty in individual shelter reports around the reasons for shelter killings, which is understandable given that many shelters are trying to protect their fundraising efforts and avoid

public recrimination. Moreover, "euthanasia" is often misapplied to cases where death is not in the interest of the animal killed. Although exact figures are currently unobtainable, that non-euthanasia shelter killings are prevalent is supported by the literature on compassion fatigue and moral stress in shelter workers, see, e.g., Andrukonis and Protopopova 2020; Arluke 1994; Frommer and Arluke 1999; Baran et al. 2009; Rogelberg et al. 2007; and Reeve et al. 2005.

13. For example, shelters and rescue organizations frequently report a public bias against black cats. This bias makes healthy black cats less likely to be adopted and more likely to be euthanized. There have been few studies on this bias, but Kogan et al. (2013) and Carini et al. (2020) show that there is some empirical evidence to support shelter workers' testimony on this problem.

14. While ringworm does not seriously undermine the well-being of those afflicted, it is a very infectious zoonotic disease, and it requires a lot of time and patience to treat (Moriello and Newbury 2006). Shelters not only face the challenge of managing this disease with limited resources but also of bearing the costs if their response is ineffective. If shelters adopt out too many animals who are subsequently diagnosed with ringworm, then "negative experiences or perceptions in the community about [them] may have a significant negative impact on adoptions, fund-raising, and donations" (Moriello and Newbury 2006, 89). All these considerations make euthanasia a regrettable yet fully appropriate response to ringworm infection in some sheltering contexts.

15. https://www.dailymail.co.uk/news/article-2254729/RSPCA-destroys-HALF-animals-rescues—thousands-completely-healthy.html; https://www.thesun.co.uk/archives/news/74549/sun-investigation-we-expose-charities-killing-1000s-of-healthy-dogs-for-growling-too-much/; https://www.telegraph.co.uk/news/11862369/RSPCA-euthanising-healthy-horses-as-cases-of-neglect-hit-crisis-point.html.

16. https://www.foxnews.com/us/peta-shelter-was-a-slaughterhouse-group-claims; https://www.nytimes.com/2013/07/07/us/peta-finds-itself-on-receiving-end-of-others-anger.html.

17. This category is similar to James Yeates's (2010) "contextually justified euthanasia." I think it is problematic to use the term "euthanasia" to describe killings of this kind because the animals in question are killed as a result of injustice, not ill health.

18. Sarcoptic mange is a highly contagious medical condition (for both humans and other animals) that is caused by mites that burrow through the skin causing acute itching and irritation. Treatment is intensive and takes several weeks to complete. It may also be necessary to quarantine the affected animal to prevent the spread of infection.

19. Sandy is not a good candidate for RTF (see Note 6) because it is never morally permissible to abandon vulnerable animals. Death is a bad outcome for any animal with an interest in continued life, but injury, starvation, dehydration,

disease, poisoning, frostbite, sunstroke are very real and probable dangers for domesticated animals without human guardians. So, although withdrawing assistance from animals is a live option, it will very rarely be a humane option. Animals with an interest in continued life have an interest in a minimally decent life, and very few abandoned animals will be capable of achieving that without human assistance. Thus, most lost and abandoned animals will not be eligible for RTF.

20. Breed-specific legislation is not uncommon. For example, in 2016, the City Council of Montreal passed a by-law banning residents from acquiring pit bulls, which were defined by the law as American pit bull terriers, American Staffordshire terriers, Staffordshire bull terriers, or crosses including one of those breeds. The law prevented people from purchasing or adopting pit bull type dogs and imposed severe and costly restrictions on people who already had such dogs. For example, guardians were required to pay for a permit and ensure that, when in public, their dog was muzzled at all times, always under the observation of someone aged 18 or older, and kept on a short leash of no more than 1.25 meters. The law was repealed in 2018.

21. Indeed, the Montreal SPCA refused to comply with the by-law (see previous note), they threatened to withdraw dog-control services (https://www.cbc.ca/news/canada/montreal/montreal-pit-bull-ban-spca-1.3751462), they mounted legal action against the City of Montreal (https://www.cbc.ca/news/canada/montreal/montreal-appeals-pit-bull-bylaw-suspension-1.3804 130), and gave their support to a mayoral candidate who agree to repeal the ban (https://dailyhive.com/montreal/montreal-spca-pleased-plantes-mayo ral-win).

22. I don't mean to suggest that there are no other agents who are responsible for the wrong in such cases. If a human guardian inexcusably abandons, neglects, or abuses their animal companion, then they, too, bear responsibility for the fate of the animal (as well as the initial wrong). However, as I noted above, even if a human caregiver is responsible for placing an animal in a situation of vulnerability, the state has a responsibility to satisfy the animal's right to rescue. If you are doubtful of this, consider the analogous responsibility of the state to rescue and care for human children who are failed by their caregivers.

23. Depending on the precise details of the case, the shelter workers may be able to save some but not all of the ten cats.

24. See Angela Martin's contribution to this volume (Chapter 3). Martin argues that, given the similarities between shelter work and triage scenarios in the human medical context, shelters ought to implement triage protocols to guide decision-making.

25. Triage decision-making processes are commonplace in healthcare systems, not just in the context of disasters. I have chosen to focus on the disaster context because that's when resources are likely to be most limited and "the fact

that some patients will die because there are not enough resources to save all severely injured people is what differentiates disaster triage from normal emergency department triage" (Greenacre and Fleschner 2017, 35). To my mind, disaster triage in human healthcare systems most closely corresponds to the daily struggle faced by many underfunded open-admission animal shelters.

26. One obvious difference between disaster triage and open-admission shelters is that active euthanasia is not widely endorsed in the context of disaster triage. Treatment may be withdrawn or withheld but the idea that some patients might be killed to make room for others is widely condemned. (That said, in real-life disaster situations doctors and nurses have been known to euthanize patients instead of leaving them to die painful and terrifying deaths alone. For an example, see Lisa Tessman's discussion of events at Memorial Medical Centre when hurricane Katrina devastated New Orleans in 2005 [2017, 1–8].) I don't think this difference is morally salient. Although doctors and nurses merely allow their patients to die in disaster triage, the truth of the matter is that the lives of those patients are sacrificed to keep some others alive, which makes disaster triage sufficiently similar to the situation often faced in open-admission shelters.

27. One might argue that people who have not adopted animals from animal shelters are more morally responsible for the tragic circumstances facing shelter workers than those who have. If more people adopted animals, then there would be less pressure on shelter resources. However, I think we should resist the claim that there is a moral duty to adopt. Since adopting an animal changes one's life in significant ways and is not a decision that should be made lightly (see Valéry Giroux and Kristin Voigt's contribution to this volume [Chapter 6]), would-be adopters must be sure that they have the time, resources, energy, and desire to enter into that kind of relationship. Placing people under moral duress to adopt animals not only compromises their autonomy but may lead to bad outcomes for all concerned. People who do not adopt or foster animals can discharge their duties to animals in need of rescue in other ways, including through political mobilization and campaign. I thank Valéry Giroux for pressing me on this point.

28. There are other things that we might do to practically support local shelters so that fewer animals will need to be wrongfully killed. This support can take many forms: volunteering at the shelter, fostering animals, supporting a palliative care program, and providing resources such as food and medicine. It's important to note that while these actions are certainly laudable and may be welcomed by shelters, they are not a permanent solution that would ensure that animals always receive what they are rightfully entitled to. Only social and structural change will make sure that resources are distributed appropriately and that fewer animals enter shelters in the first place.

References

Andrukonis, A., and A. Protopopova (2020) "Occupational health of animal shelter employees by live release rate, shelter type, and euthanasia-related decision." *Anthrozoös* 33(1), 119–131.

Arluke, A. (1994) "Managing emotions in an animal shelter." In Aubrey Manning and James Serpell (eds.), *Animals and Society: Changing Perspectives.* London: Routledge, 145–165.

Baran, B. E., J. A. Allen, S. G. Rogelberg, C. Spitzmüller, N. A. DiGiacomo, J. B. Webb, N. T. Carter, O. L. Clark, L. A. Teeter, and A. G. Walker (2009) "Euthanasia-related strain and coping strategies in animal shelter employees." *Journal of the American Veterinary Medical Association* 235(1), 83–88.

Bays, D., B. Kortis, K. Little, and S. Richmond (2019) *Return-to-Field Handbook.* Washington, DC: The Humane Society of the United States in collaboration with Neighborhood Cats, Inc., and Alley Cat Advocates.

Carini, R. M., J. Sinski, and J. D. Weber (2020) "Coat color and cat outcomes in an urban US shelter." *Animals* 10(10), 1720.

Cochrane, A. (2012) *Animal Rights without Liberation: Applied Ethics and Human Obligations.* New York: Columbia University Press.

Cormier, A., and M. Rossi (2018) "The problem of predation in Zoopolis." *Journal of Applied Philosophy* 35(4), 718–736.

DeGrazia, D. (2016) "Sentient nonpersons and the disvalue of death." *Bioethics* 30(7), 511–519.

Frommer, S. S., and A. Arluke (1999) "Loving them to death: Blame-displacing strategies of animal shelter workers and surrenderers." *Society and Animals* 7(1), 1–15.

Frowe, H. (2018) "Lesser-evil justifications for harming: Why we're required to turn the trolley." *The Philosophical Quarterly* 68(272), 460–480.

Gardner, J. (2007) *Offences and Defences.* Oxford: Oxford University Press.

Greenacre, M., and K. Fleshner (2017) "Distributive justice in disaster triage." *University of Western Ontario Medical Journal* 86(1), 35–37.

Johannsen, K. (2020) *Wild Animal Ethics: The Moral and Political Problem of Wild Animal Suffering.* New York: Routledge.

Keulartz, J. (2016) "Should the lion eat straw like the ox? Animal ethics and the predation problem." *Journal of Agricultural and Environmental Ethics* 29(5), 813–834.

Kogan, L. R., R. Schoenfeld-Tacher, and P. W. Hellyer (2013) "Cats in animal shelters: Exploring the common perception that black cats take longer to adopt." *Open Veterinary Science Journal* 7(1), 18–22.

Korsgaard, C. M. (2018) *Fellow Creatures: Our Obligations to the Other Animals.* Oxford: Oxford University Press.

McMahan, J. (1994) "Self-defense and the problem of the innocent attacker." *Ethics* 104(2), 252–290.

McMahan, J. (2008) "Eating animals the nice way." *Daedalus* 137(1), 66–76.

McMahan, J. (2018) "Nonresponsible killers." *Journal of Moral Philosophy* 15(6), 651–682.

Milburn, J. (2015) "Rabbits, stoats and the predator problem: Why a strong animal rights position need not call for human intervention to protect prey from predators." *Res Publica* 21(3), 273–289.

Moriello, K. A., and S. Newbury (2006) "Recommendations for the management and treatment of dermatophytosis in animal shelters." *Veterinary Clinics: Small Animal Practice* 36(1), 89–114.

Nussbaum, M. C. (2000) "The costs of tragedy: Some moral limits of cost-benefit analysis." *Journal of Legal Studies* 29, 1005–1036.

O'Laughlin, D. T., and J. L. Hick (2008) "Ethical issues in resource triage." *Respiratory Care* 53(2), 190–200.

Otsuka, M. (1994) "Killing the innocent in self-defense." *Philosophy & Public Affairs* 23(1), 74–94.

Quong, J. (2009) "Killing in self-defense." *Ethics* 119(3), 507–537.

Raz, J. (1986) *The Morality of Freedom*. Oxford: Clarendon Press.

Reeve, C. L., S. Rogelberg, C. Spitzmüller, and N. DiGiacomo (2005) "The caring-killing paradox: Euthanasia related strain among animal-shelter workers." *Journal of Applied Social Psychology* 35(1), 119–143.

Regan, T. (2004) *The Case for Animal Rights*. Berkeley: University of California Press.

Rodin, D. (2011) "Justifying harm." *Ethics* 112(1), 74–110.

Rogelberg, S. G., C. L. Reeve, C. Spitzmüller, N. DiGiacomo, O. L. Clark, L. Teeter, A. G. Walker, P. G. Starling, and N. T. Carter (2007) "Impact of euthanasia rates, euthanasia practices, and human resource practices on employee turnover in animal shelters." *Journal of the American Veterinary Medical Association* 230(5), 713–719.

Rollin, B. E. (1986) "Euthanasia and moral stress." *Loss, Grief and Care* 1(1–2), 115–126.

Rollin, B. E. (2011) "Euthanasia, moral stress, and chronic illness in veterinary medicine." *Veterinary Clinics: Small Animal Practice* 41(3), 651–659.

Simmons, A. (2009) "Do animals have an interest in continued life? In defense of a desire-based approach." *Environmental Ethics* 31(4), 375–392.

Spehar, D. D., and P. J. Wolf (2019) "Integrated return-to-field and targeted trap-neuter-vaccinate-return programs result in reductions of feline intake and euthanasia at six municipal animal shelters." *Frontiers in Veterinary Science* 6, 1–13.

Spehar, D. D., and P. J. Wolf (2020) "The impact of return-to-field and targeted trap-neuter-return on feline intake and euthanasia at a municipal animal shelter in Jefferson County, Kentucky." *Animals* 10(8), 1–18.

Tessman, L. (2017) *When Doing the Right Thing Is Impossible*. Oxford: Oxford University Press.

Tolchin B., S. C. Hull, and K. Kraschel (2020) "Triage and justice in an unjust pandemic: Ethical allocation of scarce medical resources in the setting of racial and socioeconomic disparities." *Journal of Medical Ethics*. doi:10.1136/medethics-2020-106457

Thomson, J. J. (1991) "Self-defense." *Philosophy & Public Affairs* 20(4), 283–310.

Yeates, J. (2010) "Ethical aspects of euthanasia of owned animals." *In Practice* 32(2), 70–73.

Young, I. M. (2011) *Responsibility for Justice*. Oxford: Oxford University Press.

3

Decision-Making Under Non-Ideal Circumstances

Establishing Triage Protocols for Animal Shelters

Angela K. Martin

3.1 Introduction

Free-roaming animals are a problem in many countries. Free-roaming animals are defined here as being either (i) stray animals, that is, animals who were once socialized and lived with humans but were subsequently lost or abandoned, and/or (ii) members of companion animal species, such as cats or dogs, who were directly born on the street and who often are not socialized (henceforth: feral animals). Their living conditions are frequently harsh: many free-roaming animals suffer from preventable diseases caused by worms and parasites, as well as from malnutrition and thirst. Their health, welfare, and even life may also be threatened by traffic and extreme weather conditions, such as cold winters and hot summers. In addition, they may live in constant fear for their offspring and be distressed about finding food and defending their territory.

I start here from the assumption that sentient nonhuman animals (henceforth: animals) count morally for their own sake. I furthermore take as a premise that these animals have a claim for assistance and protection by moral agents. This is even more the case given the fact that humans often brought these animals into such

Angela K. Martin, *Decision-Making Under Non-Ideal Circumstances* In: *The Ethics of Animal Shelters.* Edited by: Valéry Giroux, Angie Pepper, and Kristin Voigt, Oxford University Press. © Oxford University Press 2023. DOI: 10.1093/oso/9780197678633.003.0005 miserable situations: it was humans who domesticated and bred them throughout history. However, many humans fail to properly take care of domesticated animals. For example, humans frequently buy a dog or cat as a companion from a breeder but then abandon the animal for various reasons. As Clare Palmer has argued, if we create dependencies and vulnerabilities in animals, for example, by domesticating them and thus making them dependent on our care, then we also owe them special obligations in the form of assistance and help (Palmer 2010).

Many animal protection nongovernmental organizations (NGOs), public authorities, and societies for the prevention of cruelty to animals (SPCAs) operate or establish animal shelters. They have different aims: to rescue animals from neglect and abuse; to take in relinquished and found animals, treat them for their ailments, and reunite them with their owners or find a forever home for them; to establish *trap-neuter-return-maintain* (TNRM) programs for feral animals who cannot be socialized; to educate the general public about issues related to animal welfare; and to publicly speak up about animal abuse and organize political campaigns about the legal standing of animals.

In an ideal world, all abused, lost and found, abandoned, and relinquished animals would find a loving home and be taken care of. However, the reality is different: there are often more animals in need than there is space in shelters and—ultimately—in forever homes. Furthermore, many SPCAs operate with restricted budgets, are understaffed, and do not have enough space for all the animals who need a shelter place and medical care. As a consequence, charity-based and not-for-profit animal shelters face many ethically challenging situations in their day-to-day operation. For example, decisions have to be made in a short amount of time about euthanasia, killing animals who cannot be adopted, abortions, expensive treatments for individual animals (such as dental surgery), and the like. However, responsibilities are frequently unclear, and diverging values and opinions among different groups (such as veterinarians, animal caregivers, the board of directors, etc.) may make it difficult to find agreement on specific situations. Under these non-ideal circumstances, there often does not seem to be one best solution, but rather many different options with apparently similarly bad outcomes. Nonetheless, shelter staff have no choice but to make critical life-and-death decisions in these highly non-ideal circumstances.

In what follows, I outline the diverse difficulties shelters face when making such decisions. I argue that these difficulties are similar in nature to those situations in medicine where triage is needed—that is, in situations with restricted resources, such as money, medical utilities, space, and trained staff. In order to resolve these issues, I propose that animal shelters should establish decision-making procedures with requirements similar to those outlined in triage protocols. In this chapter, I take a closer look at eight widely accepted morally relevant considerations for triage protocols in human medical care. These are (i) maximizing benefit, (ii) justice, (iii) consideration of medical criteria, (iv) life-span considerations, (v) fair decision-making, (vi) patient will, (vii) re-evaluation of triage decisions and changes in the therapeutic goal, and (viii) burden of triage and staff support (Jöbges et al. 2020). My aim is to flesh out how these requirements can be extended and applied to the context of nonprofit animal shelters. Establishing such triage protocols will help to make ethically justifiable decisions which are acceptable (or at least comprehensible and transparent) for everyone involved. Finally, I outline how an external Ethics Board can support and improve decision-making in SPCAs by providing advice and help. That is, when specific decisions are the source of persistent conflict between staff members, consulting an external board of experts may help to shed light on the problems and rationales for the different options. Calling in external ethics advice may help staff members to better understand other points of view and find a compromise or agreement on specific cases without negatively affecting the work atmosphere.

3.2 Animal Shelters and the Challenge of Making Decisions Under Non-Ideal Circumstances

Animal shelters are often nongovernmental and nonprofit organizations that are financed by donations. Frequently, they operate with a limited budget or with a budget that is unpredictable and changes over time. Furthermore, shelters may lack space for the animals; there may be an insufficient number of staff members to feed, clean, and take care of the animals; there may be an insufficient number of veterinarians to undertake surgeries and medical procedures, or medical treatments may be too costly; and, ultimately, there may not be enough foster homes and adoption families for all animals in need. For all these reasons, shelters commonly do not have the means to take in, treat, and feed all animals who need care.

A further issue is that *time* is also a limited resource: decisions about important issues have to be taken in a short amount of time. For example, shelter staff may need to determine whether individual animals should receive costly therapies even though more animals could be saved for the same amount of money. Or, they must decide whether and which animals should be saved and which ones should be killed or euthanized (either because the shelter is overpopulated and has no space or because the suffering of an individual animal has become unbearable).[1] They also have to decide whether abortions are conducted to avoid overpopulation. In many cases, there is not enough time to extensively discuss all the options thoroughly. Instead, executive decisions have to be taken by, for example, the management or the head of the veterinary unit. That is, despite (or, in some cases, because of) this lack of resources (in particular, money, space, staff, and time), the staff of animal shelters face hard ethical decisions on a regular basis.

These are difficult decisions for various reasons. First of all, it is not always clear who is responsible for making decisions about a particular animal. In some cases, it is unclear who should take the decision and carry the responsibility and accountability in the first place. In addition, there may be disagreement about specific decisions among staff members and animal caretakers, members of the board of directors, and veterinarians. For example, animal caretakers may see the potential in a litter of feral cats to be socialized and rehomed with humans. The management team, on the other hand, may urge that these cats be killed because they occupy urgently needed space that could be occupied by cats who already are used to contact with humans and who could be adopted more quickly. Such diverging opinions may result in conflicts among staff, causing a negative or tense work atmosphere which is mentally strenuous for all involved. In short, often overworked staff members have to take decisions in animal shelters under absolutely non-ideal circumstances (i.e., situations of distress, with little time and not enough resources) about the life, health, and death of many animals.

To facilitate decision-making in animal shelters, basic guidelines should be in place. The benefits would be plentiful: ethical principles and guidelines would prevent continuous, exhausting debates among staff members about the right decision to take in similar cases; precious time would be saved that could be used for other purposes, such as caring for individual animals, lobbying work, educational campaigns, necessary administrative work, and the like; clear criteria for decision-making would also allow for the ethical use of resources in the shelter as their allocation would be optimized and can be defended against potential criticism; and, finally, transparent and fair procedures and principles for decision-making would allow for the quick alleviation of animal suffering in emergency situations. That is, guiding principles would avoid to some degree debates about right and wrong in regularly recurring situations. In addition, decision-making guidelines would help to make responsibilities clearer and more transparent, and, along with them, accountability for decisions.

3.3 Triage: Its Importance and Underlying Principles

There is another domain in which decisions about life and death have to be taken under similarly difficult circumstances: triage situations. The term "triage" comes from the French word *trier*, which means "to sort" or "to select." The concept of triage is associated with the French military surgeon Baron Dominique Jean Larrey (1766–1842), who established a wartime system to sort soldiers' injuries according to their gravity and urgency regardless of morally irrelevant factors such as a person's military rank or nationality (Blagg 2004; Skandalakis et al. 2006).

Triage guidelines exist in medical care and wartime hospitals to guide fair and transparent decision-making in times of highly limited means. Their aim is to optimize the outcome for all affected. Therefore, triage goes further than mere healthcare rationing. In everyday practice, healthcare practitioners have to decide which incoming patients they treat first and how far they go with their treatment. Imagine, for example, that two patients arrive at a hospital: first, patient A with a cold and a sore throat, then patient B, who was the victim of a severe motorcycle accident. Obviously, healthcare providers should first treat patient B, as her condition is much worse than patient A's. That is, priority has to be given to the sickest patients. If the condition of patient B substantially deteriorates, doctors furthermore have to decide how many life-saving procedures to use and at what point all hope is lost and patient B's condition will not substantially improve.

Triage is a more extreme form of healthcare rationing. Healthcare rationing is about deciding whom to treat in what order and how to best allocate medical resources. Triage, as I understand it here, is needed if "demand for essential resources surpasses availability" (Muensterer et al. 2021: 1). This is, for example, the case if there are more incoming patients with severe health issues than hospitals can admit and treat—because they are understaffed, lack precious medical resources, or space. That is, triage is rationing of care in what can be called "hard times" (Repine et al. 2005). During triage, decisions have to be taken about whom to save, whom to leave untreated, and whom to let die, which is not or only rarely needed during "normal" times in Western societies. In triage situations, some patients will not be admitted to hospital to receive treatment because their prognosis is too negative or because they will likely survive even without medical assistance (Singer 2011: 205). This means that, in triage situations, healthcare professionals sort patients according to the severity of their condition, and they care for those patients who are most likely to benefit from the treatment.

Triage protocols became a topic of public importance, attention, and urgency during the COVID-19 pandemic. The respiratory disease caused by the SARS-CoV-2 virus brought hospitals and healthcare providers worldwide to their limits. During the pandemic, many hospitals struggled due to a shortage of intensive care unit beds, staff, and medical equipment (such as ventilators and extracorporeal life support technologies, but also personal protective equipment for healthcare professionals). All of these would be necessary to adequately treat patients and thus to save lives. In many countries, governments and healthcare providers feared that the healthcare system would be overwhelmed and collapse. As Ehni et al. (2021: 126) note: "The scarcity of medical resources means prioritizing some patients over others, who then remain untreated and in the worst case may die as a result." The question is then: How can we ethically justify such choices about life and death? And how can we determine who receives treatment and who loses out?

Triage decisions face an inherent challenge, which is to maximize benefits while still respecting basic rights and avoiding discrimination.

> Relevant principles and values may conflict with one another, such as maximizing benefits and respecting equal rights. From a consequentialist perspective, treating patients equally might be hindering when trying to achieve the best outcome. From a deontological perspective, maximizing benefits may lead to discrimination or violations of individual rights. The fundamental ethical problem is how to combine both perspectives and justify the best outcome as well as the procedures by which they should be achieved, while still respecting individual rights. (Ehni et al. 2021, 126)

That is, there is a conflict between maximizing benefit for as many individuals as possible (using resources as efficiently as possible) and respecting basic requirements of justice.

At the beginning of the COVID-19 pandemic, many countries lacked in-depth triage guidelines about what to do if hospitals were overwhelmed by an influx of patients. Medical associations and medical academies in many countries hastily had to either establish or improve and adapt their already existing triage protocols because they proved insufficient for the situation in early 2020. To date, there is no general agreement on ethical triage principles. Instead, there are different guidelines in place in different countries.

What morally relevant considerations can be found in triage protocols? A good starting point are comparative literature reviews of triage protocols implemented during the COVID-19 pandemic. While these were specifically designed for the medical domain, an overview of the categories discussed in that literature provides a useful starting point for developing decision-making and triage protocols for animal shelters.

While there is a lot of disagreement about specific principles in triage protocols worldwide, there is also some basic agreement. Jöbges et al. (2020) reviewed triage guidelines from Australia/New Zealand, Belgium, Canada, Germany, the United Kingdom, Italy, Pakistan, South Africa, Switzerland, the United States, and the International Society of Critical Care Medicine. The authors identify the following eight areas of agreement: (i) maximizing benefit, (ii) justice, (iii) consideration of medical criteria, (iv) life-span considerations, (v) fair decision-making, (vi) patient will, (vii) re-evaluation of triage decisions and changes in the therapeutic goal, and (viii) burden of triage and staff support.[2] I develop these criteria in the following section and show how they can be fruitfully applied to animal shelters.

3.4 Extending Triage Criteria to Animal Shelters

The eight categories of morally relevant considerations listed above can serve as a useful starting point to develop triage guidelines for animal shelters, where decisions frequently have to be taken under non-ideal circumstances similar to those that make triage necessary for human patients. However, before I outline what these considerations mean and how they can be applied in practice to improve decision-making in animal shelters, some remarks on the ethics of triage in animal shelters are necessary.

Animal shelters are in a situation which makes constant triage necessary due to restricted means, time, staff, and space (see also Chapter 2, this volume, 151). However, one may object that this is problematic because it allows triage to become the norm in shelters, whereas, in human healthcare, it is limited to exceptional circumstances. That is, one may claim that I introduce here a double standard regarding the treatment of animals and humans and that my proposal is therefore *speciesist* (i.e., that I discriminate on the basis of a morally arbitrary criterion: namely, species membership). After all, how can we justify "normalizing" triage guidelines for animals, while they remain an exception for humans?

To counter this argument, recall the fact that I am concerned here with decision-making under *non-ideal circumstances*. Ideally, animal shelters would only be concerned with rationing questions about the optimal allocation and use of resources, and questions about the killing and letting die of animals would never arise—this would be the ultimate aim. However, reality presents itself differently, and solutions have to be found for shelters operating in a speciesist world where animals are not yet treated as they should be. In order to avoid arbitrary decisions under the non-ideal circumstances that shelters face, it is necessary to have some guiding triage principles. I outline these principles in the following.

3.4.1 Maximization of Benefit

A first requirement in the triage context concerns the maximization of benefit. According to Jöbges et al. (2020: 949), this can mean many different things.

[I]t could refer to saving as many people as possible, to saving the greatest possible number of life years, or to saving the greatest amount of quality-adjusted life years (QALYs), with the resources available. Depending on which criterion is applied, resource allocation will look quite different. Saving as many life years as possible would favour young people, whereas maximizing QALYs would favour those with a capacity to lead long, healthy, independent lives.

Which interpretation of "maximizing benefit" is promising for animal shelters?

A first interpretation of benefit maximization is *to save as many animals as possible*. However, note that the language of "saving lives" is misleading in the case of animal shelters. Animal shelters have to make triage decisions about a range of topics at different moments in time: How many animals can they neuter? How many abortions can they undertake? How many animals suffering from diseases or accidents can they treat? How many animals can shelters take in? How should the shelter decide which animals can be socialized to join a forever home and which ones may be too feral to be adoptable and may need to be killed? That is, in many cases, the challenges for animal shelters do not solely revolve around *saving* lives, but also around prioritization for care and treatment in the first place.

This may lead to an inadequate interpretation of "benefit maximization" in the case of shelter animals: animal shelters should not and cannot only "save" lives (understood as keeping as many animals as possible alive). Rather, they also have a further mission: they should think about what will happen to the animals *after* their stay at the shelter. For example, should some animals only be neutered and treated for minor ailments (such as parasites), but then be put back on the street? After all, they could die a few months later due to the bad living conditions on the street (such as harsh winters with no adequate food and water supply, injuries, or diseases). Might some feral cats be socialized in a way that makes them attractive candidates for adoptive families? On the other hand, if a shelter takes in a feral cat and improves her medical condition, but then shortly after kills her because there is not enough space or no potential foster or adoptive family, the cat may have been better off on the street. To weigh these different options can be challenging. That is, shelters cannot solely focus on *saving* as many lives as possible. Rather, they must keep the whole picture in mind, including the potential placement and welfare of animals *after* their time in the shelter.

A second interpretation of benefit maximization is to save the *greatest possible number of life years*. This would imply that *young* animals be given preference. However, this is morally problematic: some ethicists consider this to be unjustified discrimination based on age (called "ageism"), which is usually deemed unacceptable in the case of humans.[3] After all, some humans in the middle or near the end of their life could look forward to the prospect of many happy years if they received medical treatment. To prioritize the young in medical care *solely* due to their age and regardless of other, medical factors amounts to an unjustified form of discrimination.

The same consideration should apply to animals: the focus should lie on individual animals and factors such as their medical prognosis and their likelihood of socialization, regardless of their age. Maximizing life years could lead to the counterintuitive consequence that priority should be given to pregnant animals, and abortions avoided, in order to save as many young lives as possible. However, while kittens probably have a higher likelihood of being adopted, there is still the risk that many will not find a home and thus eventually have to be killed or put back on the street.

A third, rather promising interpretation of benefit maximization concerns the *greatest amount of quality-adjusted life years* (QALYs). QALYs have been developed in the field of health economics to assess a year in relation to the quality of life experienced. QALYs multiply the *years saved* with the *quality of life* experienced by a subject. This way, a QALY maximization approach would avoid a scenario in which humans (and animals) are saved who have many years left but who would experience a rather low quality of life for their remaining years.

QALY maximization approaches have been criticized for several reasons (Bickenbach 2021). The most prominent criticism from an ethical perspective concerns the fact that QALYs may be discriminatory against both the *elderly* and the *disabled*. First, if *life years* count, then the elderly will lose out because they do not have as many years left as a young person. As outlined above, the *exclusive* reliance on remaining life years to determine who should receive scarce medical resources, regardless of, for example, patients' physiological condition, has been criticized on ethical grounds (Harris 1987; Evans 1997; Rivlin 2000). Second, disabled individuals may have a good quality of life but not so many years left due to an impairment—or they may have the same life expectancy as able-bodied individuals but a lower quality of life. If we understand benefit maximization as maximization of QALYs, the disabled may find themselves disadvantaged in comparison to able-bodied individuals. That is, they may be discriminated against due to a condition which is not their fault and over which they do not have any control, which seems unfair. In addition, our moral intuition may actually point us in another direction: that we should prioritize the worse-off (Parfit 1997). According to such a Priority View, "[w]e should not give equal weight to equal benefits, whoever receives them. Benefits to the worse off should be given more weight" (Parfit 1997: 213). That is, understanding benefit maximization as QALY maximization may be at odds with our moral intuitions. We typically regard it as highly unfair if those worse off through no fault of their own are deprioritized. Furthermore, we may even be convinced that we should prioritize the worse-off. However, note that Parfit does not defend the view that priority is absolute. Rather, it may be outweighed by sufficiently important benefits for the better-off (Parfit 1997).

A third problem of QALY maximization is that such an interpretation of benefit maximization may *indirectly* harm disabled individuals. The disabled are frequently the target of stigmatization and prejudice. This can involve false assumptions about their quality of life and health status, which in turn can lead to problematic consequences for them, especially in triage situations (Scully 2020). However, this problem can be overcome if more attention is paid to potential biases and false assumptions about the quality of life of the disabled during decision-making.

These ethical issues regarding QALY maximization also arise with respect to animals. Various studies investigating the health status and welfare of stray cats have shown that these animals frequently live with impairing conditions and diseases, such as ear problems, gingivitis, lost incisor teeth, blindness, underweight, cat flu, anemia, flea burden, viral diseases (including feline immunodeficiency virus [FIV] infection and respiratory disease), and the like (Marston and Bennett 2009; Castro-Prieto and Andrade-Núñez 2018; Seo et al. 2021). Treating these conditions sometimes comes at a high cost or requires a substantial time commitment from veterinarians. Examples include dental treatments and teeth removals, as well as amputations. This means that staff at shelters will have to face the challenge of deciding which animals will receive which treatment and what will happen to them afterward.

In practice, this means that the staff in shelters have to weigh the short-term prognosis and benefits of a treatment for animals against the long-term health prognosis, which may be influenced by age and comorbidities. That is, it has to be determined how likely it is that an animal will actually benefit from a treatment in the short and long run. Furthermore, the likelihood of socialization and eventually adoption after treatment also has to be taken into account. In case adoption is not possible, it has to be assessed whether the animal is better off back on the street or whether killing the animal is the better option because the hardship experienced on the streets would be too problematic.[4] This may vary from one situation to another.

In addition, the Priority View has further implications for shelter animals: it may in some situations be morally permissible to prioritize animals who are worse off from a health perspective. In many situations, humans caused the dire situation of animals. Humans breed some animal species and bring into existence offspring with impairments but then fail to properly care for them or even abuse them. In such cases, moral agents may owe a positive duty of compensation and reparation to these animals. That is, it may be ethically justifiable to prioritize animals with a history of abuse (group A) over other animals (group B) with similar or even better health prospects if treatment and continued existence is in the best interest of group A—even if this does not maximize QALYs.

Further factors to be taken into account in shelters concern the number of staff and space available. Shelters can only operate with veterinarians and caregivers who treat, feed, clean, and socialize the animals. Moreover, the available space also determines how many animals can be reasonably hosted within a shelter. Overcrowding negatively affects the welfare of animals present in shelters (Turner et al. 2012; Karsten et al. 2017). To avoid over-occupancy of shelters, I suggest that shelters determine how many animals they can host under good conditions at a given time with the available staff members, space, and budget. This is a very specific number for each shelter and may vary over time. The needs of different animal species also have to be taken into account in this calculation. After all, some exotic animals (such as iguanas, turtles, and snakes) may need large, heated terrariums for themselves, and this has to be accounted for when assigning space and budgets for future animals.

Furthermore, for periods when shelters expect a higher number of incoming animals, they may fix a higher maximum number of incoming animals. This may be necessary for regions where there are national moving days once per year (such as Montreal, Canada) when people are more likely to abandon their companion animals because their new home does not allow for animals, or during summer vacation. By freeing up office space, more animals could be hosted, which, in turn, may make it possible to save the lives of more animals (e.g., with the hope that people may adopt animals after vacation season). However, this would also mean that the animals and staff may be living and working under less ideal circumstances for a while. For the sake of the well-being of staff and animals already present, this number should not be exceeded at any point.

To sum up, maximizing benefit in the case of shelters does not mean "just" saving as many animals as possible: the bigger picture must be kept in mind, including what will happen to animals *after* they are admitted to the shelter. Furthermore, I argued that the maximization of benefit has some possible limits in shelters—namely, when it comes to animals with a history of abuse and neglect. In their case, it may sometimes be morally justified to prioritize them, although this may be at odds with the principle of maximizing benefit.

3.4.2 Justice

These considerations about the ethics of maximizing benefit bring me to the next point relevant for triage guidelines: justice. In the case of humans, the criterion of justice usually demands *equality* and *equity*. According to Jöbges et al. (2020), equality requires that individuals with relevantly similar medical characteristics and prognosis—regardless of the specific diagnosis—should have the *same access* to medical treatment during a crisis. Equity prohibits unjustified unequal *treatment* (i.e., unjustified forms of discrimination) based on characteristics such as age, race, sexual orientation, socio-economic status, and the like.[5] I explain these two considerations in more detail in the following, and I outline how they can be extended to the shelter context.

Let us turn first to *equality*. Questions of equality largely depend on whether the shelter operates under an open-admission or a limited-admission policy. Open-admission shelters usually take in *all* animals who are brought to them or who are brought to their attention (e.g., animals suffering from abuse or neglect in a private home or on a farm). This means that open-admission shelters are usually not allowed to refuse animals and thus have to grant access to all animals in need. In turn, this implies that these shelters may need to kill some animals because of lack of space, lack of caregivers and veterinarians, the animals' medical condition, or because they are too feral to be socialized, which then raises issues about equity. Limited-admission shelters, on the other hand, select the animals they take in. That is, they may restrict themselves to animals of certain species and also may give priority to animals who have, for example, a high likelihood of being adopted (Humane Society of the United States 2012). As a consequence, limited-admission shelters do not need to kill animals as frequently as open-admission shelters.[6]

Equality may appear to be a particular challenge for limited-admission shelters. After all, they select the animals they take in and consequently make decisions about who will eventually be rescued. At the same time, though, these shelters may be specialized in some species and therefore may increase the chance of admitted animals eventually finding a forever home. Therefore, even though limited-admission shelters do not grant all animals equal access to a shelter space, this appears to be ethically legitimate at first sight.

But let us look a bit closer at this issue and turn to the role of *equity* in the shelter context. Equity demands that unjustified forms of discrimination be avoided: unequal treatment on grounds of morally irrelevant characteristics such as age, gender, sexual orientation, disability, or socioeconomic status are not allowed.[7] If discrimination based on morally arbitrary features is ethically problematic, then the same is true for discrimination based on species membership—in short, speciesism. Different definitions of speciesism and its wrongness can be found in the literature (see, e.g., Singer 2009; Horta 2010; Jaquet 2019; Horta and Albersmeier 2020). For the purpose of this chapter, I understand speciesism as the "unjustified disadvantageous consideration or treatment of those who are not classified as belonging to one or more particular species" (Horta 2010, 247). This definition is particularly useful for two reasons: first, it accounts for the fact that speciesism is an *unjustified* and thus morally problematic form of discrimination. Second, it shows that not only humans can benefit from speciesist discrimination: as Horta's definition outlines, individuals who do not belong to one *or more* particular species can be subject to unjustified discrimination.

In our society, some animals are frequently deemed worthier of moral consideration than others. For example, more publicly visible animals—such as companion animals—commonly benefit from better legal protection than more "invisible" animals, such as farm animals destined to be a source of food (O'Sullivan 2012). Animal shelters usually admit a wide range of different species. The question to be addressed now is: Can species membership play a role when admitting new animals? Or is it always ethically illegitimate?

Some animal species—such as dogs—generally have a higher likelihood of being adopted than other species, such as large farm animals (e.g., cows and pigs) and exotic animals who need special settings, such as heating lamps and terrariums or saltwater aquariums. Furthermore, some animal species—such as dogs—benefit more from public appreciation than liminal animals (such as injured rats and pigeons) and feral cats, who are regarded as a nuisance in some regions.

The question is then: How can we decide who should be granted access to shelters in the first place while avoiding arbitrariness, inequities, and speciesism? After all, for most animals, being admitted to an animal shelter is a valuable good: it may significantly improve their health and likelihood of survival because they receive treatment, food, and care and can potentially find a forever home. While open-admission shelters usually accept (or at least *should* accept) all animals in need, regardless of species, limited-admission shelters can select the animals they take in. Is this an ethical problem? No. The reason lies in the distinction between speciesist discrimination and species-based discrimination. Speciesist discrimination is an *unjustified* disadvantageous consideration. Discrimination based on species membership, on the other hand, can be justified in some situations. It seems legitimate that limited-admission shelters can freely choose which animals they take in, for example, because they are particularly well trained to take care of specific species. As argued before, shelters may refuse animals once their occupancy is maxed out. Furthermore, shelters should, whenever possible, maximize the benefits for all animals concerned. Therefore, when they find themselves in the situation of choosing between taking in a stray animal of species X and a stray animal of species Y, and all other aspects (such as health status and chances of survival) are relevantly similar, then the shelter may give priority to the species with the *higher likelihood of finding a forever home* (thereby leaving new space for future animals).

This means that, contrary to the case of humans, the shelter context makes some inequities permissible. This is due to fact that shelters ought to maximize the use of resources. Saving animals with a very low likelihood of being adopted who then eventually have to be killed is often a suboptimal use of resources. Such unequal treatment of some species is not per se an instance of speciesist discrimination. The animals saved are not chosen because of their species membership per se, but rather because of their likelihood of adoption: there is more demand for adoption of certain animals, and shelters should optimize their use of resources. That is, given the non-ideal circumstances under which shelters operate, I deem it legitimate to save those species who are more likely to be adopted in order to maximize benefit and to free up space for additional animals to be treated and saved.[8]

This view may result in even more drastic consequences: it can justify shelters' prioritizing those species who cause the least harm overall to other animals. Let us assume for the sake of the argument that farmed animals are killed to produce food for both humans and shelter animals, and this causes considerable harm to farmed animals. Assume furthermore that some species of domesticated animals—such as cats—are carnivorous and cannot as easily flourish on a plant-based diet than other species, such as dogs. If a group of dogs and a group of cats have the same medical prognosis and the same likelihood of being adopted, then, according to the view presented here—which does not preclude decisions based on species membership—it is ethically justified to prioritize dogs, the reason being that they can more easily flourish on a plant-based diet (for a more in-depth defense of this view, see Chapter 4, this volume, 215–217).

In sum, I have shown that decisions based on species membership may sometimes be justified in the shelter context due to the non-ideal circumstances under which shelters operate.

3.4.3 Consideration of Medical Criteria

Linked to the arguments listed above about justice is a third requirement for triage: consideration of medical criteria, such as prognosis and comorbidities. This means that *medical* criteria should be used to assess patients' mortality risk (Jöbges et al. 2020). Applied to the shelter context, it is useful to distinguish between short- and long-term survival rates: while one may directly save the lives of some animals in the short term by taking them into the shelter and providing them with the medical care they need, they may have a rather poor long-term prognosis because they have further comorbidities and are thus unlikely to live much longer. If they are treated, the costs may be particularly high, which then takes away valuable resources from other animals with a higher likelihood of survival and a decent quality of life.

Conversely, an animal may have a rather negative short-term prognosis but may lead a happy and long life afterward once means are invested into caring for her health. Therefore, short- and long-term prognoses have to be carefully balanced while also taking into account the costs and living situations of the animal in the long term. That is, not only the likelihood of being soon adopted counts, but also the general *medical* state of an animal both in the short and long term.

This may in some cases be a hard decision. After all, many stray animals live deplorable lives and are affected by impairing and debilitating conditions and diseases. However, instead of letting them just continue to face hardship on the street, eventually leading to their death, the shelters may be justified in taking these animals in and killing those animals who have—due to diseases and comorbidities—a negative long-term survival likelihood from a medical perspective.[9] This is an option that is not too costly and at the same time saves the animals concerned from unnecessary long-term suffering.

3.4.4 Life-Span Considerations

Let us now turn to considerations about life span. Triage protocols regarding humans usually refrain from considering age *alone* as a criterion for triage decisions (Jöbges et al. 2020), as this amounts to ageist discrimination. However, age may be linked to other factors, such as comorbidities and a negative medical prognosis, which can be taken into account in decision-making.

What should we do with these considerations in the case of shelter animals? Elderly animals may still have a good medical prognosis and may lead happy and fulfilling lives in forever homes. Therefore, they should not be disadvantaged based on age alone. Some people may actually prefer to adopt an elderly animal with a shorter life span because the animal is potentially calmer or because the adoption family does not want to commit to ten or more years of caregiving.

There is another reason why reliance on life span alone is problematic as a basis for decision-making in the case of shelter animals: life expectancy varies from one species to another and even within a given species. For example, small dogs have a longer life expectancy than larger dogs (Višak 2018). Turtles have an extremely long life expectancy (up to 100 years), while rodents, for example, have a shorter life expectancy. If age was used as a determinant for decisions in shelters, one would first need to establish which threshold counts exactly: The potential life span of the species? The life span of the specific breed? Basing decisions on life expectancy in animals would have the problematic consequence of potentially disadvantaging species with shorter life spans over others.

To illustrate this, imagine that a shelter has to choose between admitting an 8-year-old cat with a potential life span of 14 years and a large, 8-year-old dog with a life expectancy of 10 years. If life-span considerations count, then the dog would lose out because he is older than the cat in relation to his potential life span. Such considerations may thus lead to unjustified discrimination against some animal species. For these reasons, it makes sense to focus, first and foremost, on the medical condition, the cost and efficiency of treatment, both the short- and the long-term prognosis, and the probability of adoption of the individual animal. Only if all these factors are relevantly similar should remaining life span potentially become a criterion for triage in the case of animals.

3.4.5 Fair Decision-Making

A further consideration in triage is *fair decision-making*. This includes, among other things, transparency, respect for the patient's preferences, and an assessment of the burden of treatment and its potential benefits for the individual (Jöbges et al. 2020). Applied to the case of shelter animals, this may involve the regular assessment of the prognosis of admitted animals: Does their condition and sociability improve or worsen? Treatment and therapy may be stopped if there are no benefits or if the harm–benefit ratio is negative and the burden clearly outweighs the potential benefits. In such cases, palliative care or killing the animals may become justifiable options.

I suggest that, if possible and available, two staff members, including a veterinarian, should be involved in decisions about the death of an animal. This reduces the risk of biases and personal preferences for individual animals, and it also respects the requirement of transparency.[10] Decision-making should be conducted while keeping in mind *all* animals at the shelter, as well as further potential incoming animals. That is, opportunity costs also have to be considered. After all, it could be that another animal may benefit more from a specific treatment, a place at the shelter, and the care provided. In such a case, it is justified to withdraw treatment and a shelter place from an animal and to provide it to another animal. Furthermore, I suggest that the final decisions and rationales for them are communicated to the caregiving team to secure transparency and allow team members to come to terms with decisions that affect animals under their care.

Two options are conceivable regarding end-of-life decisions: if animals are suffering and have a low quality of life, euthanizing them is justified. If the animal still has a rather good quality of life, but likely will not recover, palliative care in foster families may be justified. Palliative care for shelter animals is resource- and cost-intensive. Therefore, one may be tempted to eliminate it altogether. However, if it can be pursued by devoted foster families who otherwise would not take care of animals, it can be justified: it sends a signal to the general public that animals matter in their own right, even if they are terminally ill or afflicted with chronic diseases that cannot be treated. That is, foster families who provide a home for animals in palliative care can be seen as ambassadors who change the public norms and attitudes about animals (see also Part I, this volume, 80). Because space within shelters is restricted, I suggest that palliative care be exclusively conducted in private foster families, not at the shelter itself. This way, valuable space can be saved for those animals who have a higher chance of survival and eventually adoption.

3.4.6 Respect for the Patient's Will

A further requirement for triage in the case of humans is respect for the will of patients, for example, to withdraw from critical care. This requirement seems notoriously hard to apply to animals. After all, animals cannot give proper informed consent or write advance directives. However, there are two other ways in which the (presumed) will of animals can be respected. First, over the past few years, a considerable body of literature in animal ethics has emerged which takes the embodied agency of animals seriously. That is, there is the view that animals can assent and dissent *with their behavior*. Second, humans—for example, caretakers in the shelter—can act as surrogate decision-makers on the animals' behalf as they usually know the animals quite well. I develop these thoughts in the following.

In recent years, the agency and self-determination of animals have received considerable attention in the literature (see, e.g., Donaldson and Kymlicka 2011; Fenton 2014; Kantin and Wendler 2015; Donaldson and Kymlicka 2016; Healey and Pepper 2021). Many philosophers agree that animals can, with their actions and bodily reactions, show dissent and, in some situations, even assent. In the shelter context, this could mean that veterinarians and caretakers closely observe critically ill animals: How are they reacting to their treatment? Are they resisting therapy for several consecutive days? Are they apathetic over an extended period of time? Have they basically given up on themselves, such that they hide in a corner and react violently to any treatment? Or, after a few days, do they show both improvement and interest in the medication and therapy?

In addition, caretakers and veterinarians who have been treating and closely following animals, as well as their medical history in the shelter, can act as surrogate decision-makers on their behalf. That is, they can assess whether a treatment is really in the best interest of an animal or whether they are better euthanized (see Chapter 1, this volume, 121–125). Therefore, their voices should, if possible, be heard when it comes to decisions about the life and death of individual animals.

3.4.7 Re-evaluation of Triage Decisions and Changes in the Therapeutic Goal

A further requirement is to re-evaluate triage decisions on a regular basis and restrict therapy if resources are too scarce. Note that withholding *some treatment* does not necessarily imply withholding *all therapy* (Jöbges et al. 2020). In the case of shelter animals, this may mean that more affordable therapy options for animals could be explored or that at least some of their suffering should be alleviated if the medical resources available are not enough to provide treatment of all conditions. To illustrate this, consider expensive and time-consuming dentistry surgeries for cats. Stray cats frequently suffer from periodontal disease, gingivitis, and lost teeth, as studies from Japan and Germany show (Kalz et al. 2000; Seo et al. 2021). These conditions are rather painful, negatively affect the well-being of the animal, and are often "hidden" by the animal patient (Gengler 2013). In situations of scarce medical resources and space in the shelter, it should be evaluated whether it is proportionate to spend money on individual dental surgeries or whether the money is better spent on other (less expensive) procedures, such as sterilizations. This may imply that not all bad teeth conditions are treated if they are too costly, but that other alternatives—for example, painkillers—are discussed.

Furthermore, sudden changes in the well-being of an animal patient also have to be considered. If an animal is doing better for a while, but then her condition suddenly deteriorates, it may be justified to withdraw therapy. That is, it may be justified to kill some animals (e.g., those with extremely bad teeth conditions or those who do not react to therapy) to treat and save other animals. An additional option would be to find a palliative care foster family for those animals whose treatment would be too costly, but whose suffering does not yet outweigh the benefits of being alive.

3.4.8 Burden of Triage and Staff Support

A final consideration in many triage guidelines is psychological support for staff. In hospitals, for instance, the consequences of triage decisions can be psychologically burdensome for healthcare professionals. Therefore, many triage protocols recommend psychological support for medical staff (Jöbges et al. 2020). In animal shelters, the situation for caregivers, veterinarians, and the like may also be very challenging and involve occupational stress and mental exhaustion, also called "compassion fatigue" (Scotney et al. 2015; Andrukonis et al. 2020). To ease the mental burden of individual caregivers, ensure cohesion necessary for the proper functioning of the shelter, and minimize conflicts and power games among different departments and individuals, I suggest that the decision-making responsibilities be clearly distributed. In addition, frequent training sessions with professionals (such as psychologists) about how to deal with compassion fatigue may help the shelter staff to continue their work while staying mentally healthy.

Furthermore, in regular team meetings (e.g., once per month), the caregiving team and veterinarians can inform each other about recent decisions (e.g., about therapy withdrawals or about animals who had to be killed). This may improve the team spirit and cooperation among staff members and foster better understanding of decisions taken by different units. If possible and needed, caregivers should be allowed to spend time with those animals with whom they have formed bonds before they are killed.

So far, I have fleshed out how triage considerations proposed in the context of the COVID-19 pandemic can be fruitfully extended and applied to animal shelters to ensure transparency, fairness, equality, and equity in decision-making processes. Note, however, that these are broad rules of thumb. Depending on the specific shelter conditions, abiding by them is possible and in some situations probably even necessary. If conflicts and fundamental disagreements about what to do in a specific situation persist, discussion with an Ethics Board may be necessary and useful to reduce tensions and conflicts among team members. I discuss this issue next.

3.5 The Need for Animal Ethics Boards in Shelters

Ethics consultation plays a rather minor role in triage protocols developed during the COVID-19 pandemic (Ehni et al. 2021). This is surprising because there may be diverging opinions about what to do in specific triage situations in hospitals—as in animal shelters. In what follows, I suggest that animal Ethics Boards are essential in the case of shelters to avoid and minimize disagreements and tensions among staff. Conflict among team members may impair the proper · functioning of shelters. Furthermore, the more staff members suffer from occupational distress, burnout, and compassion fatigue, the more likely they are to quit their job (Rogelberg et al. 2007; Turner et al. 2012; Anderson et al. 2013). If there is no consistency among staff members, this may harm the proper functioning and communication process at the shelter, which ultimately is detrimental to animal welfare. Therefore, a good working atmosphere and transparency in the decision-making process are crucial for shelters.

Caregiving shelter staff (e.g., those working on a daily basis with animals, cleaning, feeding, walking and playing with them) may develop relationships with particular animals over time. They may form bonds with and affinities toward individual animals. If it is then decided that this particular animal does not receive a needed treatment for budgetary reasons or will be killed to free up space for animals who will more likely benefit more from the care, this may result in bitterness and distress in shelter workers: after all, their work suddenly looks futile—all the care they provided was for nothing because the animal could not be saved.

I argued before that decision-making responsibilities have to be clearly distributed. Decisions to withdraw or withhold treatment should be taken by at least two staff members (including a veterinarian) and should be communicated to the team in regular meetings. Nonetheless, disagreements may arise within teams or even among decision-makers themselves. In such cases, it may be useful to bring in an independent ethics committee or ethics consultants.

I suggest that shelters form a pro bono ethics committee with a few members. Ideally, the committee members should be acquainted with both the difficulties under which shelters operate and ethical issues related to animals. The team could, for example, be composed of—minimally—an animal ethicist (or at least an ethicist) from a nearby university and an independent veterinarian. If needed, they can be called in to look more closely at specific cases, discuss them with the team (online or in person), and outline the rationale and reasons for different decisional options.

There may be two worries related to ethics committees. First, shelter staff may be against an Ethics Board because such ethics consultation may create an additional workload and require more time for shelter collaborators. However, note that the Ethics Board should only be brought in when the staff members find themselves in an impasse and deem an ethics consultation to be useful. That is, the committee should only be brought in when staff members need it to resolve actual conflicts. Reducing conflicts between groups with the help of an external committee may then save more time overall. A second worry is that the shelter collaborators are bound by the suggestions of the Ethics Board. However, this is not the case. Importantly, the Ethics Board should *not* have overriding decision-making power. Rather, the role of its members is to serve as *consultants* who may meet up with the team and discuss the different options at stake as well as their advantages and disadvantages. This may help to reduce some of the burden related to decision-making and disagreements and diminish tensions between different groups and individuals.

3.6 Conclusion

In this chapter, I argued that considerations used in triage guidelines in medical ethics can—with some adaptations—be fruitfully extended to animal shelters. After all, hospitals during periods of triage and animal shelters share some similarities: namely, restricted resources such as money, medical equipment, staff members, and space for patients. The triage requirements put forward by medical associations in many countries during the COVID-19 pandemic prove a useful starting point for developing principles that can guide animal shelters in the decisions they have to take on a daily basis.

While I have argued that the considerations outlined here are necessary for guiding decisions at shelters, they are likely insufficient and probably should be complemented with other considerations. These may vary from one shelter context to another. Shelters often deal with highly complex questions: For example, what should be done with dangerous animals who need a lot of resources (e.g., training) over an extended period of time (Benedetti et al. 2019)? How should shelters deal with confiscated animals who need a lot of space but cannot be adopted until a trial takes place? And how should the general budget be allocated to different activities, such as TNRM programs, prevention, and public awareness and education programs? That is, the requirements proposed here need to be complemented with further considerations to be responsive to the context and complexities in which particular shelters operate.

One may, however, criticize my general proposal here. One may argue that, within medicine, triage only happens in extraordinary situations, as for example during the COVID-19 pandemic. My suggestion of extending triage criteria to the shelter context, or so one may contend, normalizes the dire situation of stray and feral animals. One may thus argue that it is speciesist to apply triage guidelines in "normal" times to shelter animals, whereas, in the case of humans, triage protocols only are used in rare circumstances. Furthermore, one may claim that it is speciesist that I advocate the active killing of some shelter animals due to restricted means because we would never accept such a conclusion in the case of humans.

I already discussed this objection briefly at the beginning of Section 3.4. Note that questions about letting die also arise in triage decisions about humans. If we accept that there is no fundamental moral difference between killing and letting die (Singer 2011), then my proposal may seem less provocative. I furthermore agree that decisions about which animals should be taken in, treated, aborted, killed, or euthanized in shelters should ideally become obsolete in a non-speciesist world (for an opposing view, see Chapter 7, this volume, 286–300). Ultimately, the goal should be to reduce the numbers of unwanted animals in shelters by eliminating relinquishment, abandonment, mistreatment of animals, and irresponsible breeding practices (Turner et al. 2012). That is, people's general attitudes toward sentient animals have to be fundamentally altered. However, we currently live in a deeply speciesist society: animals are frequently deemed to have a lower moral status than humans. Therefore, in our current non-ideal society in which shelters operate with restricted means, staff members, and space, the considerations proposed here are urgently needed: they contribute to making decisions in a morally challenging situation less arbitrary, more transparent, and fairer for all involved—both humans and animals.

Acknowledgments

I would like to thank Valéry Giroux, Angie Pepper, and Kristin Voigt for their helpful comments on an earlier version of this Chapter. I also wish to thank Élise Desaulniers and the staff at the Montreal SPCA for sharing their experiences with our group of researchers.

Finally, I wish to thank the Swiss National Science Foundation (grant number 179826) for its generous support of my work.

Notes

1. I use here the term "euthanize" if death is in the best interest of an animal; otherwise, I use the term "kill."
2. Other bioethicists and medical doctors undertook similar reviews of triage protocols and focused on other categories, such as equity and ethical theories, triage criteria, respecting patients' dignity, and decision-making and quality of care (Perin and Panfilis 2021). For a further review, see Ehni et al. (2021). However, for the purpose of this chapter, I decided to focus on the requirements outlined by Jöbges et al. (2020).
3. For a discussion of some of the ethical issues related to ageism in triage during the COVID-19 pandemic, see, e.g., Ehni and Wahl (2020) and Rueda (2021). I furthermore discuss life-span considerations regarding animals in more detail in Section 3.4.4.
4. If the animal has to be returned to the street, steps could be taken to reduce hardship. For example, someone could be assigned the responsibility to feed and provide shelter for cat colonies.
5. Jöbges et al. (2020) note that concepts such as "equality" or "equity" are often defined differently in academic discourse. They explain these terminological differences in the following way: "Variation and at times a certain vagueness or unclarity was also prevalent in the guidance texts we studied. Many of them were put together quickly with a focus on practical utility, and terminology may not have been a prime concern" (Jöbges et al. 2020, 952).
6. I do not take a stance here on the justifiability of open-admission and limited-admission shelters. They both serve important purposes, and neither is superior. They have different advantages and disadvantages and face different challenges.
7. Admittedly, some of these factors may have an *impact* on the health status and thus prognosis of a person and lead, for example, to comorbidities. But taken *alone*, properties such as disability status or age should not be used as a proxy for prognosis and health status of a person.
8. This is in disanalogy to cases involving humans, in which equity must be respected. Note, though, that triage cases with humans rarely happen in a context in which a long-term placement plays a role. Therefore, they are not really comparable.
9. Whether this amounts to euthanasia is an open question. For diverging views on this issue, see Chapter 2, this volume (140–152) and Chapter 4, this volume (210–212).

10. One may argue that the reliance on two staff members to take decisions may make the decision-making process overly demanding and time-consuming. However, note that, in the case of humans, medical cases are frequently discussed by several physicians. Given that I focus here on decision-making regarding the *life and death* of animals, I claim that fair and transparent decision-making in the case of animals requires at least a short discussion of the options and opportunity costs.

References

Anderson, K. A., J. C. Brandt, L. K. Lord, and E. A. Miles (2013) "Euthanasia in animal shelters: Management's perspective on staff reactions and support programs." *Anthrozoös 26*(4), 569–578. https://doi.org/10.2752/175303713X13795775536057.

Andrukonis, A., N. J. Hall, and A. Protopopova (2020) "The impact of caring and killing on physiological and psychometric measures of stress in animal shelter employees: A pilot study." *International Journal of Environmental Research and Public Health 17*(24). https://doi.org/10.3390/ijerph17249196.

Benedetti, R., A. Malfatti, and A. Marchegiani (2019) "Difficulties in making the ethically correct choice in the management of a case of proven dangerousness of a shelter dog." *Journal of Applied Animal Ethics Research 2*(1), 76–84. https://doi.org/10.1163/25889567-12340020.

Bickenbach, J. (2021) "Disability and health care rationing." In Edward N. Zalta (ed.), *Stanford Encyclopedia of Philosophy*. https://plato.stanford.edu/archives/spr2021/entries/disability-care-rationing.

Blagg, C. R. (2004). "Triage: Napoleon to the present day." *Journal of Nephrology 17*(4), 629–632.

Castro-Prieto, J., and M. J. Andrade-Núñez (2018) "Health and ecological aspects of stray cats in Old San Juan, Puerto Rico: Baseline information to develop an effective control program." *Puerto Rico Health Sciences Journal 37*(2), 110–114.

Donaldson, Sue, and W. Kymlicka (2011) *Zoopolis: A Political Theory of Animal Rights*. Oxford: Oxford University Press.

Donaldson, S., and W. Kymlicka (2016) "Comment: Between wild and domesticated: Rethinking categories and boundaries in response to animal agency." In B. Bovenkerk and J. Keulartz (eds.), *Animal Ethics in the Age of Humans: Blurring Boundaries in Human-Animal relationships*. Cham: Springer International Publishing, 225–239.

Ehni, H., and H. Wahl (2020) "Six propositions against ageism in the COVID-19 pandemic." *Journal of Aging & Social Policy 32*(4–5), 515–525. https://doi.org/10.1080/08959420.2020.1770032.

Ehni, H., U. Wiesing, and R. Ranisch (2021) "Saving the most lives: A comparison of European triage guidelines in the context of the COVID-19 pandemic." *Bioethics 35*(2), 125–134. https://doi.org/10.1111/bioe.12836.

Evans, J. G. (1997) "The rationing debate: Rationing health care by age: The case against." *British Medical Journal 314*(7083), 822–825. https://doi.org/10.1136/bmj.314.7083.822.

Fenton, A. (2014) "Can a chimp say 'no'? Reenvisioning chimpanzee dissent in harmful research." *Cambridge Quarterly of Healthcare Ethics 23*(2), 130–139. https://doi.org/10.1017/S0963180113000662.

Gengler, B. (2013) "Exodontics: Extraction of teeth in the dog and cat." *Veterinary Clinics of North America. Small Animal Practice 43*(3), 573–585. https://doi.org/10.1016/j.cvsm.2013.02.008.

Harris, J. (1987) "QALYfying the value of life." *Journal of Medical Ethics 13*(3), 117–123. https://doi.org/10.1136/jme.13.3.117.

Healey, R., and A. Pepper (2021) "Interspecies justice: Agency, self-determination, and assent." *Philosophical Studies 178*(4), 1223–1243. https://doi.org/10.1007/s11098-020-01472-5.

Horta, O. (2010) "What is speciesism?" *Journal of Agricultural and Environmental Ethics 23*(3), 243–266. https://doi.org/10.1007/s10806-009-9205-2.

Horta, O., and F. Albersmeier (2020) "Defining speciesism." *Philosophy Compass 15*(11), 1–9. https://doi.org/10.1111/phc3.12708.

Humane Society of the United States (2012) All shelters are not alike: The important differences that can affect the mission. https://www.humanesociety.org/sites/default/files/docs/all-shelters-are-not-alike.pdf.

Jaquet, F (2019) "Is speciesism wrong by definition?" *Journal of Agricultural and Environmental Ethics 32*(3), 447–458. https://doi.org/10.1007/s10806-019-09784-1.

Jöbges, S., R. Vinay, V. A. Luyckx, and N. Biller-Andorno (2020) "Recommendations on COVID-19 triage: International comparison and ethical analysis." *Bioethics 34*(9), 948–959. https://doi.org/10.1111/bioe.12805.

Kalz, B., K. M. Scheibe, I. Wegner, and J. Priemer (2000) "Gesundheitsstatus und Mortalitätsursachen verwilderter Hauskatzen in einem Untersuchungsgebiet in Berlin-Mitte." *Berliner und Münchener tierärztliche Wochenschrift 113*(11-12), 417–422.

Kantin, H., and D. Wendler (2015) "Is there a role for assent or dissent in animal research?" *Cambridge Quarterly of Healthcare Ethics 24*(4), 459–472. https://doi.org/10.1017/S0963180115000110.

Karsten, C. L., D. C. Wagner, P. H. Kass, and K. F. Hurley (2017) "An observational study of the relationship between Capacity for Care as an animal shelter management model and cat health, adoption and death in three animal shelters." *Veterinary Journal 227*, 15–22. https://doi.org/10.1016/j.tvjl.2017.08.003.

Marston, L. C., and P. C. Bennett (2009) "Admissions of cats to animal welfare shelters in Melbourne, Australia." *Journal of Applied Animal Welfare Science 12*(3), 189–213. https://doi.org/10.1080/10888700902955948.

Muensterer, O. J., E. A. Gianicolo, and N. W. Paul (2021) "Rationing and triage of scarce, lifesaving therapy in the context of the COVID-19 pandemic: A cross-sectional, social media-driven, scenario-based online query of societal attitudes."

International Journal of Surgery: Global Health 4(1), e47–e47. https://doi.org/10.1097/GH9.0000000000000047.

O'Sullivan, S. (2012) *Animals, Equality and Democracy.* New York: Palgrave Macmillan.

Palmer, C. (2010) *Animal Ethics in Context.* New York: Columbia University Press.

Parfit, Derek (1997). "Equality and priority." *Ratio* 10(3), 202–221. https://doi.org/10.1111/1467-9329.00041.

Perin, M., and L. de Panfilis (2021) "Among equity and dignity: An argument-based review of European ethical guidelines under COVID-19." *BMC Medical Ethics* 22(1), 36. https://doi.org/10.1186/s12910-021-00603-9.

Repine, T. B., P. Lisagor, and D. J. Cohen (2005) "The dynamics and ethics of triage: Rationing care in hard times." *Military Medicine* 170(6), 505–509. https://doi.org/10.7205/MILMED.170.6.505.

Rivlin, M. M. (2000) "Why the fair innings argument is not persuasive." *BMC Medical Ethics* 1(1), 1. https://doi.org/10.1186/1472-6939-1-1.

Rogelberg, S. G., C. L. Reeve, C. Spitzmüller, N. DiGiacomo, O. L. Clark, L. Teeter, A. G. Walker, P. G. Starling, and N. T. Carter (2007) "Impact of euthanasia rates, euthanasia practices, and human resource practices on employee turnover in animal shelters." *Journal of the American Veterinary Medical Association* 230(5), 713–719. https://doi.org/10.2460/javma.230.5.713.

Rueda, J. (2021) "Ageism in the COVID-19 pandemic: Age-based discrimination in triage decisions and beyond." *History and Philosophy of the Life Sciences* 43(3), 91. https://doi.org/10.1007/s40656-021-00441-3.

Scotney, R. L., D. McLaughlin, and H. L. Keates (2015) "A systematic review of the effects of euthanasia and occupational stress in personnel working with animals in animal shelters, veterinary clinics, and biomedical research facilities." *Journal of the American Veterinary Medical Association* 247(10), 1121–1130. https://doi.org/10.2460/javma.247.10.1121.

Scully, J. L. (2020) "Disability, disablism, and COVID-19 pandemic triage." *Journal of Bioethical Inquiry* 17(4), 601–605. https://doi.org/10.1007/s11673-020-10005-y.

Seo, A., Y. Ueda, and H. Tanida (2021) "Health status of 'community cats' living in the tourist area of the Old Town in Onomichi City, Japan." *Journal of Applied Animal Welfare Science* 25(4), 1–17. https://doi.org/10.1080/10888705.2021.1874952.

Singer, P. (2009) *Animal Liberation: The Definitive Classic of the Animal Movement.* New York: Ecco Book/Harper Perennial.

Singer, P. (2011). *Practical Ethics.* Cambridge: Cambridge University Press.

Skandalakis, P. N., P. Lainas, O. Zoras, J. E. Skandalakis, and P. Mirilas (2006) "'To afford the wounded speedy assistance': Dominique Jean Larrey and Napoleon." *World Journal of Surgery* 30(8), 1392–1399. https://doi.org/10.1007/s00268-005-0436-8.

Turner, P., J. Berry, and S. MacDonald (2012) "Animal shelters and animal welfare: Raising the bar." *Canadian Veterinary Journal* 53(8), 893–896.

Višak, T. (2018) "Engineering life expectancy and non-identity cases." *Journal of Agricultural and Environmental Ethics* 31(2), 281–293. https://doi.org/10.1007/s10806-018-9724-9.

4

What If They Were Humans?

Non-Ideal Theory in the Shelter

François Jaquet

4.1 Introduction

It is a trivial observation that we treat animals in all sorts of ways in which we would never treat our conspecifics. Virtually everyone agrees that it would be wrong to raise and slaughter humans to eat their flesh, yet most people condone animal agriculture. Virtually everyone agrees that it would be wrong to subject humans to painful experiments without their consent, yet most people buy products that were tested on animals before being commercialized. Virtually everyone agrees that it would be wrong to confine and exhibit humans for the sake of entertainment, yet many people visit animal zoos and circuses. As far as conventional wisdom is concerned, humans and animals pertain to separate moral categories.

When someone asks what could justify such unequal treatment, the demand is often met with a blank stare. Why treat humans better than other animals? Well, they are humans. For millennia, most philosophers did not question this common attitude to animals, but this is no longer the case. In recent decades, this form of discrimination has been challenged. Many ethicists now consider the notion that being humans somehow grants us a superior moral status to be a prejudice akin to the view that being males or being White confers males and White people with a higher moral status. The property of

François Jaquet, *What If They Were Humans?* In: *The Ethics of Animal Shelters.* Edited by:
Valéry Giroux, Angie Pepper, and Kristin Voigt, Oxford University Press. © Oxford University Press 2023.
DOI: 10.1093/oso/9780197678633.003.0006

being a human is just as ethically irrelevant as the properties of being a male and being White.

The latter claim has become a powerful tool to question the moral permissibility of certain widespread activities. Some have argued that, since we should not perform painful experiments on humans who are incapable of giving free and informed consent in order to gain scientific knowledge, we should not run such experiments on nonhuman animals to the same end. Similarly, it has been argued that, as we should not breed and kill humans to eat their flesh, we should not breed and kill animals for the same purpose. If the fact that we must be protected from being used in these ways has nothing to do with our being humans, then some nonhumans should enjoy the same protections.

While the existence of slaughterhouses and animal labs rests entirely on the idea that we owe animals less than we do humans, other institutions initially appear less biased. A telling example is animal protection organizations, which are created for the very sake of nonhumans and generally managed by people who truly care about animal welfare. It must be the case, one might think, that humane societies give animals their fair due. But this overlooks how deeply anthropocentrism is entrenched in our societies. Even people who dedicate their entire lives to animals are not spared the effects of this ideology. As a result, certain activities that are commonplace within humane societies might well be objectionable. In this chapter, I discuss three such activities: killing healthy shelter animals for lack of resources, building partnerships with animal agriculture, and feeding meat to shelter animals.

The chapter proceeds as follows. In Section 4.2, I argue that the property of being a human is morally irrelevant. In Section 4.3, I explain how this claim can be leveraged to draw substantial ethical norms and principles and, more specifically, how it could be used to establish principles prohibiting management euthanasia, cooperation with animal agriculture, and meat-based pet food. In Section 4.4, I introduce the distinction between ideal and non-ideal theory—two ways of theorizing our moral duties that are respectively designed for ideal and non-ideal circumstances. In Sections

4.5 and 4.6, I argue that management euthanasia and cooperation with animal agriculture are unobjectionable as far as non-ideal theory is concerned, even though they would be condemned by ideal theory. Finally, in Section 4.7, I argue that meat-based pet food should be rejected even in non-ideal theory.

4.2 The Ethical Irrelevance of Being a Human

Prevailing public attitudes presuppose that being a human is a morally relevant property, one that provides its bearers with certain moral rights or moral agents with certain moral duties toward them. Why do we have a right not to be killed that cows and chickens lack? On the face of it, it's because we are humans and they aren't. Why do scientists have a duty not to perform painful experiments on their colleagues while they have no such duties toward rats and monkeys? On the face of it, it's because their colleagues are humans, but rats and monkeys aren't.

The predicate "human" is notoriously ambiguous (Singer 2011, 73–74). On the one hand, it expresses a biological concept when it refers to members of the species *Homo sapiens*. On the other hand, it expresses a psychological concept when it refers to those subjects who are both rational and self-conscious. While the two concepts are often confused due to this ambiguity in the predicate "human," they are not co-extensive. Some members of the species *H. sapiens* are not rational and self-conscious—for instance, babies and people with profound mental disabilities. And it may be that not all rational and self-conscious subjects belong to *H. sapiens*—think about chimpanzees.

Once this distinction is in place, it should be clear that conventional wisdom appeals to the biological concept of human. Most people believe that it is wrong to kill and experiment on members of the species *H. sapiens* regardless of their cognitive abilities. By contrast, they rarely object to the killings and experiments performed on nonhuman animals, whether or not these happen to be rational and self-conscious. Common-sense morality is thus committed to the view that all and only *biological* humans have certain rights and are owed certain duties. From now on, I will therefore use the word "human" to refer to *H. sapiens*, setting aside its second meaning.

Most animal ethicists agree that, so understood, the property of being a human is ethically irrelevant in the sense that it makes no difference to how we should treat individuals. This conclusion can be reached via three different arguments. The first argument rests on the observation that being a human is a merely biological property (Jaquet 2022b; McMahan 2005; Rachels 1990). What does it take for a property to be merely biological? Some properties are psychological in the sense that we can instantiate them inasmuch as we have a mind. One could cite being generous, having a good memory, or being in pain. Other properties are biological in the sense that we can instantiate them inasmuch as we have a body. Examples include being bald, being tall, and being a female. According to identity theorists in the philosophy of mind, all psychological properties reduce to biological properties. For instance, being in pain might be identical to having one's C-fibers firing. Should that be the case, the property of having one's C-fibers firing would be both psychological and biological—it would not be *merely* biological. Be that as it may, most biological properties are merely biological. They may be statistically correlated with psychological properties, but that is another matter.

Being a human is a merely biological property in this sense. Admittedly, it is correlated with psychological properties. For the most part, humans are rational, self-conscious, and capable of language. They make long-term plans and remember the distant past. Other animals, not so much. But there are exceptions; while it may be true that these differences distinguish most humans from most nonhumans, they do not distinguish all humans from all nonhumans. For one thing, many animals possess at least some of the abilities just listed—pigs and crows are self-conscious, and dolphins have impressive memories. What's more, some humans lack these abilities altogether, either because they are too young or due to a mental disability. At the end of the day, these features are only statistically correlated with being a human. Being a human is a merely biological property.

The worry is that merely biological properties do not seem to matter morally. In and of itself, the fact that someone is tall or has White skin does not provide us with more stringent moral duties toward him. In and of itself, the fact that someone is a female or has only one arm does not provide her with more constraining moral rights. For, surely, women might well have rights that men lack (e.g., a right to abortion or a right to ovarian cancer screening). And we might well owe duties to the physically disabled that we don't owe to the physically abled (e.g., a duty to provide them with adapted access to public facilities). But these special rights and duties are not due to the mere fact that these people are female or disabled. They're due to the fact that these people often possess interests that others lack. And having these interests is certainly not a biological property. Merely biological properties are morally irrelevant, and this applies in particular to the property *being a human*.

The second argument has to do with the evolution of humanity (Dawkins 1993; Ebert 2020; Rachels 1990). Evolutionary theory entails that there is no objective boundary between humans and nonhumans. Imagine a chain of individuals holding hands: at one end is a woman, next to her mother, next to her own mother, and so on; at the other end is a female chimpanzee, next to her mother, next to her own mother, and so on; more or less in the middle stands the last ancestor shared by humans and chimpanzees. Where does the human species end? One could cut the chain between two links and declare, "It does here." But this boundary would be arbitrary. There is absolutely no reason to draw the line between a given individual and her mother rather than between the latter and her mother. By contrast, the boundary surrounding those to whom one owes strong moral duties cannot be arbitrary in this way. It has to be an objective feature of reality. Membership in the human species can therefore not be morally relevant.

The third argument rests on the following thought experiment:

Due to a series of accidents involving genetic mutations and natural selection, a new species emerged from *Homo sapiens*: *Almost sapiens*. As its name suggests, members of this new species are like us in every possible respect except their species. As a matter of fact, they resemble us much more than White people resemble Black people or men resemble women.

This scenario suggests the following lesson. Since the boundaries of race and gender are morally irrelevant, it is very unlikely that the difference between *H. sapiens* and *Almost sapiens* is morally relevant. But this difference consists in the property of being a human. Accordingly, it is very unlikely that the property of being a human matters morally.

On second thought, then, we should reject the intuitive suggestion that this property confers on its bearers a higher moral status for it has three unwelcome implications. It implies that some merely biological properties are morally relevant, that some arbitrary properties are morally relevant, and that members of *H. sapiens* have rights that members of *Almost sapiens* lack. From now on, I will therefore assume that whether or not a subject is a human is morally irrelevant. In the next section, we will see how this conclusion can be put to work in the selection of moral principles.

4.3 The Selection of Moral Principles

The irrelevance of *being a human* has a significant methodological implication. It provides us with a test we can use to identify the moral principles governing our treatment of nonhuman animals. Whenever we consider a certain moral principle specifying that we should treat some animals in a certain way, we should ask, "What if these animals were humans?" If the principle is plausible when applied to this counterfactual scenario, we can accept it; if it's implausible when applied to this counterfactual scenario, we must reject it.

This test must be handled with care or misuses will be all too frequent. Suppose I wonder whether dogs should be granted the right to vote and I decide to address this issue by asking, "What if they were humans?" I might then think: since humans should be granted the right to vote, so should dogs. Obviously, something's wrong with this piece of reasoning. The mistake, I want to suggest, is to think that dogs should have the right to vote if they were humans. And it rests on a misunderstanding of the counterfactual in which we're interested. We are not interested in what should happen if dogs were humans with typically human mental abilities and interests. We're interested in what should happen if dogs were humans and yet kept (as far as is conceivable) their actual mental abilities and interests. If dogs were humans in this sense, they would be more similar to young children than they would be to normal adults. Accordingly, they should not be granted the right to vote.

In that case, our test results in a rather intuitive principle—most people have the intuition that dogs should not be allowed to vote. However, some of its outcomes will be much less intuitive. Suppose I wonder whether it is okay to farm and slaughter pigs for food, and I decide to address this issue by asking, "What if they were humans?" In light of the above, I should not wonder whether it is okay to farm paradigmatic humans. Instead, I should wonder whether it would be okay to farm humans with mental abilities and interests similar to those of a pig. But, in this case, this qualification changes nothing. The answer is the same: it is wrong to farm and slaughter human beings for food regardless of their mental capacities.[1] Conclusion: farming and killing pigs for food is wrong.

Here is a possible objection to this test. Assuming that the property of being a human is morally irrelevant, there is another question one might ask, this time about humans: "What if they were not humans?" Asking this question instead would result in the selection of very different principles. For instance, the intuitive principle that human babies should not be farmed would not pass the test for the intuitive answer to the question "What if they were not humans?" is that they could be killed. Thus, much hinges on whether we should test the principles governing our treatment of animals with the question "What if they were humans?" or rather test our principles governing our treatment of humans with the question "What if they were not humans?" Why go for the first option rather than the second?

This is because we have independent reasons to distrust the widespread intuition that animals do not count for much. This intuition is epistemically defective because it is due to a mixture of two irrelevant influences. On the one hand, it is largely a reaction to the cognitive dissonance that we experience as a result of the "meat paradox." Most people love animals, don't want to harm them, yet harm them by consuming meat. As is now well documented, this practical paradox generates a state of dissonance, which is unpleasant. To ward off this unpleasantness, people form all sorts of beliefs whose only function is to resolve the paradox. For instance, they start to believe that humans need to eat meat or that animals do not suffer that much (Loughnan et al. 2014). Another belief they adopt is the belief that animals do not count a lot from the ethical point of view (Jaquet 2021).

On the other hand, this belief very much appears to be shaped by our tribalistic psychology. Roughly, tribalism is a sort of group-level selfishness. It proceeds in three steps (Machery 2016). First, we scan our environment to detect those social groups that are most salient. Then, we classify individuals in our environment into ingroup members and outgroup members. Finally, we discriminate against outgroup members and form the belief that they matter less than ingroup members. As it happens, most people seem to follow this pattern in their relationships with nonhuman animals (Jaquet 2022a; Kasperbauer 2017). Tribalism appears to shape not only the way we treat animals but also our intuitive understanding of what we owe to them.

Importantly, these explanations undermine the epistemic credentials of the widespread intuition that animals do not count for much (Jaquet 2021, 2022a). As a general rule, we should not trust moral intuitions that we have because they are psychologically comfortable or because of our general tendency to discriminate against outgroup members. These belief-forming processes are unreliable in the sense that many of the beliefs they generate are false (e.g., the belief that meat is healthy and the belief that members of other races are lazy). But then, if we should distrust our intuitions about what we owe to animals, it looks like we should not assess the principles governing our duties to humans in light of our intuitive response to the question, "What if they were not humans?" On the contrary, we should assess our principles governing our duties to animals in light of our intuitive response to the question, "What if they were humans?"

In the following, I focus on three practices that are common within animal shelters and seem to fail this test. The first is euthanasia for lack of resources, which is sometimes called "management euthanasia."[2] Millions of animals, mostly cats and dogs, are killed in shelters every year. Some are euthanized in their own interests, narrowly construed, because an illness or an injury makes their life no longer worth living. This does not raise too serious moral issues. Others, however, are killed even though they are healthy because nobody wants to adopt them. Shelters work with highly limited resources in terms of time, space, and food. They cannot afford to keep animals on their premises indefinitely as this would take away resources from others. When the animals in question cannot survive on their own, releasing them into the wild is simply not an option. All this presents shelters with a dilemma: either they accept all the animals that are brought to them, but then they have to kill those who cannot get adopted or be released, or they refuse to kill the animals they host, but then they have to close their doors to many others. It's either open-admission or no-kill, but not both.

To assess the practice of killing shelter animals for lack of resources, we need to ask, "What if they were humans?" What should we think of, say, an orphanage that, in order to be able to foster new children, would kill those who have been there for a long time and were not adopted? Intuitively, that would be terribly wrong. The orphanage should rather refuse entry to new kids as long as all the beds are occupied. As a first approximation, this suggests that animal shelters should adopt a no-kill policy even though that would mean giving up their open-admission policy.

Many humane societies are not concerned with companion animals only. They also aim to help farm animals. A second practice that is widespread among animal protection organizations is meant to do just that: cooperate with animal agriculture to improve the welfare of these animals. This kind of cooperation often takes the form of welfare certifications and labeling programs. The farmers who participate in the programs receive a certification insofar as they respect certain norms typically meant to foster the UK Farm Animal Welfare Council's "five freedoms": freedom from hunger and thirst; freedom from discomfort; freedom from pain, injury, and disease; freedom from fear and distress; and freedom to express normal behaviors. The corresponding labels are then used to help consumers make better-informed and less unethical choices. In addition, shelters recruit animal welfare experts who then negotiate with farmers to improve animal welfare legal codes.

To assess this kind of cooperation with animal farmers, we need to ask, "What if these farmers were exploiting human babies?" And the answer is straightforward: it would be plainly intolerable to cooperate with people who would raise and kill humans for food—even human babies, whose mental abilities do not exceed those of animals. The appropriate response to such an industry would be uncompromising struggle for its abolition rather than modest attempts to reform it. As a first approximation, this suggests that animal shelters should not cooperate with animal agriculture.

A third common practice concerns both farm animals and the animals who await a possible adoption at the shelter. Obviously, the latter animals must be fed. Given that some of them are obligate carnivores, they are often fed meat (i.e., the flesh of dead animals). While this should come as no surprise, it is nonetheless paradoxical. How can an organization that is entirely dedicated to helping animals support an industry that routinely causes their suffering and death? In response, some will maintain that, to the extent that shelter animals need to eat meat to survive, animal shelters have no other option than to feed them meat. Although this is not true of dogs—who are flexible omnivores rather than obligate carnivores—it may be true of cats.

Again, the suggestion is that we approach this issue via the question, "What if they were humans?" Suppose an animal shelter ordered meat coming from a farm that raised and killed human babies to sell their flesh. Not only would it be blatantly immoral for the farmers to produce such food; it would also be clearly wrong for the shelter to buy it. And we would not be impressed should they reply that the cats who are waiting to be adopted are obligate carnivores. As a first approximation, this suggests that animal shelters should not feed meat to their animals.

4.4 Ideal and Non-Ideal Theory

The above seems to indicate that humane societies are doing three things wrong. They should not practice management euthanasia, they should not cooperate with animal farmers, they should not feed meat to the animals they shelter. And all this seems to follow from the ethical irrelevance of the property of being a human combined with common intuitions about our duties to human beings. In the remainder of this chapter, I want to take a different look at these issues. While all these conclusions are compelling as long as we assume that humans and other animals face roughly similar circumstances, this assumption is false. The circumstances faced by humans and nonhumans differ in a crucial respect: while the former are generally more or less ideal, the latter are by and large highly non-ideal. As a result, the principles that govern our treatment of fellow humans and those that govern our treatment of other animals pertain to different kinds of theory: respectively, ideal and non-ideal theory.

The distinction between ideal and non-ideal theory traces back to John Rawls's *Theory of Justice* (1971). While it has been applied to the issue of moral demands (Murphy 2003) and to the treatment of animals (Garner 2013), to this day, it remains primarily used in political philosophy. In this area, an important debate opposes those philosophers who favor ideal theory and those who favor non-ideal theory. In the first camp, authors such as Rawls himself are happy to theorize almost exclusively about idealized circumstances. Members of the second camp object that this makes their work too detached from the world as it is and, a fortiori, practically irrelevant. We will not be concerned with this debate, which I mention only to set it aside. Instead, I will side with a third group, according to which philosophers should investigate both ideal and non-ideal theory. This conciliatory view should provide an adequate framework for our discussion.

Ideal theory applies to ideal circumstances, whereas non-ideal theory applies to non-ideal circumstances.[3] This raises a question: What is the difference between ideal and non-ideal circumstances? Ideal circumstances are generally understood to meet two criteria: full compliance (all or most agents comply with their duties) and favorable conditions (the economic and social conditions necessary for justice are in place). Non-ideal circumstances, by contrast, are taken to fail to meet at least one of these criteria (Valentini 2012, 655). For the sake of argument, I will follow a long tradition of focusing on the first criterion and distinguish ideal from non-ideal circumstances in terms of whether most agents do or do not comply with their duties. In the sense in which I will use these labels, then, ideal theory tells us what we should do if most others did what they should, whereas non-ideal theory tells us what we should do if most others fail to do what they should.

Following Rawls (1999, 89), many philosophers (e.g., Garner 2013; Simmons 2010) accept three desiderata for non-ideal theories. First, a non-ideal theory must be feasible in the sense that it can be achieved under current, non-ideal circumstances. Second, it must be permissible, which it is if its achievement would reduce what the related ideal theory identifies as the most serious and urgent injustices in the current circumstances.[4] Finally, it must be effective, such that its achievement would move society from the current, non-ideal circumstances toward the ideal circumstances in which the related ideal theory can be implemented. This is the model we will work with. I will therefore assume that a satisfactory non-ideal theory of our duties to nonhuman animals must be feasible, permissible (in this specific sense), and effective.

Before applying this model to the issues raised in Section 4.3, three points are worth dwelling on. First, as indicated by the third desideratum, non-ideal theory is supposed to be transitional; it must take us, step by step, from the current situation all the way to the circumstances that are more hospitable to the ideal theory. Second, non-ideal theory does not amount to second-best theory. The suggestion is not that, because our ideal is currently unfeasible, we should settle for a close approximation. For a state of affairs that most resembles our ideal might take us astray. Sometimes, picking a third- or fourth-best option leads us more effectively to our destination. Third, any non-ideal theory should build on an ideal theory. This follows from the second and third desiderata. We need at least a vague idea of the principles that would apply in ideal circumstances to identify both the most serious current injustices and the most effective way to get there (Simmons, 2010, 33–34).

Having said that, I will not take a stand for a specific ideal theory concerning our duties to animals. Rather, my argument will rest on a formal principle that all ideal theories ought to accommodate: we should treat animals as well as we would if they were humans. As we have seen, this formal principle is well established and can be used to support many stringent duties to animals. Now, it should be clear that most people do not comply with these duties and are unlikely to do so anywhere in the near future. Insofar as animals are concerned, then, the current circumstances are *highly* non-ideal. By comparison, we are much more advanced on the way to our ideal when it comes to humans. This is not to say that all humans face ideal circumstances—one only has to look at global statistics for child trafficking, domestic violence, and extreme poverty to see that many face miserable conditions. But the fact remains that humans are not killed for food by tens of billions each year.

In saying all that, I take it that the opposition between ideal and non-ideal circumstances is a continuum rather than a dichotomy. People can comply with their duties to various degrees, and, as a matter of fact, they comply with their duties to humans far more than they do with their duties to other animals. Accordingly, humans are by and large in much more ideal circumstances than other animals. This fact has crucial importance for the present questions. For it means that we should not test the moral principles governing our duties to animals by wondering how we should treat them if they were humans *in typically human circumstances*; we should test these principles by wondering how we should treat animals if they were humans *in typically animal circumstances*.

Accordingly, these principles ought to be assessed in light of the three desiderata mentioned above. First, they should be feasible, meaning that it should be possible to realize them under current circumstances, where most people do not comply with their duties to animals. Second, they should be morally permissible, meaning that they should remove what our vague ideal theory identifies as the most serious injustices done to animals, those that disadvantage animals most significantly as compared to humans. Finally, they should be effective, meaning that they should move society toward the ideal position vaguely described by our ideal theory, where animals are treated as well as humans. What does such a non-ideal theory have to say about management euthanasia, collaborations with animal agriculture, and meat-based pet food?

4.5 Management Euthanasia

Consider management euthanasia first, and remember the dilemma faced by animal shelters. On the one hand, they can endorse an open-admission policy, but they will then have to euthanize the many animals whom no one wants to adopt. On the other hand, they can endorse a no-kill policy, but then they will have to close their doors to many animals in need. In short, they must choose between two unappealing combinations: open-admission plus management euthanasia (OAME) or no-kill plus limited access (NKLA). I will defend the first option. If I am correct, the situation faced by animal shelters is not an ethical dilemma in the philosophical sense of the phrase: it's not that, no matter which alternative they opt for, animal shelters will do something wrong. In my opinion, there is nothing wrong with management euthanasia in this situation. All the wrongness there is lies within the series of acts that resulted in this situation.

At first glance, there is a case to be made to the contrary. Consider again an orphanage that would endorse a policy of open admission and consequently had to kill healthy children on a regular basis. That would be morally awful. Everyone will agree that this orphanage should rather endorse a no-kill policy, even though that meant restricting access to further children in need. Assuming that we should treat animals as we should treat them if they were humans, we are led to the conclusion that OAME is wrong and that animal shelters should rather opt for NKLA. I want to suggest that this argument by analogy is misguided because it ignores a crucial difference: while the situation of the orphans in this thought experiment is far from enviable, it would be quite exceptional. In our societies, children's circumstances are incomparably more ideal than those of animals.

No plausible ideal theory would favor OAME. But this is beside the point. What we face here is a choice between two non-ideal theories: one favoring OAME, the other favoring NKLA. Ultimately, we should therefore choose that which best satisfies our three desiderata for non-ideal theories. Which one is that? For a start, it should be clear that both theories are feasible, as indicated by the observation that both OAME and NKLA are already in place in many shelters. Turning to the second desideratum, permissibility, the issue is which policy would best contribute to remedying the most egregious injustices suffered by shelter animals. And I maintain that it is OAME. While NKLA would satisfy the interest in continued existence of the few animals who were lucky enough to access a shelter, OAME would satisfy the stronger interest of many more animals not to die of hunger, diseases, and injuries alone on the streets. Finally, the issue of effectiveness is more complicated. While neither policy would clearly hinder independent efforts to reach our ideal, it is unclear that either would help us get there. Still, it seems to me that OAME would be slightly more likely to do so than NKLA. Indeed, the greater availability of adoptable animals together with publicity of the necessity to kill some of them when resources are scarce might reduce abandonment rates.[5] Of course, this policy is compatible with the deployment of other efforts mobilized to get people to comply with their duties to animals. In any case, it is highly unlikely that it would prevent the advent of a society free of abandonments.

All in all, OAME is feasible, permissible, and effective. By contrast, while feasible, NKLA is neither permissible nor effective. Our non-ideal theory should therefore favor management euthanasia. If one carefully distinguishes the act of killing from the series of events that led to this predicament, there is nothing wrong with such a practice in the highly non-ideal circumstances faced by animals. Of course, something is wrong in the whole process ending with the killing of these animals. What's wrong is the behaviors that lead to this situation: namely, the numerous acts of agents who violate their duties to animals, be they individual dog or cat owners who abandon their pets or political institutions that failed to protect these animals' fundamental interests. Although management euthanasia would be wrong under more or less ideal circumstances, it isn't under the current highly non-ideal circumstances faced by shelter animals.

4.6 Cooperation with Animal Agriculture

Consider next the practice of cooperation with animal agriculture. In order to improve the welfare of animals who are raised and killed for food, some humane societies set up welfare certifications and labels, which farmers receive insofar as they respect certain norms. Because these certifications and labels help consumers choose products that were created more ethically, they provide an incentive for farmers to meet higher welfare standards. There is no denying that these standards are insufficient. Animal suffering is arguably inherent to animal agriculture—whether or not milk cows are allowed to roam free, they are separated from their calves. Nevertheless, it should be acknowledged that these standards have the potential to reduce the amount of animal suffering drastically, provided that they are implemented strictly.

Yet there is a prima facie case to be made that humane societies should not collaborate with animal agriculture, a case based on the question "What if they were humans?" If these farmers exploited human beings—even human beings comparable to farm animals in terms of their interests and mental abilities—it would be manifestly wrong to cooperate with them and give them any kind of formal endorsement. We should not help them exploit humans more humanely; instead, we should get them to stop exploiting humans at all. At the very least, we ought to publicly condemn these practices. This suggests that animal shelters should not cooperate with animal agriculture. I want to suggest that this argument is misguided because it ignores the extent to which the circumstances of farm animals are non-ideal.

No plausible ideal theory would favor cooperation with an industry that exploits and kills sentient beings. But this is beside the point. What we face is another choice between two non-ideal theories: one favoring cooperation with animal agriculture, the other opposing such cooperation. We should therefore choose that which best meets our three desiderata. For a start, both policies would be feasible: cooperation is already in place between humane societies and animal agriculture, and non-cooperation has to be feasible since doing nothing is always an option. (Of course, proponents of this policy do not advocate doing nothing; they advocate demanding the end of human agriculture. But this recommendation is prima facie compatible with the cooperation policy. What's distinctive about their position is that it supports not doing something, and *that* is always an option.)

Turning to the second desideratum, permissibility, the issue is really which policy would most reduce the worst injustices suffered by farm animals. And I surmise it is cooperation. Few things can be worse than living on a factory farm, with insufficient space to walk, let alone access to the outside. The cooperation policy promises to reduce these harms, whereas the no-cooperation policy promises no such thing. This is contested territory, of course. No doubt some will deny that cooperation with animal agriculture has such positive effects in the short run. Gary Francione (2010), for instance, argues that the animal industry would improve its practices even in the absence of legal reforms because the new practices involve lesser costs. He might press the same argument against welfare labels. But this argument is weak. Although some new practices are less expensive, this observation cannot be generalized (Balluch 2008; Garner

2010; Sentience Institute 2020). Farmers only adopt higher welfare standards that are in their best economic interest. In many cases, however, the new practices are more costly and make economic sense only because farmers expect to sell their products better or at a higher price thanks to the label. They would stick to their old habits without the incentive of a label.

Finally, the cooperation policy would be effective and increase the likelihood that animal exploitation will one day be abolished. This is for two main reasons (Sentience Institute 2020). First, reforms contribute to raising public interest for the ethical and legal status of animals. As they are widely publicized, they place the animal question at the heart of the public discussion. Second, welfare reforms tend to raise the production costs and the market prices of animal products. Reforms after reforms, these are less and less competitive on the food market, hopefully up to a point where they will be unable to compete with alternatives such as plant-based substitutes and cultured meat. Of course, this process is gradual and slow to a point that can be frustrating. But it is much more likely than purist abolitionism to lead us to a world devoid of animal exploitation.

Some will inevitably deny these effects. Thus, Francione (2010) maintains that welfare reforms and labels allow people to consume animal products with a clear conscience by conveying the idea that using animals is morally okay. Most extant evidence goes in the other direction (Sentience Institute 2020). Three facts in particular must be highlighted. First, countries with stringent welfare standards have higher levels of vegetarianism. Second, empirical studies suggest that people who read about welfare reforms are more likely to reduce their consumption of animal products. Third, meat consumption was negatively associated with media coverage of farmed animal welfare in the United States from 1982 to 2008. While these facts constitute only defeasible evidence, they are hard to reconcile with the claim that welfare reforms allow people to consume animal products by giving this habit an air of moral respectability. Further research is needed before we can judge the issue with any confidence, but a significant majority of experts on animal advocacy believe that welfare reforms are effective (Reese Anthis 2017).

Importantly, humane societies that choose to cooperate with the animal industry need not renounce issuing an abolitionist message for all that. The concession that some forms of exploitation are less immoral than others is perfectly consistent with the denunciation of all forms of animal exploitation. Some will worry that, while all this is logically consistent, it makes little psychological sense. Looking at an SPCA label on a pack of meat, aren't consumers likely to believe that the Society condones this product and that everything must therefore be fine with it? I doubt that. Some organizations that implement a reformist strategy in the short run have met significant success in conveying an abolitionist message for the longer run. L214 is a good example. This French organization supports higher welfare standards and promotes producers who have adopted these standards as well as distributors who require that from their suppliers (L214 2021). Yet it is well known to oppose all animal use on grounds of principle.

All in all, a cooperation policy appears to be feasible, permissible, and effective. By contrast, while non-cooperation is feasible, it is unlikely to be permissible or effective. Accordingly, although cooperating with animal farmers would be wrong under more or less ideal circumstances, it seems to be the way to go under the current highly non-ideal circumstances faced by farm animals.

4.7 Meat-Based Pet Food

Let's finally turn to the policy of feeding meat to shelter animals. While this issue arises for companion animals generally and is therefore by no means marginal, it has received only little philosophical attention (Donaldson and Kymlicka 2011, 149–153; Milburn 2016, 2017, 2019). What should we make of it within our methodological framework?

As was the case with management euthanasia and cooperation with animal agriculture, a prima facie case can be made that animal shelters should not feed meat to the animals they host. Suppose that, in the neighborhood of a shelter is a farm in which human babies are farmed and killed early enough that they do not get to develop mental capacities above those of typical farm animals. Their flesh is then used to make perfectly nutritious pet food and sold to the shelter. Intuitively, it would be horribly wrong both for the farmers to produce that meat and for the shelter to buy it. If pets needed to eat human meat, we would not hesitate one second before saying, "Too bad for them!" But then, assuming that we should treat farm animals as well as we should treat humans with similar interests, this seems to entail that animal shelters must not feed meat to their animals. Once again: this reasoning is misleading in that it leans on the way we should treat animals if they were humans in more or less ideal circumstances. What we need to ask instead is whether it is okay for animal shelters to feed meat to their protégés in the highly non-ideal circumstances that non-human animals currently face.

Before answering this question, one might want to consider possible alternatives. The most obvious one is to feed shelter animals a plant-based diet. But this suggestion has its limits. As far as meat consumption is concerned, it is customary to distinguish two types of animals: flexible omnivores and obligate carnivores. Dogs exemplify the first type: they surely can eat meat, but all their nutritional needs will easily be met on a plant-based diet. Cats, on the other hand, are different beasts. Though they do not need meat per se (Knight and Leitsberger 2016, 3–4), some of the nutrients on which their survival depends are naturally present only in meat.[6] For the sake of argument, let's assume that cats cannot do without meat. Sue Donaldson and Will Kymlicka discuss other solutions: letting cats hunt or feeding them eggs, scavenged corpses, or cultured meat (2011, 149–153). And Josh Milburn adds a couple more: modifying cats genetically so that they no longer need meat to survive (2017, 197) or feeding them with the flesh of non-sentient animals (2016, 455–458). These authors also consider the extinction of cats, but only as a last resort.

As my aim is not to defend any one of these alternatives but only to argue that animal shelters should not feed meat to the animals they have under their care, let's work with the worst-case scenario: the only feasible alternative is eliminating the cats. On this assumption, we face another choice between two non-ideal theories: one favoring the policy of feeding cats meat, the other favoring the policy of killing them. Let's then see how these policies fare in terms of our three desiderata.

Considering the first desideratum, we've already established that both policies would be feasible. Meat-based pet food is already in place, and the extermination of cats is by assumption the only feasible alternative. Turning to the second desideratum, only the latter policy is permissible. While the interests of companion animals are neglected in many ways, there is no denying that by far the worst injustices are inflicted on farm animals. At least eliminating shelter cats would contribute somewhat to alleviating these injustices. And, while it would frustrate their interests in continued existence, this harm would be negligible in comparison to that inflicted on farm animals.[7] Finally, only the policy of killing cats is effective in the sense that is relevant to our third desideratum. Remember that we are not looking for a second-best theory but for an approach that is most likely to lead us to our ideal—in this case, a society devoid of animal exploitation. By feeding meat to cats, animal shelters would jeopardize the advent of this ideal.

Again, this is all on the worst-case assumption that cats can be fed only with the flesh of other sentient animals. It is quite possible that cats could be fed cultured meat or the flesh of non-sentient animals. However, this would not undermine my claim that they should not be fed the flesh of sentient animals raised and killed to produce meat. All in all, then, feeding meat to shelter animals is feasible, but it is neither permissible nor effective. Our non-ideal theory should therefore condemn such a policy. Not only would feeding meat to shelter animals be wrong under more or less ideal circumstances; it is wrong under the current highly non-ideal circumstances faced by farm animals.

4.8 Conclusion

We have considered the ethics of three practices that are widespread within humane societies and animal shelters: management euthanasia, cooperation with animal agriculture, and meat-based pet food. All three practices would be wrong should they involve human beings instead of nonhuman animals, so all are wrong in ideal theory. Under actual circumstances, which are far from ideal for animals, things are different. Management euthanasia and cooperation with animal agriculture are morally okay because they are feasible, permissible, and effective. As for feeding meat to shelter animals, it is neither permissible nor effective, which makes it just as wrong in non-ideal circumstances as it is in ideal circumstances.

Acknowledgements

I am grateful to Valéry Giroux, Angie Pepper, and Kristin Voigt for their kind invitation to participate in this project and for their helpful comments on earlier drafts of this paper.

Notes

1. If you don't share this widespread intuition, then this line of argument isn't for you.
2. The use of the term "euthanasia" is contested when it comes to animals who are killed for lack of resources. Here's a common objection: euthanasia is best defined as killing an individual for his or her own good, yet animals who are killed for lack of resources are not killed for their own good; therefore, they are not euthanized. I am not convinced by this objection. As I see it, the important question concerns the available alternatives. If the alternative is freeing animals and letting them starve, then death is in their best interest. Of course, one might object that another available alternative is to dedicate more resources to them. However, the issue of resource allocation should be addressed separately. How to allocate resources is one question; whether to kill an animal for whom we lack resources is another. If we have previously decided that a certain animal will not

receive resources, then giving her more resources is no longer an option. And if killing her is the best remaining available alternative, then death is in her best interest, and this will be a case of euthanasia.

3. Ideal theory's focus on idealized circumstances is not to say that it is utopian, for the idealized circumstances it deals with must remain consistent with the constraints imposed by the laws of nature and human psychology. Ideal theory must be achievable in principle even though, by definition, it cannot be achieved in the short run.

4. I'm following Robert Garner's interpretation of Rawls: "The moral permissibility of a course of action, for Rawls, is a function of the degree to which it removes the most grievous or most urgent injustice, the one that departs the most from the ideal theory" (2013, 13).

5. In July 1980, the French magazine *Paris Match* published a picture of the bodies of 140 dead dogs deposited on a road. These dogs had been collected in only two days by the Société Protectrice des Animaux (SPA), the French equivalent to the SPCA. Such campaigns can be powerful in raising public awareness of the tragedy represented by animal abandonment.

6. The main example is taurine, whose deficiency in cats can result in serious digestive issues, blindness, cardiomyopathy, and ultimately death. While certain plant-based preparations for cats are expressly supplemented in taurine, many veterinarians advise cat guardians not to restrict their animals' diet in this way. As the American Society for the Prevention of Cruelty to Animals puts it on its website, "meat absolutely needs to be on the table when you are feeding a cat" (retrieved from https://www.aspca.org/news/why-cant-my-cat-be-vegan).

7. Pet food is often made from the waste products of meat intended for humans. One might therefore object that refraining from feeding cats with meat would not reduce the worst injustice done to farm animals. However, whether or not meat-based pet food is made from waste, the money spent on it supports the meat industry more generally and gets further invested in animal exploitation (Milburn 2019, 1972).

References

Balluch, M. (2008) "Abolitionism vs reformism." https://vgt.at/publikationen/texte/artikel/20080325Abolitionism/index_en.php

Donaldson, S., and Kymlicka, W. (2011) *Zoopolis: A Political Theory of Animal Rights*. Oxford: Oxford University Press.

Ebert, R. (2020) "Are humans more equal than other animals? An evolutionary argument against exclusively human dignity." *Philosophia* 48(5), 1807–1823.

Francione, G. L. (2010) "The abolition of animal exploitation." In G. L. Francione and R. Garner (eds.), *The Animal Rights Debate: Abolition or Regulation?* New York: Columbia University Press, 1–102.

Garner, R. (2010) "A defense of a broad animal protectionism." In G. L. Francione and R. Garner (eds.), *The Animal Rights Debate: Abolition or Regulation?* New York: Columbia University Press, 103–174.

Garner, R. (2013) *A Theory of Justice for Animals: Animal Rights in a Nonideal World.* Oxford: Oxford University Press.

Jaquet, F. (2021) "A debunking argument against speciesism." *Synthese 198*(2), 1011–1027.

Jaquet, F. (2022a) "Speciesism and tribalism: Embarrassing origins." *Philosophical Studies 179*(3), 933–954.

Jaquet, F. (2022b) "What's wrong with speciesism." *Journal of Value Inquiry 56*, 395–408.

Kasperbauer, T. J. (2017) *Subhuman: The Moral Psychology of Human Attitudes to Animals.* New York: Oxford University Press.

Knight, A., and Leitsberger, M. (2016) "Vegetarian versus meat-based diets for companion animals." *Animals* e Moral Psychology of Human Attitude (9), 57.

L214 (2021) "Pourquoi des campagnes réformistes?" https://www.l214.com/agir/pourquoi-des-campagnes-reformistes/.

Loughnan, S., Bastian, B., and Haslam, N. (2014) "The psychology of eating animals." *Current Directions in Psychological Science 23*(2), 104–108.

Machery, E. (2016) "The evolution of tribalism." In J. Kiverstein (ed.), *The Routledge Handbook of Philosophy of the Social Mind.* New York: Routledge, 104–117.

McMahan, J. (2005) "Our fellow creatures." *Journal of Ethics 9*(3–4), 353–380.

Milburn, J. (2016) "Not only humans eat meat: Companions, sentience, and vegan politics." *Journal of Social Philosophy 46*(4), 449–462.

Milburn, J. (2017) "The animal lover's paradox? On the ethics of 'pet food.'" In C. Overall (ed.), *Pets and People: The Ethics of Companion Animals.* New York: Oxford University Press, 187–202.

Milburn, J. (2019) "Pet food: Ethical issues." In P. M. Thomson and D. M. Kaplan (eds.), *Encyclopedia of Food and Agricultural Ethics.* Dordrecht: Springer, 1967–1973.

Murphy, L. B. (2003) *Moral Demands in Nonideal Theory.* Oxford: Oxford University Press.

Rachels, J. (1990) *Created from Animals: The Moral Implications of Darwinism.* Oxford: Oxford University Press.

Rawls, J. (1971) *A Theory of Justice.* Oxford: Clarendon Press.

Rawls, J. (1999) *The Law of Peoples.* Cambridge, MA.: Harvard University Press.

Reese Anthis, J. (2017) "Effective animal advocacy researcher survey June 2017." https://www.sentienceinstitute.org/blog/eaa-researcher-survey-june-2017.

Sentience Institute (2020). "Summary of evidence for foundational questions in effective animal advocacy." https://www.sentienceinstitute.org/foundational-questions-summaries

Simmons, A. J. (2010) "Ideal and nonideal theory." *Philosophy & Public Affairs* 38(1), 5–36.

Singer, P. (2011) *Practical Ethics*, 3rd ed. Cambridge: Cambridge University Press.

Valentini, L. (2012) "Ideal vs. non-ideal theory: A conceptual map." *Philosophy Compass* 7(9), 654–664.

5

Being Popular and Being Just

How Animal Protection Organizations Can Be Both

Agnes Tam and Will Kymlicka

5.1 Introduction

The Los Angeles Animal Services (LAAS) has more than a hundred years of history serving animals in the city, running one of the largest municipal shelter systems in the United States, and it is widely regarded as a leader on progressive animal issues in the country. In line with its mandate and history of progressive reform, LAAS in 2017 proposed to the City Board of Animal Services that shelter dogs should be fed plant-based not meat-based diets. LAAS had done its homework to show that this proposal was morally desirable, scientifically sound, and economically viable. Scientific evidence of its nutritional sufficiency was presented. Sponsorship from reputable plant-based dog food companies was secured. Sound moral arguments were given. As Commissioner Roger Wolfson put it,

> We are the department of animal services, not the department of animal companion services. So we need to start from a place of avoiding unnecessary killing of animals. We already shelter pigs and chickens and turkeys and we wouldn't think about killing them unnecessarily. So if dogs can get their needs met without killing animals we owe it to the citizens of Los Angeles to try.[1]

Agnes Tam and Will Kymlicka, *Being Popular and Being Just* In: *The Ethics of Animal Shelters*. Edited by: Valéry Giroux, Angie Pepper, and Kristin Voigt, Oxford University Press. © Oxford University Press 2023.
DOI: 10.1093/oso/9780197678633.003.0007

Despite the evidence and arguments, the public reaction from the citizens of Los Angeles was overwhelmingly negative. The proposal was described as a display of "human arrogance," and an act of "virtue signaling" and "cruelty to animals."[2] The proposal was widely seen as a public reaction disaster for LAAS and was quickly withdrawn.

This is just one example of a chronic dilemma facing progressive animal protection organizations (APOs). Animal rights activists can afford to be radically at odds with public opinion: indeed, activist groups often deliberately flout public opinion in order to garner media attention. But many community-based APOs are heavily reliant on public support, trust and goodwill. Public backlash can lead not only to setbacks in a particular campaign—such as the plan to change shelter diets—but also can lead to a reduction in donations generally, thus undermining an organization's financial capacity to run its shelters. Animal charities already face intense competitions with other human charities.[3] Moreover, APOs often need to work collaboratively with a wide range of public officials, including legislators and law enforcement officers. Given their particular location in the institutional ecology of the animal advocacy movement, they cannot afford to ignore the constraints of public support.

In light of cases such as the LAAS proposal, many APOs have learned to be pragmatic, perhaps even conservative. To avoid repeating LAAS's mistake, many avoid taking "risky" positions on issues of animal ethics. They often decide to focus only on popular causes—for example, protecting cats and dogs from individual acts of cruelty—while setting aside less popular causes, such as the fate of farmed animals or the legal status of animals as "property." This helps preserve their institutional efficacy, although arguably at the expense of their own institutional mandates, which often refer to protecting *all* animals from unnecessary suffering. It also comes at a high cost in terms of the morale of staff and volunteers who often would like to take a more progressive stance.

As we said, this is a chronic dilemma facing many APOs. Is there anything that philosophy can do to help address it? One possible response is that the task of philosophers is to articulate more and better moral arguments for progressive change or identify and correct the relevant false beliefs that lead to the misinterpretation of moral norms. In the LAAS case, this might mean specifying more clearly what are the relevant facts and moral reasons for shifting to a plant-based diet for shelter animals in the hope that this will overcome the moral ignorance or moral inertia of the public and persuade people to support the proposal.[4]

In this chapter, we offer an alternative proposal. Scientific communication and moral argumentation are important, but we now have overwhelming evidence that scientific and moral legitimacy are often insufficient to mobilize public support for progressive agendas. This is not just because individuals are often irrational or egoistic, but also because human beings are social animals, and, as such, we are strongly oriented toward group norms and hence toward what we will call "*we*-reasons" or "reason-for-*us*." Drawing on recent work in the philosophy of social norms, we will argue that we-reasons rooted in group norms are distinct from both prudential reasoning ("reason-for-*me*") and from moral reasoning ("reason-for-*everyone*"). We also explore why these we-reasons are often powerful obstacles to progressive reform, as they were in the LAAS case. However, we will also argue that APOs can try to wield the power of "*we*-reasoning" to mobilize public support for their progressive agendas, and we conclude by considering how LAAS might have achieved a different result for the vegan shelter campaign if they had followed the logic of *we*-reasoning.

5.2 Understanding Group Norms

In this section, we briefly explore the concept of group norms and how they generate a form of *we*-reasoning that is different from both prudential reasoning and moral reasoning. We then consider why these norms are so powerful in social life, both for good and bad.

5.2.1 The Nature of Group Norms

Consider some paradigmatic cases of group norms: the norm of politeness among Canadians, the norm of wearing black to funerals in Christian societies, the norm of female genital cutting in Muslim societies, the norm of dueling among British aristocrats, the breadwinner norm for men, the norm of binding women's feet in imperial China, and the norm of playing the most embarrassing games at orientation camps among Hong Kong university freshmen. In each of these cases, an attitude or an action is prescribed for the members of a bounded community. If you belong to the relevant community, you are likely to feel that you ought to follow the norm. How can we make sense of this ought-feeling?

Some social conventions are the result of simple self-interest. To use a textbook example, it is in everyone's self-interest to have a convention in society about which side of the road to drive on. There may be no inherent reason for preferring the left or the right side of the road, but we need to pick a side, and, once the convention is established, everyone has a self-interested reason in complying with it. In these cases, we have a collective rule, but we don't need to invoke the idea of *we*-reasons to explain it: prudential reasoning is sufficient.

However, the sorts of group norms we are interested in cannot be explained in terms of prudential reasoning. Consider the norm of dueling among aristocrats. Conformity was not based on self-interest because it could easily get one severely injured or even killed. One of us was once a freshman in Hong Kong who derived no pleasure from playing the orientation games of asking "love hotels" for their price or drinking a ketchup, soy sauce, and cream mix. The reason for conformity to these silly, harmful, sometimes even immoral group norms is not reducible to self-interest. On the contrary, people feel a sense of *obligation* to comply which preempts their self-interest, and indeed refusal to comply is often criticized as a form of selfishness.

So compliance with group norms typically involves subordinating one's self-interest out of a sense of other-regarding obligation. This may sound like it involves moral reasoning since morality is our paradigmatic example of subordinating self-interest to other-regarding obligations. But in fact these group norms do not share the characteristics of moral norms, at least as "morality" is usually understood. Consider paradigmatic moral norms, such as the norms against murder, slavery, and rape. In these cases, the reason for conformity is *membership-independent*. Everyone owes it to everyone else (in the moral community) to conform to these moral oughts. These norms apply to Canadians' interactions with strangers and outsiders and in their relations to us. And everyone can hold each other accountable for complying with these norms. It is perfectly appropriate (and perhaps even obligatory) for Canadians to encourage others to abide by these moral reasons, and vice versa. This is why moral norms are seen as reasons-for-*everyone* to follow.[5]

By contrast, group norms are *membership-dependent*. Their conformity is owed *by* members *to* members. They present reasons-for-*us*, not reasons for everyone. For example, only freshmen in Hong Kong universities are expected to participate in those silly orientation games.[6] Freshmen outside of Hong Kong would not be chastised for non-conformity. Indeed, it would often be inappropriate for foreigners to demand that freshmen in Hong Kong conform to these norms because the expectation to conform is owed to their peers in Hong Kong only. Similarly, aristocrats didn't expect peasants or churchmen to comply with the group norm of dueling and didn't think of themselves as accountable to these groups for their own compliance. The obligation to duel was only owed to (and accountable to) other aristocrats. So, too, with the imperial Chinese norm of foot-binding. The Chinese didn't expect other societies to comply with this norm and did not think of themselves as accountable to other societies for their own compliance. Unlike moral norms, therefore, the "owing relation" of group norms—who owes conformity to whom—is distinctly membership-dependent.

And this in turn raises a second difference between group norms and moral norms, which is the latter's *expectation-independence*. The source of authority of moral norms is grounded in objectively valid moral principles, at least in the minds of the conforming agents.

If asked why you refrain from engaging in slavery, it would be inadequate to answer "That's what people here expect me to do." The proper answer is "That's the right thing to do." Most people believe that slavery would be morally wrong even if one found oneself in a society where slavery was common. Its wrongness is therefore expectation-independent.[7]

By contrast, the authority of group norms is *expectation-dependent*. In other words, the reason for conformity to group norms is grounded almost exclusively in the shared normative expectations themselves, at least in the mind of the conforming agents. If asked why you wear black to a funeral, it is fully adequate to answer "That's what people expect me to do here." You do not need to come up with your own reason for action (e.g., you do not need to provide some prudential or moral justification for why the color black is the appropriate way to express grief). In the case of group norms, unlike moral norms, the obligation to comply with the norm disappears if and when it no longer expresses a group's actual commitments. The reason to comply with a group norm is not its objective validity, but rather the fact that it expresses a joint commitment or will of the members of a group, and hence compliance is an expectation of group membership (Gilbert 2006, 2013).[8]

5.2.2 The Power of Group Norms

In short, group norms generate *we*-reasons that are distinct from both prudential self-interest and impartial morality. This is important, we believe, because history suggests that humans are uniquely responsive to we-reasoning. Progressive reformers often assume that the most powerful drivers of behavior are either self-interest or impartial moral reasoning, but in fact history suggests that we-reasons may prevail even when they conflict with self-interest and even when they conflict with impartial morality.

For example, the persistence of the food binding norm in Imperial China was due not to moral ignorance of its cruelty. Many parents of the elite class had moral and prudential reasons not to bind their daughters' feet, but these moral reasons were overridden by we-reasons to uphold class honor (Appiah 2010). To give another example, during the Jim Crow era, many restaurants and hotels adopted racist policies, refusing to serve African Americans, which is often attributed to moral ignorance. But we know that many of these same businesses lobbied for the Civil Rights Act of 1964 that forbade discrimination of the basis of race (Sunstein 2019). This suggests, that while aware of the moral norm of racial equality, they also felt a competing obligation to comply with the group norm of racial honor upheld by whites. Choosing to serve African Americans would be seen as allowing personal greed for African Americans' money to override solidarity with fellow whites and hence as a form of group disloyalty. Group norms of racial honor trumped both personal financial self-interest and moral reasoning.

So group norms can compete with, and sometimes override, moral reasons. But they are also powerful in a different and subtler way. According to recent psychological research, group norms often bias the way members interpret scientific evidence and moral arguments. Cultural cognition theory holds that people tend to accept or reject beliefs based on their perceived congruence with their social norms and group identities. We often consciously or unconsciously employ a range of psychological mechanisms (e.g., bias, heuristics, affect) to credit or dismiss evidence of risk so as to "fit values they share with others" (Kahan et al. 2011, 148). The predictions of the cultural cognition theory have been tested and confirmed in a wide range of issues, from nuclear power to guns, and from nanotechnology to vaccination of schoolgirls for HPV (Kahan 2010). Such cultural cognition is known to protect group norms from change, making them sticky.[9] As we will shortly see, group norms might have had similar distorting effects in the LAAS case, leading Angelenos to discount the scientific evidence and moral arguments presented by LAAS because it conflicted with their received norms.

5.2.3 The Normativity of Group Norms

But why are group norms so powerful? And is this something we should regret and seek to minimize? Is the tendency to engage in we-reasoning a deficiency or pathology that we should seek to overcome? Is it a form of servility to subordinate oneself to the views of one's own group?

Even philosophers who acknowledge the power of group norms in social life often express skepticism that there is anything genuinely normative about *we*-reasoning. For example, Cristina Bicchieri writes,

> we have an ingrained tendency to move from *what is* to *what ought to be*, and conclude that "what is" must be right or good. Yet, apart from our longstanding habits of performing and expecting others to perform certain actions, there is no deeper foundation to these presumed "rights and obligations," however intensely felt they might be. (2014, 210, emphasis in original)

We do not share this cynical view. We believe that group norms are of fundamental significance to human life because they make groups and give meaning to group life.

The first thing to understand is that group life, for most people, is the center of human life. Human beings, like other social species, are group-making animals, and norms are fundamental to making groups. We orient our lives in terms of groups, and orienting ourselves to groups is first and foremost about orienting ourselves to the norms that constitute the group. In this sense, social animals are "normic" or "normatropic"—as we move around in the world, we orient ourselves to the norms that define the groups we belong to (Lorini 2022).

Ask yourself this: What are you doing this weekend? Where do you begin to answer this question? For most people, the answer starts with the group identities we affirm. We are members of our families, our work teams, our professions, our cities, and our cultural community. When we plan our weekend, we consider our roles and membership in each of these groups and the norms that regulate them. This does not mean we necessarily endorse each of the norms in these groups. We do not. But without these group norms, these groups can hardly exist in their current shape. And without group life, humans live their life in the void.

But group norms do not just constitute groups and anchor human life, they make them meaningful as well. They enable a wide range of social goods, including group belonging, group trust, group honor, and group identification. To see this point, consider what makes a meaningful friendship. Surely, it is not one in which two friends act according to their own individual points of view as a matter of routine. To show love, concern, and trustworthiness to our friend, we meet the normative expectations of our friend *because* they are our friend's, as a matter of routine. By contrast, if our friend decides when to meet, what to do, and where to explore all on her own terms, however reasonable they might be, this friendship may leave us feeling alienated. There is no united "We" in this friendship, just two separate individual "I." Group norms play the same role as these interpersonal normative expectations in groups (Scheffler 2018). The larger the group, the harder it is for each individual member to meet each individual member's expectations. In large-scale cultural communities, some members may never get to meet each other in life. So group trust, group belonging, and group honor are all mediated by these group norms. And to show trust, express belonging, and maintain honor as a member is to conform to these group norms. Put differently, to be a good member is to put aside the "I" and think and act from the "We"-constitutive of group norms as a matter of routine. This is what it means to be a *committed* member. And when members jointly commit to the group by conforming to their group norms, their group life becomes meaningful to them.

None of this suggests that members cannot or should not revise their group norms. Orienting oneself to group norms does not mean blindly deferring to them. We believe that we-reasoning is indeed a form of reasoning and judgment, not mindless conformity, although it is distinct from the logic of impartial moral reasoning. We return to this question in Section 5.4 as it is key to changing group norms.

But any effort to revise group norms must start from the recognition that group norms are an inescapable feature of human life, offer weighty reasons for action, and are resistant to change. Unless moral reformers understand this, they will always be on the outside of the groups with which they seek to engage.

5.3 Implications for Animal Protection Organizations

What does all of this entail for APOs? In this section, we argue that their room for maneuver is often constrained by group norms. If APOs are seen as breaking these group norms, or as failing to show that their decisions are *we*-reasonable, disapproval from members is likely to follow. To illustrate, we return to the LAAS case.

The extent to which group norms constrain APOs depends in part on whether they are *community-based*. International animal advocacy groups are not necessarily beholden to particular *we*-groups. For example, People for the Ethical Treatment of Animals (PETA) prides itself on taking an "uncompromising, unwavering view on animal rights."[10] By defining its mission "to stop animal abuse worldwide," PETA explicitly disavows its readiness to be bound by the norms of particular social or cultural groups. Their central commitment is to universal moral norms.

By contrast, the LAAS, like most APOs, is community-based. The mandate of these organizations often contains explicit manifestations of their readiness to be bound by the shared values and principles of the particular communities they are rooted in. On the LAAS's website, it is stated that they "envision a day when every pet born has a good home and is cared for all its life, when no person is ever endangered by an animal and when all Angelenos are actively engaged in making Los Angeles the most humane city in the nation."[11] The constituents of LAAS are *Angelenos* and their animals, as opposed to every person and animal in the world. In this way, LAAS expresses its readiness to bind itself to Angelenos. And in return, members of the public reciprocally express their readiness to bind themselves to LAAS through their participation in LAAS's practices, such as making donations, volunteering, and collective appreciation of their service.[12]

In this sense, LAAS is built around a model of joint commitment, linking the APO to a community. We will return to the precise object of this joint commitment in a moment. We would like to first highlight the significance of the fact that LAAS situates itself as a member of an Angeleno community that is held together by joint commitments. If LAAS is a member, by the logic of joint commitment, it is bound by the group norms of Angelenos. Its practices are not merely constrained by moral norms, epistemic norms, or other "reasons for everybody."

We believe that this helps explain why the vegan diet proposal was deemed illegitimate. Public backlash against the proposal may partly reflect disagreements about impartial morality or about scientific findings. But it may also involve the perceived violation of Angeleno group norms. What exactly are these norms? The content of group norms is often implicit and not codified. But we can try to isolate these group norms by thinking about those members of the Los Angeles public who are supporters of the LAAS (e.g., the people who make donations to LAAS, write letters to city council to support them, and encourage schools and families to send children for shelter visits). These are the people who see themselves as linked to the LAAS through joint commitment involving mutual expectations.

At the most general level, these supporters of the LAAS are people who think of themselves as "animal lovers" and who take pride in the city's image as the most humane city in the nation. But, as a vast literature reveals, "animal lovers" come in different shapes and sizes (e.g., Joy 2020). The supporters of a wildlife rescue sanctuary who admire free-living animals, for example, may have quite derogatory attitudes toward "tame" domesticated animals. In the case of LAAS, by contrast, we are dealing with the sort of "animal lovers" whose focus is specifically on companion animals and whose image of a "humane city" is tied up first and foremost with norms of "responsible pet care" and "responsible pet ownership."[13] And their support for LAAS is tied to its role as guardian and embodiment of this particular set of norms. As a humane city of responsible pet owners, people who associate with this community expect its members, including the LAAS, to mutually commit to keeping the city pet-safe and pet-friendly; to ensuring that dogs and cats find good homes (and that dogs and cats are protected from bad owners); to ensuring appropriate food, exercise, and companionship for their pets; grieving for the loss of pets; and so on.

It is in this context, we believe, that the proposal for changing the diet of shelter animals needs to be considered. Most public supporters of the LAAS feed meat to their dogs and cats, often with the advice and encouragement of other loyal members of the Angeleno pet-loving community, including veterinarians and trainers, and view this as instantiating the norm of responsible pet care. The proposal for dietary change is, therefore, an important change to the existing practices that form the bedrock of people's self-identity as responsible pet owners. Angelenos—particularly those who view themselves as mutually committed to the LAAS—will ask themselves whether the LAAS's decision is compatible with *our* ideas of responsible pet care, or whether it is instead seen as a betrayal of *our* norms.

Viewing the proposal in this way has two important implications. First, dietary practices are not a mere norm of prudence, and changing them without justifying the change with reason-for-*us* can seem like an attack on *our* norms and *our* identity. To deviate from these membership expectations is, prima facie, to violate a joint commitment and implicitly to betray the community built around that commitment. It seems to us that this indeed is how the vegan diet proposal was perceived by many in the LA public. It was seen not only or primarily as lacking adequate reasons-for-*everyone*, but also and more powerfully, as a betrayal of the *we*.

So the backlash can be viewed as a direct result of the violation of group norms constitutive of the LA community of animal lovers. But group norms might also have worked in subtler ways against the vegan reform. As we noted earlier, reasons-for-*us* are powerful not only in *trumping* impartial moral and scientific reasons, but also in *shaping* how people respond to moral and scientific arguments. And this, too, was visible in LAAS. People raised doubts about the evidence for the sufficiency of a vegan diet. But as cultural cognition theory would predict, this doubt is best understood not as a purely scientific disagreement but as a reflection of the fact that Angelenos trusted those scientific authorities who aligned with their group commitments (to responsible pet ownership and responsible pet care) and distrusted those who didn't.

Seeing the dietary practice as a group norm not only helps to make sense of the public backlash, but also helps explain why moral argumentation and scientific information was insufficient. As we have argued, group norms are distinct from moral norms in the sense that the former operate in the space of reason-for-*us* and not exclusively in the space of reason-for-*everyone*. In our view, the LAAS made compelling moral arguments that farmed animals are owed moral consideration and shouldn't be treated as resources to feed companion animals. Similarly, the LAAS provided compelling factual information about how unnecessary this suffering is because dogs can thrive on a vegan diet. But these moral and scientific reasons-for-*everyone* by themselves are not yet reasons-for-*us* to act differently. As we explained, joint commitments carry their own group legitimacy that is not reducible to their moral or scientific legitimacy, and the latter does not automatically trump the former. To ensure support for progressive reform, therefore, we need to engage with this space of reasons-for-*us* and show how proposed reforms are *we*-reasonable in the light of our joint commitments.

5.4 An Alternative Strategy of Moral Reform: We-Reasoning

While group norms are powerful, and powerful obstacles to change, they are not fixed or static. The fact that feeding meat to dogs is currently part of the Angeleno group norm of responsible pet ownership does not mean that this will always be so. We can and should hope to change group norms. But if the analysis above is correct, this is unlikely to simply be a matter of piling up new and better moral arguments or scientific information. We need to tackle the group norm directly. In what follows, we introduce an account of norm-change that honors the group perspective while providing critical resources for members to re-interpret their norms. We further believe that we-reasoning can offer a new strategy for progressive APOs to implement moral reform without compromising ethical integrity nor losing public support. We show this by applying it to the LAAS case.

5.4.1 An Account of Joint Interpretation

Identifying reasons to revise group norms seems paradoxical. After all, if a group norm is reason-for-*us* to follow simply *because it is ours*, what reason-for-*us* is there to reject it? Group norms seem to bootstrap their own authority. However, this paradox arises only when we evaluate a group norm in isolation. In reality, group norms fit into a larger web of norms, and it is this larger web that constitutes a group's joint commitment (Tam 2020c). For example, the norm of holding the door for the elderly in Canada is authoritative because it coheres well in a web of norms of respect for the elderly, politeness, norms of civility, and so on. Some group norms are more peripheral to the joint commitment; others are more central. And these relations and meanings are not static. As membership changes, and as background circumstances change, the meanings of these norms as well as their relations might change as well. Which customs, values, and principles are jointly accepted is a result of an ongoing joint interpretation of who *we* are and of the extent to which those customs, values, and principles "fit" with our collective understanding. Philosopher Michael Walzer likens this joint interpretation to literary reading.

> The best reading . . . illuminates the poem in a more powerful and persuasive way. Perhaps the best reading is a new reading, seizing upon some previously misunderstood symbol or trope and reexplaining the entire poem. (Walzer 1987, 27)

Following Walzer's analogy, a joint commitment constitutive of group norms is like a poem—inchoate, imprecise, and incoherent by itself. Its meanings require interpretative efforts. The more a reading can clarify the imprecise meaning of a norm; resolve the indeterminacy of its application; bring to light untold connections between members, norms, or circumstances; or give coherence to the webs of norms and beliefs in which it is embedded, the more persuasive a reading is. Good we-reasoning aims at a good reading of a joint commitment, making possible and meaningful the best version of ourselves. The legitimacy of a group norm stems from good we-reasoning. If a better reading of a given group norm can be given, then the current reading ought to be changed.

For this process to be effective, certain distinctive features of *we*-reasoning must be respected. One of these features is *standing* to interrogate group norms. As we explained earlier, group norms and moral norms differ in this respect. The authority to interrogate moral norms are membership-independent and expectation-independent: reasoning about moral norms should be inclusive of everyone. Not so for group norms. Outsiders or apostates are unlikely to have any standing when interpreting what *we* should commit to since they are neither willing nor able to be bound by the joint commitment. Standing to interrogate group norms is limited to those who express loyalty to the group. There is an epistemic dimension here as well about who possesses the hermeneutical resources to interpret joint commitments. A foreigner usually cannot accurately read members' level of readiness to be bound by a particular value or custom expressed in their action and symbols. We-reasoning requires we-standing—being "one of us," one who is both willing and able to commit.

Assuming we can identify reasons-for-*us* for change, how can these be communicated to other members? This can be very challenging. By virtue of their joint commitment, members expect deference to prevailing interpretations. Any new interpretation can be easily perceived as a rejection of the existing joint commitment and of the membership constituted by it. Communicating a new interpretation therefore requires the speaker to be willing and able to demonstrate her *trustworthiness*, such that she is seen as merely dissenting, as opposed to seceding or rebelling, and that her interpretation manifests her loyalty to the group. The distinction between dissent and secession/rebellion is important. If someone argues for a norm-change not out of concern for the joint commitment, but out of concern for her personal moral understanding and judgments, this could mean rejecting her membership and, at the same time, undermining the authority of joint commitment by not doing her part. Dissent is different. Dissent does not imply disrespect for joint commitment. A dissenter suggests a different way of reading a joint commitment from the we-perspective, without any intention to terminate their membership. Whether someone is dissenting or rebelling/seceding cannot simply be read off of her action. As soon as someone acts differently from the existing norm, questions will arise about how to interpret the underlying intention.[14] This is why trustworthiness becomes essential. Trustworthiness reflects a commitment on the part of the dissenter to go out of her way to remove epistemic and emotional obstacles of trust, including misunderstanding and mistrust. Put differently, it requires the norm-entrepreneur to be able to demonstrate that she is speaking to *us* from *us* about *us*.

In short, to be consistent with we-reasoning, proposals for reform must be attentive to issues of standing/loyalty and trustworthiness. We believe that this sheds light on the LAAS case. To successfully appeal to reasons-for-*us*, APOs would need to fulfill two conditions:

1. To establish their *we*-standing—that is, their loyalty to the community, and hence their standing to speak for "We Angelenos" (or more specifically, "we members of the Angeleno community of responsible pet owners").
2. To identify *we*-reasons for the proposal—that is, reasons that are reasons from *us* to *us* about *us*.

The first step is for organizations like LAAS to show their *we*-standing to participate in we-reasoning. This requires manifesting one's readiness to be bound by the norms of joint commitment.

Whereas PETA can say it will be accountable only to universal morality, if LAAS wants to mobilize *we*-reasoning, then it needs to show that it identifies as Angeleno and is ready to be bound to Angeleno norms.

In this respect, LAAS may have made a strategic mistake in choosing celebrities (e.g., Moby) who were outspoken about veganism to be the face of the campaign. As we've seen, veganism is not a norm that the majority of Angelenos, including pet owners, have accepted. There is of course a strong community of vegans in LA, with their own joint commitments, and by choosing vegan celebrities as the face of the campaign, LAAS could be seen as throwing in its lot with that community. But that is a different community from the community of Angelenos who are invested in ideas of responsible pet care, who are the traditional constituency and supporters of the LAAS. The two communities differ not only with respect to what they feed companion animals, but also with respect to the very legitimacy of companion animals. The vegan community contains a strong stand of "extinctionist" thinking which argues that companion animals should go extinct, which has deepened the gulf between the two communities.[15] Vegan activists are therefore seen, among the broader pet-owning community, not only as outsiders, but as threats to the very moral practice of responsible pet care/ownership that underpins their identity. Anti-pet and pet-extinctionist claims by vegans are in fact carefully collected and circulated within the pet community as alleged evidence of the "hidden agenda" of animal rights activists not only to abolish relations of exploitation, but also to abolish the very practice of caring for companion animals.[16]

In this sense, far from taking special efforts to show themselves as loyal members of the Angeleno responsible pet care community, the LAAS in fact was seen as aligning itself with outsiders, even enemies, of that community. It thereby lost the we-standing to speak to the rest of us about who we ought to be. To signal *we*-standing, it might have been more effective for the LAAS to appeal to spokespeople who are known above all for their commitment to the Angeleno pet community, including vets and trainers and those who have been

involved in creating dog parks or other pet-friendly initiatives—
people whose loyalty to the relevant *we* is unquestioned.

Once *we*-standing and a *we*-perspective are established with
members, the next step is to identify good *we*-reasons to reconfigure
group norms in such a way that the vegan dog shelter proposal is
appropriate by their light. As we said, the norm of trustworthiness
dictates that the norm-entrepreneur be competent and willing in
reinterpreting joint commitment. Offering only impartial moral
reasons and scientific data for the proposal is not sufficient to show
trustworthiness in relation to the group's identity since by themselves these are outside the group's values.

An alternative starting place would have been the norm of responsible pet ownership itself. LAAS could have demonstrated readiness to be bound to this norm but offer a new and better reading of
the norm. There are many possibilities here. One possibility is that
LAAS could have translated the relevant scientific arguments and
moral arguments for the vegan diet into a *we*-argument. Reasons-
for-*us*, as we have explained, are not reducible to scientific truths
or impartial moral arguments. They are not reasons-for-*everyone*.
But they are not inherently incompatible with them either. After all,
reasons-for-*us* are built on raw materials, such as interests, desires,
moral principles, values, and truths, and they offer a particular
reading of their relations and meanings for a group. Think of the *we*-
perspective as a lens through which we view the world with particular colors and shapes so that it becomes meaningful to us. Applying
this point to LAAS, it would require LAAS to present the scientific
and moral arguments for a vegan diet as a joint interpretation of
responsible pet care and as an appropriate evolution in a long and
honorable tradition of Angeleno pet ownership, thus keeping faith
with its core members and core values.[17] This shows trustworthiness
that they know what Angelenos are committed to and value in their
we-identity.

We do not want to understate the challenges to rereading joint
commitments. As we've noted, group norms form a complex web,
and it is difficult to pull out one thread without changing the surrounding norms. In this case, norms about feeding dogs and cats

are of course inextricably related to norms about feeding humans. All of the moral and scientific arguments the LAAS provided for feeding dogs a vegan diet can also be marshalled for feeding human children a vegan diet. If avoiding unnecessary animal cruelty is a good reason to feed dogs a vegan diet, it is also a good reason to feed humans a vegan diet. Some of the resistance to the vegan dog diet may in fact come indirectly from the perception that this implicitly challenges deeper group norms about human diet or even deeper norms about species hierarchy (Kymlicka 2018). At the end of the day, gaining public acceptance for a vegan diet in animal shelters may require changing public attitudes toward veganism generally.

If so, then proposals for a vegan animal shelter face an uphill battle: proposals for a vegan-friendly dog shelter would need to be embedded in a broader campaign for a vegan-friendly LA. But even this broader project, we would argue, would need to be tied to joint commitments. If joint commitment is indeed like a text, new readings are always possible relative to new circumstances, new readers, and new relations between readers and authors. It takes creative work. For example, LAAS might argue that LA as a city has a distinctive history of inclusiveness. The LAAS could point to the city's history of expanding rights to the LGBTQ community, migrant communities, and racial minorities as evidence of Angelenos' distinctive joint commitment to inclusion. The creation of a multispecies community which views formerly farmed animals as members of society, not as resources to be exploited by the community, could then be proposed as an extension of this long-standing group commitment and identity. The key is to speak to Angelenos' concern about their own norms, not just to impartial moral requirements or scientific evidence.[18]

5.5 Conclusion

In this chapter, we showed that different types of norms are important for APOs that seek to reform our treatment of animals. As community-based organizations, APOs are constrained by group norms in addition to moral norms, scientific truths, and legal norms. These group norms present membership-dependent and expectation-dependent reasons-for-*us*. These reasons-for-*us* are often what make or break reforms. On the one hand, they constrain what APOs can do because violations of them can trigger severe public backlash. On the other hand, they can also mobilize public support for reforms.

As Delon (2018) notes, this distinction between different types of norms is often overlooked both by practitioners and philosophers. There is a common tendency among philosophers and reformers to speak solely with the voice of impartial reason. When the public are unmoved, they assume that people are irrational or egoistic. Nothing can be farther from the truth. People are fundamentally social or groupish, and they filter impartial moral arguments through the lens of group identity. This can be seen from moral progress in other domains. Research has shown that widespread moral understanding was achieved long before the abolition of the British slave trade (Tam 2020b), the end of female genital cutting in Sudan (Bicchieri 2016), and the abandonment of dueling (Appiah 2010). What made progress in these cases ultimately possible is that moral awareness was supplemented with we-reasoning that revised group expectations. Animal advocates and practitioners need to take seriously these shared expectations and identify ways to align them to justice. And this in turn is likely to require much greater attention to questions of standing and trustworthiness within the particular communities that APOs serve.

Acknowledgments

We would like to thank Sue Donaldson, Valéry Giroux, Angie Pepper, and Kristin Voigt for their helpful feedback on earlier drafts. Thanks are also due to Élise Desaulniers and the staff at the Montreal SPCA for sharing their insights with us.

Notes

1. https://www.theguardian.com/us-news/2017/dec/29/los-angeles-vegan-dog-diet-animal-shelters-moby

2. https://ethicsalarms.com/2017/12/18/q-what-do-you-get-when-you-cross-human-arrogance-virtue-signalling-and-cruelty-to-animals-a-a-vegan-ani mal-shelter/. The negative public reaction was reinforced when the City's Chief Veterinarian, Dr. Jeremy Prupas, issued a report—citing testimony from three unnamed veterinarians and an unnamed pet food representative—that a vegan diet might cause diarrhea to some dogs during transition and the po-tential cleaning involved might add burdens to currently understaffed shelters. However, as we will discuss, these concerns—which could easily be addressed in the transitional phase—were not the basis on which the public viewed the proposal as "cruel."

3. https://faunalytics.org/giving-to-animals-new-data-who-how/.

4. This is sometimes called the "Philosopher's Model" of moral progress, exemplified by Peter Singer (2011) and Dale Jamieson (2002). For a discussion of the Philosophical Model, see Tam (2020a, chap. 1).

5. We are here assuming that morality and "the moral point of view" are defined by some idea of impartiality, as is common in the moral philosophy literature. There is a more capacious definition of "morality," found particularly in the so-cial sciences, which essentially includes any and all social norms that are seen as authoritative within a community. On this broader view, what we are calling "group norms" would qualify as one dimension of a society's "morality." (On this broader view, many nonhuman animals also have moral norms since they have authoritative group norms—see, e.g., Andrews 2020.) Nothing in our ar-gument depends on this semantic question. What matters for our argument is the distinction between "reasons for us" and "reasons for everybody." For those who prefer the broader definition, everything we argue about the importance of attending to group norms alongside impartial moral norms can be rephrased as an argument about the importance of attending to "reasons for us" alongside "reasons for everybody" within the meta-category of "morality."

6. Non-members might be expected to comply with a group's norms under spe-cific conditions. For example, a non-Christian guest might owe it to a Christian family to wear black at a family funeral. But, in such cases, the non-member complies out of respect for group members, not out of a direct sense of obli-gation to the norm, which would indeed not be binding in their regular non-Christian context.

7. If we distinguish group norms from moral norms in this way—in terms of membership-dependence and expectation-dependence—it is clear that a norm can evolve from one category to the other (Brennan et al. 2013, 101–102). What began as a group norm for us can become "moralized" and seen as a matter of

impartial moral obligation. Conversely, what was once seen as a moral norm binding on all can become un-moralized and seen as a matter of group norm. On our account, norms are not defined by their evolutionary origins but by the structure of the underlying expectations as experienced by the participants. There are, of course, other ways of developing typologies of norms which may be better suited to other philosophical purposes (e.g., O'Neill 2017). If our goal is to understand resistance to progressive reform, however, we think it is important, and indeed essential, to distinguish reasons-for-us from reasons-for-everybody.

8. Explaining conformity to group norms in terms of intrinsic recognition of group membership is a hallmark of the shared agency tradition. Alternatively, the rational choice tradition explains norm conformity in terms of convergence of conditional preference. Cristina Bicchieri (2006, 42) famously argues that "fear, benevolence, and the desire to fulfill others' legitimate expectations" can all be reasons for conformity. For a good discussion of these two traditions and an attempt to integrate the insights from both, see Brennan et al. (2013).

9. For example, when a woman who cut young girls was told the health risks associated with the norm of female genital cutting, she responded by saying very few of the girls she cut fell ill. For those who were infected, she believed that it was the existence of magic, dismissing scientific explanation (Bicchieri 2016, 130).

10. https://www.peta.org/about-peta/why-peta/

11. https://www.laanimalservices.com/about-us-2/

12. An interesting example of how making and accepting donations creates normative expectations to obey wider commitments of the community comes from a recent backlash against the Hong Kong office of Doctors Without Borders (Médecins Sans Frontières, MSF). The office was among the second largest beneficiary of donations by Hong Kong citizens. In 2019, the office refused to send medical help to the pro-democracy protests, citing political neutrality and a duty of care to its own personnel. Their response was legally permissible and, on some interpretation, morally permissible. But it was fiercely criticized by local Hong Kong citizens, resulting in a massive drop in donations and membership. Why were the Hong Kong people so angry? It cannot be reduced to claims about the requirements of universal morality. After all, many international humanitarian organizations also failed to send help, and the same level of anger was not directed at them. Hong Kong people felt that when MSF refused to help the wounded protesters, it was betraying a joint commitment that bound them as "We-the-Hongkongers."

13. We use the terms "pet care" and "pet ownership" because this is likely to be the prevalent self-identity of the group. Many animal rights theorists argue for abolishing the status of animals as "property" which is "owned" and hence replacing the term "pet" with "companion animal" and replacing ideas of "ownership" with ideas of, say, "guardianship" or "family member." Philosophically,

we endorse these arguments (Kymlicka 2017). But our focus here is on how members of the Angeleno public understand their joint commitment, and we suspect that they view it in terms of ideas of responsible pet ownership.

14. The norm of trust is highly important here, although we don't have the space to explore it. When an act is open to interpretation, trust disposes one to give a favorable interpretation of its intention, to give it the benefit of the doubt. For a more detailed discussion of trust and its relation to trustworthiness, see Tam (2021).

15. For discussion of the extinctionist position and how it has impeded coalitions in favor of animal rights, see Donaldson and Kymlicka (2011, 77–82).

16. More generally, vegans often identify themselves as outsiders of or non-conformists to their society, which again raises the challenge of how to invoke veganism while still emphasizing one's standing as a solidaristic member.

17. In rethinking the idea of "pet care," it is worth noting that both concepts—"pets" and "care"—are ripe for reinterpretation. With the rise of microsanctuaries, there are increasing numbers of formerly farmed animals who are now effectively becoming companion animals, as in "Esther the Wonder Pig." As more and more people become aware of the possibility of having relationships of companionship with pigs or goats or chickens, one could imagine that the hard distinction between "pets" and "food animals" or "farm animals" will start to dissolve.

18. What about APOs located not in progressive urban California but in, say, the conservative rural South? There is no guarantee that prevailing group norms can always be (re-)interpreted in a way that will support progressive reform, and in some cases there may be no alternative but to rely solely on prudential self-interest and impartial moral reasoning. But we shouldn't preclude the possibility that group norms in conservative communities have their own pro-animal resources. See the fascinating discussion by Matthew Scully—one of George Bush's speech-writers—who argues that conservative Christians in the United States have abandoned their fundamental joint commitments by supporting animal exploitation (Scully 2003).

References

Andrews, K. (2020) "Naïve normativity: The social foundation of moral cognition." *Journal of the American Philosophical Association* 6(1), 36–56.

Appiah, K. A. (2010) *The Honor Code: How Moral Revolutions Happen*. New York: W. W. Norton.

Bicchieri, C. (2006) *The Grammar of Society: The Nature and Dynamics of Social Norms*. Cambridge: Cambridge University Press.

Bicchieri, C. (2014) "Norms, convention, and the power of expectation." In Cartwright N. and Montuschi E. (eds.), *Philosophy of Social Science: A New Introduction*. Oxford: Oxford University Press, 208–232.

Bicchieri, C. (2016) *Norms in the Wild: How to Diagnose, Measure, and Change Social Norms*. Oxford: Oxford University Press.

Brennan, G., L. Eriksson, R. Goodin, and N. Southwood (2013) *Explaining Norms*. Oxford: Oxford University Press.

Delon, N. (2018) "Social norms and farm animal protection." *Palgrave Communications* 4(1), 1–6.

Donaldson, S., and W. Kymlicka (2011) *Zoopolis: A Political Theory of Animal Rights*. Oxford: Oxford University Press.

Gilbert, M. (2006) *A Theory of Political Obligation: Membership, Commitment, and the Bonds of Society*. Oxford: Oxford University Press.

Gilbert, M. (2013) *Joint Commitment: How We Make the Social World*. Oxford: Oxford University Press.

Jamieson, D. (2002) *Morality's Progress: Essays on Humans, Other Animals, and the Rest of Nature*. Oxford: Oxford University Press.

Joy, M. (2020) *Why We Love Dogs, Eat Pigs, and Wear Cows: An Introduction to Carnism*. Newburyport: Red Wheel.

Kahan, D. (2010) "Fixing the communications failure." *Nature* 463(7279), 296–297.

Kahan D., H. Jenkins-Smith, and D. Braman (2011) "Cultural cognition of scientific consensus." *Journal of Risk Research* 14(2), 147–74.

Kymlicka, W. (2017) "Social membership: Animal law beyond the property/personhood impasse." *Dalhousie Law Journal* 40(1), 123–156.

Kymlicka, W. (2018) "Human rights without human supremacism." *Canadian Journal of Philosophy* 48(6), 763–792.

Lorini, G. (2022) "Animal norms: An investigation of normativity in the non-human social world." *Law, Culture and the Humanities* 18(3), 652–673.

O'Neill, E. (2017) "Kinds of norms." *Philosophy Compass* 12(5), 1–15.

Scheffler, S. (2018) "Membership and political obligation." *Journal of Political Philosophy* 26(1), 3–23.

Scully, M. (2003) *Dominion: The Power of Man, the Suffering of Animals, and the Call to Mercy*. New York: Macmillan.

Singer, P. (2011) *The Expanding Circle: Ethics, Evolution, and Moral Progress*. Princeton: Princeton University Press.

Sunstein, C. (2019) *How Change Happens*. Cambridge, MA: MIT Press.

Tam, A. (2020a) *Norms, Reasons, and Moral Progress*. PhD thesis, Queen's University.

Tam, A. (2020b) "Why moral reasoning is insufficient for moral progress." *Journal of Political Philosophy* 28(1), 73–96.

Tam, A. (2020c) "The legitimacy of groups: Toward a we-reasoning view." *Analyse & Kritik* 42(2), 343–367.

Tam, A. (2021) "A case for political epistemic trust." In K. Vallier and M. Weber (eds.), *Social Trust*. New York: Routledge, 220–242.

Walzer, M. (1987) *Interpretation and Social Criticism*. Cambridge, MA: Harvard University Press.

6
Companion Animal Adoption in Shelters

How "Open" Should It Be?

Valéry Giroux and Kristin Voigt

6.1 Introduction

For most shelter animals, quick adoption is the desired outcome: it takes animals out of the cramped, stressful conditions of the shelter and offers them the opportunity to live and bond with an individual or family who will be concerned with their needs and well-being. Ensuring quick adoption also means that space and resources are freed up for other animals who urgently need care. At the same time, shelters must ascertain that adopters can and will provide decent homes for the animals they adopt. This requires that shelters be selective and prepared to turn down would-be adopters if there are reasons to think that they will not make good caregivers. Exercising discretion in this way can make the adoption process longer and, in some cases, disappointing for would-be adopters. Those who are denied adoption may turn to pet shops or breeders instead. How should shelters approach the adoption process, given these different, potentially competing, concerns?

This chapter identifies a range of relevant considerations that should inform the design of a shelter's adoption process. These

Valéry Giroux and Kristin Voigt, *Companion Animal Adoption in Shelters* In: *The Ethics of Animal Shelters*. Edited by: Valéry Giroux, Angie Pepper, and Kristin Voigt, Oxford University Press. © Oxford University Press 2023.
DOI: 10.1093/oso/9780197678633.003.0008

considerations include not only the well-being of shelter animals but also the interests of animals living outside the shelter and of those who may come to existence in the future. While there is merit in the recommendation, defended by important animal organizations like the Humane Society of the United States (HSUS), that shelters favor an "open adoption" approach, which significantly reduces the amount of screening required as part of the adoption process, we suggest that the empirical evidence on which this move relies is lacking in certain respects and might not benefit the "(would-be) adoptees" as much as advocates of open adoption suggest. Moreover, the current debate is not sensitive to the fact that the adoption process sends an important message to prospective adopters and the community more broadly about the moral status of nonhuman animals: failing to properly screen would-be adopters can reinforce the belief that the lives and well-being of companion animals, and perhaps of nonhuman animals more broadly, are not very important after all. While it is difficult to assess empirically the magnitude of such broader effects, they should be taken into account when designing adoption policies. For shelters, the adoption process is one of the main points of interaction with the public, offering an important opportunity to challenge their views about nonhuman animals. This concern for what adoption policies express about the moral status of nonhuman animals, we argue, speaks against certain features of the open adoption approach.

While this chapter raises concerns about open adoption, it is important to emphasize that we do not argue for a return to traditional methods of screening would-be adopters. In particular, we share one of the central concerns that open adoption advocates have about the use of a list of strict criteria that would-be adopters are expected to meet because many of those criteria are unjustifiably discriminatory and do not help distinguish between candidates who are likely to provide a good home for the adopted animal and those who will not. We also agree with open adoption advocates that a conversation between the staff and would-be adopters is extremely important and useful and should be a central component of the adoption process. This chapter focuses on what we think are important blind spots of open adoption in particular because this approach is increasingly considered "best practice." The upshot of our discussion is not that we should reintroduce the problematic aspects of earlier adoption policies but rather that certain elements of the open adoption approach must be reconsidered.

Adoption processes have a range of different components. Even though we will try in the last section of this chapter to offer concrete suggestions, our goal isn't so much to outline the "perfect" adoption procedure but rather to highlight that some of the current discussion, and in particular the push toward more "open" adoptions, does not reflect a sufficiently broad range of criteria. We offer suggestions on how specific aspects of adoption approaches should be assessed once a wider range of criteria is applied. While we refer throughout the experience at the Montreal SPCA to illustrate how individual shelters might approach choices about their adoption policies, we also highlight (in Section 6.3) that it is crucial for such choices to be sensitive to the specific circumstances in which individual shelters find themselves.

6.2 From "Protective" to "Open Adoption"

Finding a home is the primary outcome shelters seek for the animals in their care. The importance of successful adoption for shelter animals can hardly be overstated: shelter animals are "vulnerable and needy victims of a broken animal welfare system, negligent past-owners, or tragedy. Adoption gives them a critically needed benefit—that of a loving family—which will greatly improve their lives" (Rulli 2017, 174).

Adoption promises many advantages to shelter animals. In shelters that are not adapted to long-term stays, animals' living conditions are typically harsh. Individuals are often kept separate from one another, in individual cages, where they have very little space, or with other animals with whom they may not get along. The average animal does not exercise enough and suffers from boredom and lack of affection. The noise can also increase anxiety and even lead to depression. The stress they experience often even leads to respiratory problems that need medical attention. While conditions vary greatly from one shelter to another, it can be assumed that animal welfare is rarely, if ever, optimal (see, e.g., Taylor and Mills 2007 on dogs; Wagner et al. 2018 on cats). Given this background, adoption generally leads to significantly better living conditions than what shelters can offer.

Most shelters do not have the resources or capacities to keep unadopted animals in the shelter for more than a few weeks and sometimes even a few days. The network of foster families shelters work with is limited, which means that not all animals can stay outside the shelter until they are adopted. In many shelters, animals for whom no homes (temporary or permanent) can be found are simply killed as the space is needed for new animals who might be more easily adopted. Rulli quotes studies that estimate that 2.7 to 3.7 million animals are killed annually for this reason in the United States. In Canada, 40% of the cats received in shelters in 2011 (about 60,000 individuals) were killed (Canadian Federation of Humane Societies [CFHS] 2017). Therefore, when animals in shelters are not quickly adopted, they run a high risk of losing their life or being "returned to field" (following a practice sometimes called *shelter, neuter and return* [SNR]; Edinboro et al. 2016) and left to fend for themselves, facing the numerous threats, hazards, and challenges of a semi-wild life. Given this background, the benefits of quick adoption seem clear.

While shelters are keen for their animals to be adopted, shelter workers routinely deal with animals who are abused or abandoned and are acutely aware of how important it is that animals find homes that provide care and stability. When it comes to finding such homes, there is a prima facie case for taking the time to thoroughly screen prospective adopters and ensure that they have an adequate understanding of the needs of the animal they are seeking to adopt and the responsibilities they are incurring. It is reasonable to assume that the more stringent the adoption requirements and the more thorough the screening process, the greater the chances that the approved adoptive family will be able to provide for the welfare of the animal and will not abuse or neglect them. Traditionally, shelters have, therefore, applied a range of strict criteria that adoptive families had to meet if they were to adopt an animal (we call this the "protective approach").[1] For example, to reduce the risk that animals are abandoned, would-be adopters have to own their homes or demonstrate that their landlord accepts animals (Balcom and Arluke 2001). Such policies may also require that would-be adopters provide references or submit to home visits to verify that the animal is adjusting properly and is comfortable (Bahney 2006).

In recent years, however, influential animal welfare organizations such as the American Humane Association have begun to advocate minimal vetting of would-be adoptees. Two considerations in particular seem to be driving this shift. First, many of the strict criteria traditionally applied in protective approaches seem to discriminate against low-income adopters. Indeed, if adopters must have a fenced yard, a certain level of income, or be able not to leave a companion animal alone for more than a limited number of hours per day, this can make the adoption seem like a privilege for the rich. Not only is this unfair to members of vulnerable communities who could greatly benefit from adopting a companion animal, but it also deprives the shelters of a large pool of potential adopters (Ly et al. 2021).[2] These concerns are heightened when we take into account that members of marginalized groups are more likely to have to relinquish their animals in the first place (e.g., because they cannot afford veterinary care or lose their housing).[3]

Second, the criteria shelters applied for adoption were so strict that they screened out even the most suitable adopters. Troughton (2015) explains that, in the 1990s, two respected members of the animal welfare movement were denied adoption by their local shelters. This experience led the American Humane Association to organize a forum to determine a reasonable list of adoption criteria. While the meeting did not lead to agreement on the criteria that should be applied for adoption, the concept of "open adoptions" emerged:

Being "open" means we free potential adopters from unrealistic and unachievable expectations . . . expect our staff to help people and trust them . . . establish constructive relationships . . . evaluate what role our shelters play in terms of pet acquisition within our communities . . . be honest with ourselves about what we can and cannot control . . . base decisions on the needs of the animals as well as the pet-owning dynamics in our communities . . . and we will not be afraid to take some risks. (Joe Silva, then Director of Massachusetts Society for the Prevention of Cruelty to Animals Shelter Development, quoted in Troughton 2015, 270)

In a second meeting, Adoption Forum II, organized by PetSmart Charities, the "Five Essentials of a Successful Adoption" were identified as follows: (i) the match would be suited to the individual animal and family; (ii) the pet would be afforded appropriate veterinary care; (iii) the pet's social, behavioral, and companionship needs would be met; (iv) the pet would have a livable environment (including appropriate food, water, shelter, etc.); and (v) the pet would be respected and valued (see PetSmart Charities 2003, 4).

Adoption Forum II also recommended a reconceptualization of the pre-adoption interaction with prospective adopters. These interactions should, for example, "take place in a welcoming atmosphere"; assume that both staff and adopters "come from a place of commonality wanting to help animals"; "use . . . guidelines to delineate issues for discussion and education, not as inflexible mandates"; be a "discussion, rather than a series of barriers the applicant must overcome in order to get an animal"; and "look . . . for a way to make an adoption, not turn one down" (PetSmart Charities 2003, 8).

On such an approach, shelter practices should focus on finding "acceptable" homes rather than the "best" home (e.g., PetSmart Charities 2003, 4). This means that "[a]doptions became less of an issue of who could or could not adopt an animal and more a question of 'making a good match,' as the staff put it" (Balcom and

Arluke 2001, 138). On an "open" approach, shelters shift their adoption process "from screening clients according to rigid guidelines to matching clients and pets through an open conversation made possible by a climate of trust, communication and understanding" (American Society for the Prevention of Cruelty to Animals [ASPCA] and PetSmart Charities 2007, 2).

This approach emphasizes the importance of "removing barriers" to adoption and that "adoption policies should not include automatic 'no's' or 'must-haves'" (Humane Society of the United States [HSHS] 2020, 11): "Your job [as shelter staff] isn't to ferret out bad adopters, it is to help support great pet owners. Your goal is to find a way to get to yes" (HSUS 2020, 21). For example, shelters should not require landlord checks or evidence of veterinary care provided to previous companion animals or take a potential adopter's intention to declaw a cat as a reason to refuse an adoption (HSUS 2020, 11–15). This does not mean, however, that shelters with an open adoption approach *never* reject would-be adopters; for example, an applicant who appears intoxicated or has a history of animal abuse would be denied even on an open adoption policy (Balcom and Arluke 2001). At the same time, would-be adopters who might be refused on protective approaches can end up adopting an animal if a shelter adopts a more open approach to adoption. Advocates of open adoption acknowledge that this may increase the risk for individual animals but see it as the right choice overall: "instead of avoiding risks to 'protect' the animals, [the organization] would take risks for the sake of the animal" (ASPCA and PetSmart Charities 2007, 6).

In this chapter, we want to resist the conclusion that an open adoption policy will necessarily lead to a win/win situation or that its benefits outweigh the risks associated with it. While we recognize the virtues of a conversation between shelter professionals and would-be adopters, and the importance of offering help and support to adopters, we make the case for retaining some strict adoption criteria and for framing the adoption process in a way that underscores animals' moral status.

6.3 The Implications of Open Adoption for (Would-Be) Adoptees

The open adoption approach is driven by two claims: first, that the risk of a negative adoption outcome is much lower than shelter workers might assume and, second, that turning down a potential adopter has negative repercussions not only for the human who is not entrusted with an animal or the animal who might have been adopted, but also for other animals. In this section, we unpack and assess the first claim. We address the second claim in Section 6.4.

6.3.1 Risks of Inadequate Care and Relinquishment

While open adoption advocates sometimes acknowledge that open adoption increases the risks for the adopted animal, they also emphasize that these risks are significantly lower than we might anticipate and that the criteria used in protective approaches are not, in fact, good indicators of negative outcomes for adopted animals. For example, a 2014 study by two members of ASPCA staff (Weiss et al. 2014, 320) found that "moving from policy based adoptions to conversation based or policy-free (open) adoptions did not impact the risk for improper animal care. The adopted animals had no substantial differences in attachment, where they slept, vet visits and several other factors." Similarly, emphasizing the merits of open adoption, the Humane Society Boulder Valley notes that "after the first year, despite a 30% increase in adoption, the average return rate increased only from 8.4% to 9.6%" (ASPCA and PetSmart Charities 2007, 7). Should we take these findings to be decisive? Before concluding that it is best for shelter animals that shelters take up an open adoption approach, we must acknowledge some of the limitations of these studies. Indeed, if we take these limitations seriously, then it is far from obvious that the evidence for the open adoption approach is as strong as its advocates suggest.

It is extremely difficult to determine the real success of an adoption procedure. Studies often rely on self-reports from adopters who choose to participate in the study. Self-report, for example of attachment to the adopted animal or of whether the animal is still in the home, is of course not always reliable, and it is not clear whether participants would admit to socially undesirable behaviors or attitudes, such as not offering adequate veterinary care or having rehomed the animal (for more discussion of this general problem, see Powell et al. 2021; see also Scarlett et al. 1999, 52–53, on possibly inconsistent self-reports in their study). Low response rates should also weaken our confidence in the results of these studies. For example, in the study just mentioned (Weiss et al. 2014), the response rate is 54%. In a study by Weiss and Gramann (2009), which examines differences between adoptions that involve a fee and those that do not, response rates in these two groups are 34% and 30%, respectively. Moreover, rates of return to the shelter, while important, tell us nothing about the well-being of animals who are *not* returned: they might, as open adoption advocates seem to assume, live perfectly good lives in their adoptive homes—but it may also be the case that they have been put down, rehomed, or abandoned.

It is important to emphasize this point: the crucial question is how adopted animals are doing under different adoption schemes. The studies open adoption advocates refer to do not, however, offer answers to that question. Relinquishment rates and adopters' self-reports allow no conclusions about adopted animals' well-being, and, in any case, adopters can simply choose not to participate in the studies, as the response rates indicate. In the case of human adoption, social workers might visit adoptive families' homes to ensure that the child is settling in well, and any problems are likely to become apparent during these visits or during medical appointments or at daycare or school. For adopted animals, however, there is much less opportunity, if any, for potential problems to be flagged and addressed. This is not to say, of course, that adopted animals are *not* doing well; but we cannot draw any conclusions about adopted animals' well-being from the data that open adoption advocates cite.

In addition, the documents advocating for open adoption do not always cite sources for the empirical claims made, and, when they do, the cited studies lend less support to open adoption than is suggested. For example, the Humane Society of the United States encourages shelters to be open to the adoption of animals who are to be given as "gifts" to third parties.[4] It cites four studies in support of the claim that "pets received as gifts are actually more likely to remain in their homes than pets acquired in other ways" (HSUS 2020, 13; see also ASPCA and PetSmart Charities 2007, 5). A closer look at these studies suggests a more uncertain picture. Weiss et al. (2013) survey 222 individuals who had received an animal as a gift. Participants had to answer questions about their involvement in the selection of the animal (notably, the available answers to this question do not cover all possible scenarios), whether the fact that the animal was a gift affected their attachment to the animal, and whether the animal is still in the home. The study concludes that there is no association between receiving the animal as a gift, on the one hand, and, on the other hand, self-perceived attachment to the animal or whether the animal is still in the home. In addition to the concern about the reliability of self-reports, the study did not survey homes where animals were adopted by the guardians *themselves* rather than received as a gift so the authors' conclusion that "pets given as gifts are not at higher risk for abandonment" is premature. Scarlett et al. (1999) find that only a small proportion of those relinquishing their animals to the shelter cite the fact that the animal was an unwanted gift as a reason for their decision (0.3% for dogs, 0.4% for cats). However, we cannot draw any conclusions about the relative likelihood of relinquishment for gifted animals without information about how many animals in the study were in fact initially received as gifts; this information is not provided in the study.

The other two studies cited seem to lend support to some elements of the open adoption approach but call into question others. New et al. (2000, 188) find that dogs received as gifts had a lower risk of relinquishment than those who came from a shelter, a friend, or a pet shop, or who had been a stray—but they also note that "dogs obtained at no cost and with little effort are at increased risk of relinquishment" (198), which would seem to cast a negative light on other aspects of open adoption, such as waiving adoption fees. Similarly, Patronek et al. note that

> [d]ogs obtained in a manner presumed to predispose them to an increased risk of relinquishment (e.g., as gifts or from pet stores) were at decreased (gifts) or not at increased (pet stores) risk [of relinquishment], compared with that for dogs acquired for > $100 from breeders or private owners. In contrast, dogs obtained at little or no cost (< $31) were at increased risk. The amount of money an owner was willing to invest in the acquisition process appeared to be a good indicator of their future commitment to care for a dog. (Patronek et al. 1996, 579)

Since animals received as gifts are acquired without fees by their guardians, it seems that those risks would concern them as well (and also shelter animals for whom adoption fees are waived). More generally, it is not obvious that information about *non-shelter* animals received as gifts tells us anything about *shelter* animals received as gifts since these two groups could differ in relevant respects (e.g., the adopted animal's age).

What is more, other studies report more worrying outcomes for animals received as gifts. An Australian study, for example, finds that among all animals relinquished to a shelter, the rates of euthanasia were particularly high for cats and dogs who had been received as gifts (Montoya et al. 2017). Noting the contrast to North American studies on this issue that suggest that gifted animals did not have a higher relinquishment rate, they point out that "those studies . . . only considered animals deliberately given as a present, whereas in our study, animals acquired at no cost from family and friends were included in the gift category" (Montoya et al. 2017, 197). While this means that the results of the Australian study are not directly applicable to the shelter context (where the question is how to respond to adoption requests where the adopted animal *is* intended to be given as a gift), they do highlight that the North American studies do not address what is, after all, a crucial factor in assessing outcomes for these animals: What happens to them *after* relinquishment?

More broadly, the cited evidence focuses on relinquishment rates but does not offer any information on what happens to animals received as gifts who are *not* subsequently relinquished to shelters. What is their quality of life? How are these animals treated by guardians who did not, after all, choose to adopt them? Are these animals at higher risk of being rehomed without involving the shelter or of being abandoned?

All this is not to say, of course, that easing the requirements for adoption, for example by allowing animals to be given as gifts, *necessarily* leads to worse outcomes for adopted animals. However, advocates of open adoption overstate the conclusiveness of available studies, their applicability to the shelter context, and the certainty with which empirical claims can be made. There is a case for recognizing and acknowledging that some of the central empirical questions about the outcomes of different kinds of adoption are difficult to ascertain. This uncertainty adds to the complexity of choosing appropriate adoption policies.

6.3.2 Relinquishment as a Minor Issue

Another plank of the open adoption approach is that shelters should take a less negative stance on post-adoption returns. "Returning adopters" (HSUS 2020, 18) should be met without judgment. The Humane Society recommends a "satisfaction guaranteed" policy (HSUS 2020) that allows adopters to return an animal to the shelter if they are unhappy with them. Shelters should view these as opportunities to gather more information about the animal: having spent a substantial amount of time with the animal in question, anyone returning an animal can provide the shelter with more information about them and thus facilitate the identification of a more suitable adoptive home.

Open adoption advocates emphasize that the return of animals to the shelter after adoption should not be seen as a failure. For example, the HSBV document notes,

> If adopters return an animal because their adoption did not work out,
> they are trying to do the best thing for that animal, they can provide ad-
> ditional information to assist placing that animal again, and they are
> complying with our request to bring the animal back to us. We respect
> them for their honesty. We do not make them feel guilty. We offer them
> another chance. Adoption returns do not mean failure. (ASPCA and
> PetSmart Charities 2007, 7)

What they fail to consider, however, is that a failed adoption causes
instability for the animals, which can significantly increase their
anxiety, potentially surpassing the anxiety they would have experienced if they had remained at the shelter. For the animal, if the relinquishment is caused by a poor fit with the adoptive family or a
bad experience, this can also make it more difficult for the animal
to be adopted in the future. If a bad match (poor environment or
situation management) leads to the animal biting a family member,
for example, not only might the animal then be more likely to bite
again, but they might now be considered dangerous. Such a stain on
their record can lengthen their stay in their shelter or even lead to
the animal being put down if considered unadoptable. A bad adoption experience that induces trauma for the animal may also lead
to behavioral problems that will in turn diminish their chances of
finding a permanent home in a more suitable environment.[5]

6.3.3 Risk Assessment Depends on Context

A further consideration for assessing the merits of different adoption approaches is the specific characteristics of individual shelters
and the conditions in which they operate. What open adoption
proponents seem to underestimate is that the situation varies greatly
from one shelter to another. Whether an animal's well-being is
improved by a less than perfect adoption also depends on what their
well-being is in the shelter.

In cases where a shelter has exceeded its capacity and the animals being kept have a very poor quality of life—if they don't have comfortable beds and toys, if there are not enough staff to keep their cages clean and allow them to stretch their legs once a day, if the network of foster families available is limited, etc.—then it may be better to get the animal out as soon as possible, even if the adoptive home is not ideal or if there is a good chance that the animal is subsequently returned to the shelter. At the very least, she will have had a few days' break from the conditions of the shelter. But this tradeoff is very different if the shelter can offer an acceptable quality of life to its residents. The Montreal SPCA, for example, does not always operate at its maximum occupancy rate. There are periods during which there is no shortage of space and staff have the time to provide adequate exercise and enrichment for individual animals. Under such circumstances, the argument that open adoption is a means of improving adopted animals' well-being seems significantly weaker.

In addition, it is not clear how well the open adoption approach can respond to the specific needs of individual shelter animals, whose past experience of trauma or medical conditions mean that they require an adopter who has experience or the competence to provide a good home for the animal. Some of these animals may require a particularly patient guardian who is able to deal with, for example, incontinent animals or an animal with separation anxiety. The challenge is to identify a suitable adopter who is particularly devoted; willing to learn about socialization, training, and behavioral issues; or to invest considerable time and resources in medical care. While open adoption advocates emphasize the importance of matching adopters with individual animals, only a small proportion of would-be adopters would be suitable for animals with such specific needs, and shelters must turn down those who are not. If a considerable proportion of the animals in a shelter have special needs, it is not clear that the open adoption approach can offer an appropriate or helpful response.

There are good reasons to doubt the claim that adopted animals are not put at greater risk under open adoption programs than under protective ones. As we argue in the next section, there are additional reasons, perhaps more sociological or political in nature, to be critical toward open adoption.

6.4 Implications of Adoption Policies for Nonhuman Animals More Generally

While the previous section casts doubt on advocates' claim about the benefits of open adoption for adopted shelter animals, we think the open adoption approach stands on stronger ground when it comes to its benefits for other animals, both inside and outside the shelter, particularly as a result of the space and resources that are freed up when more animals are adopted. However, as we argue in this section, this perspective is too narrow: open adoption might also have worrisome effects on all companion animals and perhaps on nonhuman animals more generally because of what it signals about animals' moral status. This section highlights the positive effects of open adoption before arguing that they must be weighed against the broader impact of sending the message that animals' well-being is less important than adopters' needs.

6.4.1 The Case for Open Adoption

Three major considerations speak in favor of open adoption. Consider, first, the animals who are *not* adopted as a result of a shelter's protective adoption policy. In the context of human adoption, where adoption criteria are typically very strict, de Wispelaere and Weinstock describe what they call the "child-child" tradeoff, where "attempts to protect one set of prospective adopted children ends up putting another set of children at risk." They explain that

> [t]he vast majority of children who are presently available for adoption are living in sub-optimal conditions.... By focusing only on the potential harm of neglect or abuse by prospective adoptive parents, a regime may end up providing some children with excellent prospective parents but

at the cost of leaving other prospective adoptees in these sub-optimal
conditions. Generally speaking, the stricter the screening of prospective adoptees, the less children will be adopted and the more will end
up in institutional or foster care (or worse); conversely, the more relaxed
the screening, the more children will be adopted but the risk of neglect
and abuse within adoption families could potentially increase. (de
Wispelaere and Weinstock 2018, 220)

They argue that this tradeoff speaks in favor of more relaxed
screening processes for prospective adopters: the state has a responsibility to *all* prospective adoptees. This kind of concern seems to
be driving much of the open adoption advocates' willingness to
take risks: we must be concerned not only with the animals who *are*
adopted but also with the animals who are *not* adopted because of
overly restrictive adoption policies.

Second, in the context of animal shelters, there is also the broader
concern that shelters that adopt restrictive adoption policies can
help fewer animals overall because animals spend more time in the
shelter and therefore use more resources. Shelters often capture this
in terms of animals' "length of stay" (i.e., the time they spend in the
shelter or in foster homes before being adopted). Not only do long
stays at the shelter pose risks to residents' health and well-being, they
also mean that the shelter has fewer resources for other programs
or activities (UC Davis Koret Shelter Medicine Program 2015) like
behavioral rehabilitation for animals who cannot be easily adopted
because of behavior problems; animal welfare advocacy; animal
cruelty and neglect investigations; development of affordable sterilization services for low-income families; lobbying for improved
legal protection of animals or for better practices; or running a trap,
neuter, release, and maintain (TNRM) program for feral cats in collaboration with municipalities and volunteers. Greater length of stay
also reduces the amount of space available for other animals in need
of rescue.

Third, people who decide to adopt an animal often assume that
all they have to do is go to a shelter and choose the animal they
like. When they have to go through a relatively complex or invasive

process, and especially if their application is later rejected, they may be left feeling bitter and even humiliated or insulted.[6] This experience may cause them to give up on adopting an animal altogether, and the shelter may have missed out on a suitable home for an abandoned animal waiting in a shelter. The shelter may also garner a reputation for being unwelcoming as rejected adopters share their negative experience with friends or family. Alternatively, would-be adopters may purchase an animal from a breeder or pet shop to avoid policies they perceive as judgmental or intrusive (e.g., Sinski 2016), which in turn encourages these industries to produce more animals in need of care.[7] Some might turn to a breeder who is irresponsible or, worse, a puppy mill, where animals' welfare is seriously compromised.[8] Adoption is an important public-facing activity for shelters. Welcoming potential adopters and making sure that the visitors do not feel treated as potential threats to the animals might avoid the exploitation of purebred animals for reproduction and the potential increase in the number of animals being abandoned or otherwise needing rescue.

While these considerations speak in favor of open adoption, we must also keep in mind that adoption processes can have *indirect* effects on how people view animals. Even though such effects may be harder to measure, they are no less important than the direct impact of adoption policies and could mitigate considerably the desirability of the open adoption approach.

6.4.2 A Crucial Worry About Open Adoption: Signaling

Adoption policies can influence the moral value we attribute to animals and the consideration we give to their interests. And our representation of animals may, in turn, have very concrete effects on the companion animals who are adopted, on companion animals outside the shelter, and possibly even on animals of all species: those who already exist as well as those who will exist in the future. Despite its advantages, what open adoption signals might indirectly pose a serious threat for animals through what it suggests about their moral status.[9]

The view that nonhuman animals and their interests should count for less than human beings and their similar interests is dominant in our societies. It is also considered normal to attribute more value to some animals than to others: we are generally much more protective of the animals we find cute and to which we become attached and adopt as companions than of animals with whom we identify less easily, who seem more threatening, or from whose exploitation we can derive more benefit. That said, this ideology has never completely escaped criticism. Throughout history, some thinkers have criticized anthropocentrism and the presumption that humanity is at the heart and summit of nature. They have also emphasized the similarities between the animals we love and those we eat. Since the early 1970s, the term "speciesism" has been used to refer to discrimination based on species membership, which often takes the form of the exploitation of individuals considered morally inferior or the refusal to protect them as well as the members of the favored species, *Homo sapiens* in particular. Many philosophers have denounced speciesism as morally unjustified and likened it to racism and sexism because it is based on a morally irrelevant property (Singer 1975, 1979; Rachels 1990; DeGrazia 1996).

Shelters' adoption processes can either contribute to or challenge speciesist norms and assumptions (e.g., that animals can be "owned," that their fundamental interests are less important than even trivial human interests, or that companion animals should be better protected than farmed animals). This should be a consideration in how adoption policies are chosen and framed. This concerns not only the particular policies in place (e.g., How are would-be-adopters screened? Is there an adoption fee?) but also how adoption and specific aspects of the adoption procedure are presented to the public. For example, many shelters, including the Montreal SPCA with whom we worked for this project, have frequent "Adoption Days" when adoption fees are reduced or waived in a way similar to a commercial sale. According to open adoption supporters, shelters should go as far as to encourage the donation of animals to relatives, on their birthdays or on other festive occasions (HSUS 2020), as if they were commodities. Shelter staff are encouraged to place plants and music in the room where animals are exhibited (McHugh-Smith and Buckman 2010, 6). Employees are asked to show a positive attitude and smile at the visitors, who are described as "clients" or "customers." These strategies are meant to increase adoptions. But they might also leave would-be adopters with the impression that animals are merchandise they can shop for, purchase for their enjoyment, and eventually discard.

An important aspect of the practical recommendations we offer in this volume is that organizations such as the Montreal SPCA should make it an explicit goal of their work to challenge speciesist norms (see, in particular, Section 2.A of the Guidelines in Part I of this volume). While some shelters traditionally restrict their mission to improving animal welfare narrowly construed, many of them are already committed to challenging the way animals are considered objects, merchandise, or resources available to us for our different needs rather than individual sentient beings with their own intrinsic worth. As we have emphasized at several points in this volume, it is crucial for animal protection organizations to navigate the tension between the anti-speciesist commitments we think they should adopt and the broader, speciesist environment in which they work. But if animal welfare organizations take seriously their commitment to significantly improve the way animals are considered and treated, they shouldn't focus exclusively on short-term improvements for a very marginal proportion of all sentient animals, which is constituted by the *companion* animals who go (or could go) through their institution. They should take their mission to include the protection of *all* nonhuman animals, including the cats and dogs who do not go through the shelter, but also animals of other species, such as pigs, chickens, fishes, crocodiles, and elephants.

This might start with the language they use (see Part I of this volume, Section 2.B); for example, staff should refer to "companion animals" rather than "pets," and to "guardians" rather than "owners." As with other areas where language is used to challenge prevailing norms (e.g., gender egalitarian language), the goal is, in part, disruption: using unexpected language creates dissonance for hearers who, ideally, will reflect on why someone might object to terms such as "owner" or "pet."[10] Other practices, too, can challenge prevailing social norms, especially when they involve interactions between shelter staff and the general public. Consider the proposal we develop in Part I of this volume to move shelter residents toward a plant-based diet (see Section 6.A). While prevailing norms assume—incorrectly, for the most part—that a good diet for companion animals must include animal flesh, shelters can challenge this norm by promoting a plant-based diet for dogs in particular.

The adoption process, we argue here, presents another opportunity to challenge existing norms around nonhuman animals. Indeed, it seems reasonable to assume that the requirements of the adoption process reflect the importance placed on the welfare and interests of the animals to be adopted and perhaps even more generally on the moral status of *all* sentient animals. Carefully selecting adopters, and being open to the possibility of rejecting some applicants, quite straightforwardly reflects our concern for the adoptees. In the human context, there is little doubt that demanding adoption requirements can be explained at least in part by the seriousness attached to the fate of the children.

As mentioned earlier, in the human context, some authors have questioned the strictness of the criteria for adoption. De Wispelaere and Weinstock argue that we must strike a balance: an overly strict adoption procedure imposes costs on those children who are not adopted because not enough adopters meet the requirements; on the other hand, if the procedure is too permissive, this increases the risk of unacceptable outcomes for adopted children. However, this debate proceeds in a context where the moral and legal status of children is no longer considered inferior to that of adults. It is of course necessary to be on the lookout for abuses that are still far too frequent and to criticize adult domination of which children are still undeniably victims. But the fact remains that children have the status of rights holders, of persons in their own right, of vulnerable beings whom we must protect as a priority. This is obviously not the case for nonhuman animals—quite the contrary.

Compared to the adoption procedures in place for children, the screening process for shelter animal adoption is, of course, significantly laxer. Even if, as de Wispelaere and Weinstock suggest, the criteria for human adoption should be relaxed, adopted children would remain much better protected than companion animals. First, all children are officially identified by the state, which exercises surveillance in various ways. Children are most often born in a hospital, they attend school, they are registered with the state. Existing social norms make it the case that neighbors and relatives will be concerned if signs of abuse or neglect are discovered. Child protection agencies will intervene when their interests or welfare are threatened without running into the barriers of property rights since their parents/guardians do not own them.

Second, the administrative steps, even if they were less demanding, would still be incomparable to those applied by even the most rigorous animal shelters. For instance, the defenders of the open adoption approach for animals consider an adoption process lasting up to two days "unreasonably lengthy" (ASPCA and PetSmart Charities 2007, 4). Clearly, even advocates of easing restrictions on human adoption do not envisage that it would be wrapped up in all of two days! Participants of PetSmart Charities' adoption event identified five "hard criteria" that must be met before an adopter can be approved for adoption: the adopter must agree to have the animal spayed or neutered; they will be rejected if they have a history of animal or child abuse; if they are suspected of being drunk or under the influence of drugs at the time of adoption; if they want to use the animal as a food source; and, finally (though somewhat less important and more negotiable than the first four criteria), they must agree to keep identification on the animal (e.g., a dog tag or microchip) at all times (PetSmart Charities 2003, 9). These criteria are, of course, rather minimal and a far cry from what would be deemed acceptable in the human context, even for those who advocate for a less strict human adoption process.

Arguably, the speciesist context in which shelters operate makes it *more* important to have a selection process that does not reinforce the view that an animal's fate does not matter much. The fact that, in our society, animals have a much lower status and enjoy much less protection than human children is, in principle, a reason to have a *more stringent* adoption procedure for animals than for human children.

The goal of achieving recognition of the moral status of animals speaks in favor of adoption criteria that reflect their moral value and the importance of their interests. Admittedly, we do not have conclusive evidence to confirm that a strict adoption process will help change the way animals are viewed and treated. Even if shelters traditionally impose an invasive adoption procedure, speciesist ideology is still hegemonic in our society and animals are still considered to have a moral status far inferior to that of humans. Making it difficult to adopt animals is certainly insufficient to reverse speciesism. What reasons do we have to assume that refusing to relax the criteria for adoption would benefit animals? The answer to this question might be partly located in the fact that, even though adoption is still quite demanding, the general public is not aware of this and continues to assume that any individual willing to adopt an animal can simply show up at a shelter, pick the animal they like, and leave with them in exchange for a reasonable "price."

Shelters' decisions about designing their adoption policy should therefore be informed by the broader goal of underscoring the importance of our duties toward nonhuman animals. Nobody should take lightly the fate of the individuals who depend on us for the satisfaction of their most basic needs. Nobody should consider the choice to take in or abandon an animal as having little moral import. Would-be adopters must be prepared to demonstrate their suitability for adoption and accept that they might be challenged if they make problematic choices with regard to their animals.

The focus should certainly not be on the client's desire as much as on the interests of the vulnerable beings who need a home. Much of the language used and recommended by open adoption advocates—such as offering "great animals at a highly competitive price" (ASPCA and PetSmart Charities 2007, 5), "good customer service [that] includes instant results" (HSUS 2020, 16), with a "satisfaction guaranteed" (HSUS 2020, 18) or "no-fault return policy"

(HSUS 2020, 18)—implies that shelter animals are merchandise that adopters can purchase and, if they are unsatisfied, return for a refund, as one might a toaster or a toy. This language plays into the all too common misperception that sentient animals are property or objects that can be bought and disposed of if they don't meet our needs.

As long as nonhuman animals are viewed as having a moral status far below that of human beings, it will be difficult, if not impossible, to adequately protect even the most basic of their interests. It is therefore crucial that animal welfare organizations work to change the way we think about these individuals. To significantly improve the lot of nonhuman animals, it is necessary not only to put in place and enforce measures to protect their welfare, but also to carry out social, cultural, political, and legal actions to change the way animals are perceived. They must be seen as individuals with moral value, independent of the value that human beings place on them. The way shelter animals are generally treated is an indication of the moral value placed on them in our society. Therefore, the adoption procedures in place must reflect the seriousness with which the fate of animals must be approached. It is important not only that shelter adoption policies be sufficiently stringent to counter the wrong assumption that animals are mere commodities that human beings can trade as they want, but also that this fact is known by the general public. To help change the status of dogs and cats, and hopefully all animals in our society,[11] animal protection organizations must publicly state and show their commitment to putting the interests of those animals above human interests or desires, such as that for animal companionship.

6.5 How Should the Adoption Process Be Designed?

An important consideration that supports the case for open adoption is that living conditions in shelters are often very poor. This often leads to a significant degree of stress and anxiety for shelter animals as well as medical problems that can sometimes even require that the animal be euthanized. Open adoption policies may help address this problem but they are not the *only* response to this concern. When studies that highlight shelter residents' well-being suggest a shift to open adoption as a response to this problem, it is often only one suggestion among several. Alternative proposals for reducing residents' stress include the provision of additional space and stimulation as well as cage enrichment. Such strategies could also efficiently diminish length of stay and risks of disease (Janke et al. 2017; Karsten et al. 2017).

That said, even if the conditions in shelters were significantly improved, they would most probably never be ideal, and this needs to be taken seriously when reflecting on how an adoption procedure should be designed. In the previous sections, we outlined what strike us as the most relevant considerations that should shape shelters' adoption policies. While this, of course, doesn't settle the issue, it seems that advocates of open adoption are overly focused on the short-term benefits of a quick and simple adoption process and insufficiently sensitive to what these processes signal about animals' moral status: by adopting such policies, shelters risk contributing to the portrayal of companion animals (and perhaps even *all* nonhuman animals) as beings of low moral standing. This section assesses specific aspects of adoption policies with respect to the considerations just outlined. In this chapter, we are not arguing for any particular approach shelters should take when it comes to adoption. Rather, we are cautioning here against an approach that evaluates different adoption policies *only* with respect to how many, and how quickly, animals are adopted. Even though we have concerns about the open adoption approach and think that certain aspects of the approach need to be reconsidered, we also think it has important merits that any adoption policy should maintain. For one thing, we take the focus on conversation between staff members and would-be adopters to be a considerable improvement of the adoption procedure and see it as essential. Other aspects of the open adoption approach, we suggest, can be modified or reframed to address the concerns we raise here. The approach we favor is not a return to the rigid application of problematic adoption criteria but rather an approach that selects those aspects of the open adoption process that are (or can be made to be) consistent with anti-speciesist goals.

Some of the considerations we outlined in the previous sections seem to run contrary to each other: the harder the shelter makes adoption, the more it signals that nonhuman animals have moral status—but the harder it is to adopt, the fewer animals will actually find homes. How can such conflicts be attenuated?

6.5.1 Signaling

What remains central, in our opinion, is that adoption must be presented, both to would-be adopters who contact shelters and to the general public, as an important and likely life-changing decision with serious consequences for the animal. Potential adopters should be welcomed, encouraged, and thanked for their willingness to take on the responsibility of caring for a vulnerable being: they are, after all, helping to alleviate the injustice animals suffer in our societies. They should feel that what they are willing to commit to is an extraordinarily important thing: we are talking about nothing less than saving lives. On the other hand, adoption should also be presented as a privilege. One cannot claim to have the "right" to adopt. Precisely because it is so important for the fate not only of adopted animals but also for all animals whose perceived moral status is affected, the process must reflect the seriousness of the issues at stake. With a clearer understanding of the animals' status, adoptive families should be prepared to undergo an appropriately demanding screening process.

Concerns about signaling speak against several of the recommendations made by open adoption advocates. First, adoption fees can be part of an adoption policy but they must be described in a way that is consistent with animals' moral status, not in terms that underscores the idea that animals are objects that can be bought and sold: this means, for example, that commercial language and slogans like "adopt one, get one free" should be avoided. Discounts on the adoption fee for certain animals (e.g., those who are less "popular" because they are mixed-breed, older, or black) and/or premiums for young or purebred animals (Reese et al. 2017) should be applied only if they can be communicated in a way that reflects the importance of their fate and avoids the impression that some animals are worth more than others (Sinski 2016).

Second, some open adoption advocates argue that it must be the would-be adopters' interests that should guide the adoption conversation. Troughton (2015, 273), for example, notes that "the adopter—not the animal(s)—is the center of the counselor's positive attention. The importance of this stance cannot be overstated." This, we think, is problematic. Instead, it should be the *adoptees'* interests that are at the front and center of the adoption conversation. Importantly, this can be communicated to adopters in a way that is not judgmental: shelter staff can emphasize the importance of the animal's welfare and of finding a good and suitable home for them and encourage the adopters to see themselves as contributing to justice and animal welfare (along the lines described earlier) rather than as responding to their own needs for animal companionship.

Third, shelters should consider the message that specific adoption events send. Adoption Days that emphasize, for example, that the shelter is overpopulated in response to a particular crisis (at the Montreal SPCA, for example, this might be during kitten season or after Moving Day,[12] when many animals are lost or abandoned) and encourage adopters to help animals in need are in line with the concern for signaling that we describe here.[13] Other ways of framing Adoption Days are, however, deeply problematic. Consider, for example, the American Humane Association's suggestion that "pet contests are always popular. Contest ideas are only limited by your imagination. Some categories include smallest pet, largest pet, ugliest pet, oldest pet, celebrity pet look-alike, and best trick. Participants have fun and compete for gift certificates while the shelter promotes its adoption program and raises money" (McHugh-Smith and Buckman 2010, 24). Presenting and relating to shelter animals in this way only serves to underscore the view that animals are objects that can be used for our amusement and entertainment and is, therefore, something that shelters should avoid.

6.5.2 Checklists and Conversations to Establish Adopters' Suitability

A key aspect of the open adoption approach is the conversation between shelter employees and would-be adopters rather than a checklist of criteria that adopters must satisfy. Advocates argue that procedures that reject candidates as soon as one of the numerous boxes on a list is not checked can have quite unfortunate consequences: many potentially good and perhaps some of the best adoptive families available for particular animals wouldn't pass this type of test. For instance, even if a family doesn't have a fenced yard, they might be perfectly suitable for an energetic dog who likes playing outside if they are very active and ready to take long walks or go to dog parks every day. Similarly, the absence of a yard might not be a problem for a senior dog who does not require much exercise. A potential adopter might not have a high salary, but if she is willing to devote a sufficient proportion of her income to high-quality food and veterinary care, she can offer a better home than a candidate who has a higher income but is less disposed to spend money on his animal companion. A candidate who is inexperienced but willing to learn what there is to know about dog needs could end up being a better guardian than someone who has plenty of experience with dogs but only offers them mediocre care. A conversation seems to be a much more appropriate way to appreciate the specific intentions and potential of a would-be adopter than a strict list of yes/no answers. Such a conversation can also help avoid the discriminatory effects on socially vulnerable would-be adopters associated with a protective approach that strictly applies criteria such as income or access to a fenced yard.[14]

As should now be clear, we completely agree that conversations should be an important part of the adoption process. That said, we think of them somewhat differently from open adoption advocates. Some defenders of the open adoption approach seem to assume that a conversation can and should replace all criteria. They suggest that rejecting a would-be adopter because, for example, they admit that they plan to declaw their cat is ineffective because adopters can simply lie about their intentions. Also, denying the adoption for that reason means that the shelter misses the opportunity to educate the person about the impact of declawing on the cat's welfare. An open dialogue that allows would-be adopters to explain why they want to declaw a cat without making them feel judged increases the likelihood that they will be receptive to information about more appropriate means to protect furniture against being scratched, for instance.

Advocates of open adoption sometimes suggest that the standards of restrictive adoption policies are in tension with conversation; Weiss et al. (2014) even call the open adoption approach "conversation based" and contrast it with the restrictive, "policy based" approach (what we in this chapter have called the protective approach). But this is a false dichotomy: shelters can have *both* conversations with would-be adopters *and* a range of adoption criteria. Indeed, an adoption procedure which combines a respectful conversation and a set of strict criteria combines advantages of both open and protective adoption approaches. Nothing prevents shelter staff from explaining, in a friendly and constructive manner, why some adoption criteria are in place and why the shelter must turn down would-be adopters who intend to declaw the animal, refuse to have them sterilized, show indifference toward the animal's need for stimulation or affection, or plan on leaving them alone for extended periods of time, without making the applicant feel humiliated or inadequate.

A constructive conversation along these lines can not only help establish whether or not an adopter is suitable; it can, in fact—as open adoption advocates also highlight (HSUS 2020, 14)—address concerns that might otherwise speak against adoption. For example, the intention to declaw a cat is often based on false information about what precisely this involves; if staff explain to the adopter that declawing is, essentially, a form of amputation that has severe implications for the cat's well-being, the adopter might change their mind about declawing. Similarly, an adopter might have certain ideas about what kind of dog they want to adopt but, in consultation with shelter staff, realize that a dog who requires less exercise is more suitable for their lifestyle. In other cases, the conversation may lead the would-be adopter to realize that their current situation is not sufficiently stable to take on the responsibility for a companion animal and so postpone the adoption until a later point. But if that is not the case and if the would-be adopter still insists, at the end of a conversation, on adopting an animal even though she has not demonstrated that she would provide them with the necessary care, it is crucial that the staff feel prepared to turn down the adoption request, even if this upsets the would-be adopter.

We concur with advocates of open adoption that conversation with would-be adopters is crucial. But contrary to what is sometimes suggested in the debate, this doesn't necessarily mean making adoption "easier." Of course, it can lead to a more flexible approach that allows for specific criteria to be waived when this seems warranted by individual circumstances. But it certainly doesn't lead to doing away with them entirely.

6.5.3 Training Courses for Would-Be Adopters and Post-Adoption Programs

Another concern about open adoption and the kind of conversation between shelter staff and would-be adopters is its effects on adopters' expectations. We know that one important reason for failed adoptions (resulting, for example, in the animal's return to the shelter or abandonment) is that adopters are misinformed or have unrealistic expectations (New et al. 2000; Mondelli et al. 2004; Shore 2005; O'Connor et al. 2016; Powell et al. 2018). Even when other reasons are identified, such as the animal's behavioral problems or high veterinary costs, these reasons often hide a more fundamental one: the misaligned expectations of the adopters. The authors of a 2018 study offer the following example:

> the presence of problematic behaviors is regularly cited as a primary reason for relinquishment. However, the ability of owners to correctly identify canine behaviour is poor, despite most dog owners rating their understanding of dog behaviour highly. Therefore, relinquishment is

likely to at least partially reflect the owner's perception that a behaviour is a problem, due to unmet expectations or a disparity between owner lifestyle and the needs of the dog, rather than simply canine behavioural disorders. (Powell et al. 2018, references omitted)

This suggests that the better informed adopters are about the needs of companion animals, and the more accurate their expectations of what caring for an animal entails, the greater the chances that the adoption will be successful: "An understanding of adopters' expectations prior to adoption will help animal shelters better match, educate, and prepare adopters for their lives with companion animals" (O'Connor et al. 2016). The flipside of this is that an inexperienced prospective adopter who is allowed to adopt an animal after a conversation that emphasized the benefits of living with an animal companion over the responsibilities that come with it is more likely to have unrealistic expectations about what the guardianship of a companion animal involves.

In parallel to adjusting expectations prior to adoption, it is worth considering the role of training courses and post-adoption programs. Advocates of open adoption are certainly right to emphasize the importance of establishing relationships with adopters and the local community more broadly; animal "parenting classes" and post-adoption programs are an excellent way to establish such relationships and make it more likely that the shelter can support adopters who face issues and avoid relinquishment of the animal (see Reider 2015 for discussion of post-adoption programs). Such programs can help those guardians who are motivated to provide good care for their companions but may not have much experience or lack information. "Bad" animal guardianship is often the result of poor knowledge rather than ill will. This is important also because companion animals' lives can be improved in ways that don't require much in the way of resources. For example, people in small apartments can use wall shelves to provide vertical space for their cats to explore; everyday objects such as boxes can be fashioned into toys that provide stimulation to companion animals while their guardians are at work. In addition, these kinds of activities can signal to adopters that becoming the guardian of an animal is a serious process and that being a good guardian requires skills and knowledge.

6.6 Conclusion

Our purpose in this chapter was to discuss the question of how to choose and design adoption procedures in the animal shelter context, focusing in particular on the recent move toward "open adoption" that many organizations are advocating. We argued, first, that the evidence about the effects of open adoption on shelter animals is much less conclusive than advocates of open adoption suggest. The certainty with which advocates make a range of empirical claims about the benefits of open adoption is not warranted. Second, while the current debate and, in particular, the push for "open" adoption, has focused on a narrow set of criteria, we argued that the decision regarding which process to favor must be informed by a wider range of considerations. In particular, we highlighted that the adoption process offers a crucial opportunity to signal the moral status of non-human animals and challenge accepted norms about companion animals and, perhaps, even all nonhuman animals.

While this does not prescribe any specific approach to adoption, we argued here that shelters should take a broader perspective when it comes to their adoption procedures. In our view, shelters should have, as part of their mission, the goal of challenging dominant speciesist norms. To what extent different adoption procedures help shelters pursue this goal should then be an explicit part of decisions around the design and implementation of adoption policies. While some of the concerns we raised about the signaling effects of open adoption can be avoided by simply reframing certain aspects of the procedures (e.g., changing the presentation of Adoption Days), tradeoffs between competing goals are often unavoidable. We do not deny that open adoption could have important benefits, such as preventing would-be adopters from purchasing animals from breeders rather than adopting from a shelter.

However, any such benefits must be weighed against the possibility that open adoption reinforces the impression that decisions about the fate of animals may be taken based on the desire of the adopters rather than on the interests of the animals themselves. In addition, shelters can explore other means of reducing the number of animals waiting for adoption, such as taking a strong stance against breeding (e.g., by campaigning for legal restrictions on breeding and refusing breed identification of shelter animals), educating the public about the importance of spaying and neutering, expanding their network of foster families, and fighting against speciesism more generally. Shelters should consider the situation of all animals; we are concerned that open adoption procedures undermine the goal of gaining recognition of the moral and political status of animals and ultimately improving the legal protection of their interests.

Acknowledgments

We would like to thank Angie Pepper and Agnes Tam for their helpful comments and suggestions on earlier drafts, Amélie Martel for enlightening discussions, as well as the staff of the Montreal SPCA for the helpful insights they shared with us. While they disagreed with much of what we argue here, Gabrielle Carrière and Alexandre Ellis provided us with important input that helped us clarify our argument; we are very grateful that they were willing to share their perspective with us.

Notes

1. The terminology is inconsistent in the literature. "Non-open" adoption approaches are sometimes called "traditional" (Association for Animal Welfare Advancement 2018), "policy-based" (as opposed to conversation-based; Weiss et al. 2014), or "restrictive" (Weiss et al. 2014). We prefer the term "protective," used by Balcom and Arluke (2001), since it captures the underlying intention of protecting the adoptee.

2. See also http://blog.theaawa.org/if-your-adoption-policies-put-up-barriers-youre-part-of-the-problem/; https://www.humananimalsupportservices.org/blog/common-barriers-to-adoption-and-how-to-bust-them/.

3. It is crucial to understand the impact of structural inequality on marginalized and disadvantaged communities and not to see the choice to relinquish one's animal as an indication of "irresponsible" guardianship; see Guenther 2020, chapter 3, for more discussion.

4. One shelter actively promotes the adoption of animals as Christmas gifts by sending staff and volunteers dressed as Christmas elves to deliver the adopted animals directly to their new homes (HSUS 2020, 13).

5. This risk was reported to us by Amélie Martel, Director of Animal Welfare at the Montreal SPCA at the time our interviews were conducted.

6. Some experiences are described in a recent *New York Times* article (Bahney 2006) and in Balcom and Arluke (2001).

7. Breeding not only creates additional animals in a context where already many more animals exist (waiting in shelters or wandering the streets as strays) than can be found homes for. It is also a process that instrumentalizes nonhuman animals for human purposes. Indeed, it creates animals with particular features that are appealing to us, even if they create significant health problems for the animals. More generally, it is based on the principle that we are allowed to produce animals to satisfy our desire for companions over whom we will then exercise a property right.

8. For an argument on why people have a duty to adopt from a shelter rather than "buy" an animal from a breeder, see Rulli (2017).

9. This problem is not unique to the shelter environment; Donaldson and Kymlicka (2015) identify a similar tension in the context of farmed animal sanctuaries.

10. For discussion of the importance of language for animal liberation theory, see Wyckoff (2015). Of course, adopting language that reflects the status that animals should enjoy must be part of a broader strategy to improve the way animals are perceived. It is important to avoid simply making real injustices invisible by describing them in euphemisms.

11. Humans are generally good at putting nonhuman animals in different categories: the animals we invite into our homes (e.g., cats, dogs) are seen very differently from other animals, such as those in the wild or those we use for various purposes. The seriousness with which we treat the adoption of the shelter animals might not affect our representation of animals in general but only that of companion animals. However, even if this was the case, our worry is significant since it means that adoption policies might have implications if not for the fate of all animals, at least for the fate of all *companion* animals. That said, we believe that there is a reasonable possibility that our treatment of shelter animals affects positively the moral status of farmed, liminal, and wild animals as well. Considering how strongly we tend to oppose humans to all other animals,

it seems that we assimilate, at least to a certain degree, all nonhumans. Breaking the human–nonhuman moral divide in treating some animals with the respect we normally reserve for human beings gives us reason to hope for an eventual improvement of the fate of all animals. Additionally, we should remember that an important strategy of the animal rights movement consists in trying to get the general public to see farmed animals in a way that is similar to how they see companion animals. From this, it seems reasonable to assume that a more respectful perspective on companion animals—through the work of activists who remind people that pigs have abilities comparable to those of dogs, for example—would also lead to a more respectful attitude toward farmed animals. We thank Agnes Tam for pushing us to clarify this point.

12. In Montreal, most residential leases end on July 1, so on this day the city is filled with moving trucks as a large number of people move between residences. This leads to companion animals being lost or abandoned, especially in light of leases that prohibit companion animals.

13. For instance, the BC SPCA offered half-priced adoptions explicitly to free up shelter space in September 2021 (see Femia 2021).

14. It is of course commendable that shelters are sensitive to possible discriminatory effects of their practices on vulnerable human communities. However, we must be careful not to address the background injustices in our society on the backs of vulnerable individuals such as animals. Strategies for addressing these concerns about the possible discriminatory effects of adoption policies must not put animals at greater risk; rather, we should find strategies to ensure that everyone has the means to meet the physical and psychological needs of the animals they may be entrusted with. As we suggest in Part I of this volume, low-cost veterinary care, provided by shelters, could be an important plank in such a strategy.

References

American Society for the Prevention of Cruelty to Animals (ASPCA) and PetSmart Charities (2007) "Humane Society of Boulder Valley: Pioneers in open adoptions." https://www.aspcapro.org/sites/default/files/hsbouldervalley-prof ile-from-aspcapro.pdf

Association for Animal Welfare Advancement (2018) "Adoption best practices." www.theaawa.org.

Bahney, A. (2006) "So you think you can just adopt a dog?" *New York Times*, March 23.

Balcom, S., and A. Arluke (2001) "Animal adoption as negotiated order: A comparison of open versus traditional shelter approaches." *Anthrozoös 14*(3), 135–150.

Canadian Federation of Humane Societies (CFHS) (2017) "Cats in Canada 2017: A five-year review of cat overpopulation." https://humanecanada.ca/our-work/focus-areas/companion-animals/cats-in-canada-2017-a-five-year-review-of-cat-overpopulation/.

DeGrazia, D. (1996) *Taking Animals Seriously: Mental Life and Moral Status*. Cambridge: Cambridge University Press.

de Wispelaere, J., and D. Weinstock (2018) "Ethical challenges for adoption regimes." In A. Gheaus, G. Calder, and J. De Wispelaere (eds.), *Routledge Handbook of the Philosophy of Childhood and Children*. New York: Routledge, 213–224.

Donaldson, S., and W. Kymlicka (2015) "Farmed animal sanctuaries: The heart of the movement? A socio-political perspective." *Politics and Animals* 1(1), 50–74.

Edinboro, C. H., H. N. Watson, and A. Fairbrother (2016) "Association between a shelter-neuter-return program and cat health at a large municipal animal shelter." *Journal of the American Veterinary Medical Association* 248(3), 298–308.

Femia, V. (2021) "BC SPCA offering half-priced animal adoptions to free up shelter space." CTV News, September 26. https://bc.ctvnews.ca/bc-spca-aims-to-free-up-space-with-half-price-adoption-event-1.5601394.

Guenther, K. M. (2020) *The Lives and Deaths of Shelter Animals*. Stanford: Stanford University Press.

Humane Society of the United States (HSUS) (2020) *Adopters Welcome: Finding, Engaging and Supporting More Adopters*. Washington, D.C.: HSUS.

Janke, N., O. Berke, T. Flockhart, S. Bateman, and J. B. Coe (2017) "Risk factors affecting length of stay of cats in an animal shelter: A case study at the Guelph Humane Society, 2011–2016." *Preventive Veterinary Medicine* 148: 44–48. doi. org/10.1016/j.prevetmed.2017.10.007.

Karsten, C. L., D. C. Wagner, P. H. Kass, and K. F. Hurley (2017) "An observational study of the relationship between Capacity for Care as an animal shelter management model and cat health, adoption and death in three animal shelters." *Veterinary Journal* 227, 15–22. doi.org/10.1016/j.tvjl.2017.08.003.

Ly, L. H., E. Gorden, and A. Protopopova (2021) "Inequitable flow of animals in and out of shelters: Comparison of community-level vulnerability for owner-surrendered and subsequently adopted animals." *Frontiers in Veterinary Science* 8, article 784389. doi: 10.3389/fvets.2021.784389.

McHugh-Smith, J., and J. L. Buckman (2010) "Operational guide for animal care and control agencies: Animal adoption." American Humane Association. https://www.google.com/url?sa=tandrct=jandq=andesrc=sandsource=weban dcd=andved=2ahUKEwizhLi4q7z2AhVojIkEHY_wBIEQFnoECAUQAQand url=https%3A%2F%2Fwww.americanhumane.org%2Fapp%2Fuploads%2F2 016%2F08%2Fop-guide-adoption.pdfandusg=AOvVaw0KCgjR3GJVHGP09 jRX2N61.

Mondelli, F., E. P. Previde, M. Verga, D. Levi, S. Magistrelli, and P. Valsecchi (2004) "The bond that never developed: Adoption and relinquishment of dogs in a rescue shelter." *Journal of Applied Animal Welfare Science* 7(4), 253–266. doi:10.1207/s15327604jaws0704_3.

Montoya, A., J. Rand, R. Greer, C. Alberthsen, and D. Vankan (2017) "Relationship between sources of pet acquisition and euthanasia of cats and dogs in an animal shelter: A pilot study." *Australian Veterinary Journal* 95(6), 194–200. https://doi.org/10.1111/avj.12582.

New Jr., J. C., M. D. Salman, M. King, J. M. Scarlett, P. H. Kass, and J. M. Hutchison (2000) "Characteristics of shelter-relinquished animals and their owners compared with animals and their owners in U.S. pet-owning households." *Journal of Applied Animal Welfare Science* 3(3), 179–201. doi:10.1207/S15327604JAWS0303_1.

O'Connor, R., J. G. Coe, L. Niel, and A. Jones-Bitton (2016) "Effect of adopters' lifestyles and animal-care knowledge on their expectations prior to companion-animal guardianship." *Journal of Applied Animal Welfare Science* 19(2), 157–170. doi:10.1080/10888705.2015.1125295.

Patronek, Gary J., L. T. Glickman, A. M. Beck, and G. P. McCabe (1996) "Risk factors for relinquishment of dogs to an animal shelter." *Journal of the American Veterinary Medical Association* 209(3): 572–581.

PetSmart Charities. 2003. *Report on Adoption Forum II.* Phoenix, Arizona, January 16–17. https://spca.bc.ca/wp-content/uploads/Report-On-Adoption-Forum-II.pdf.

Powell L., D. Chia, P. McGreevy, A. L. Podberscek, K. M. Edwards, B. Neilly, A. J. Guastella, V. Lee, and E. Stamatakis (2018) "Expectations for dog ownership: Perceived physical, mental and psychosocial health consequences among prospective adopters." *PLOS ONE* 13(7): e0200276. https://doi.org/10.1371/journal.pone.0200276.

Powell, L., C. Reinhard, D. Satriale, M. Morris, J. Serpell, and B. Watson (2021) "Characterizing unsuccessful animal adoptions: Age and breed predict the likelihood of return, reasons for return and post-return outcomes." *Scientific Reports* 11(1), 8018. https://doi.org/10.1038/s41598-021-87649-2

Rachels, J. (1999) *Created from Animals: The Moral Implications of Darwinism.* Oxford: Oxford University Press.

Reese, L. A., M. Skidmore, W. Dyar, and E. Rosebrook (2017) "No dog left behind: A hedonic pricing model for animal shelters." *Journal of Applied Animal Welfare Science* 20(1), 52–64.

Reider, L. M. (2015) "Adopter support: Using postadoption programs to maximize adoption success." In E. Weiss, H. Mohan-Gibbons, and S. Zawitowski (eds.), *Animal Behavior for Shelter Veterinarians and Staff.* Oxford: Wiley Blackwell, 292–358.

Rulli, T. (2017) "For dog's sake, adopt!" In C. Overall (ed.), *Pets and People.* Oxford: Oxford University Press, 172–186.

Scarlett, J. M., M. D. Salman, J. G. New, and P. H. Kass (1999) "Reasons for relinquishment of companion animals in U.S. animal shelters: Selected health and personal issues." *Journal of Applied Animal Welfare Science* 2(1), 41–57.

Shore, E. R. (2005) "Returning a recently adopted companion animal: Adopters' reasons for and reactions to the failed adoption experience." *Journal of Applied Animal Welfare Science* 8(3), 187–198.

Singer, P. (1975) *Animal Liberation. A New Ethics for Our Treatment of Animals*. New York: HarperCollins.

Singer, P. (1979) *Practical Ethics*. Cambridge: Cambridge University Press.

Sinski, J. (2016) "'A cat-sized hole in my heart': Public perceptions of companion animal adoption in the USA." In M. P. Pręgowski (ed.), *Companion Animals in Everyday Life*. New York: Palgrave Macmillan, 73–89.

Taylor, K. D., and D. S. Mills (2007) "The effect of the kennel environment on canine welfare: A critical review of experimental studies." *Animal Welfare* 16(4), 435–447.

Troughton, B. (2015) "The adoption process: The interface with the human animal." In E. Weiss, H. Mohan-Gibbons, and S. Zawitowski (eds.), *Animal Behavior for Shelter Veterinarians and Staff*. Oxford: Wiley Blackwell, 269–285.

UC Davis (2015) "Length of Stay (LOS)." Koret Shelter Medicine Program. https://www.sheltermedicine.com/library/resources/?r=length-of-stay-los.

University of Wisconsin-Madison School of Veterinary Science (2015) "Support for open adoptions." https://www.uwsheltermedicine.com/library/resources/support-for-open-adoptions.

Wagner, D. C., P. H. Kass, and K. F. Hurley (2018) "Cage size, movement in and out of housing during daily care, and other environmental and population health risk factors for feline upper respiratory disease in nine North American animal shelters." *PLoS ONE* 13(1), e0190140. https://doi.org/10.1371/journal.pone.0190140.

Weiss, E., E. Dolna, L. Garrison, J. Hong, and M. Slater (2013) "Should dogs and cats be given as gifts?" *Animals* 3(4), 996–1001.

Weiss, E., and S. Gramann (2009) "A comparison of attachment levels of adopters of cats: Fee-based adoptions versus free adoptions." *Journal of Applied Animal Welfare Science* 12(4), 360–370.

Weiss, E., S. Gramann, E. D. Dolan, J. E. Scotto, and M. R. Slater (2014) "Do policy based adoptions increase the care a pet receives? An exploration of a shift to conversation based adoptions at one shelter." *Open Journal of Animal Sciences* 4, 313–322. http://dx.doi.org/10.4236/ojas.2014.45040.

Wyckoff, J. (2015) "The radical potential of analytic animal liberation philosophy." In A. Matsuoka and J. Sorenson (eds.), *Critical Animal Studies: Towards Trans-Species Social Justice*. London/New York: Rowman and Littlefield, 296–316.

7
Transformative Animal Protection

Sue Donaldson and Will Kymlicka

7.1 Introduction

The goal of this chapter is to address an important challenge
confronting animal protection organizations (APOs): their immediate mandate is to rescue and protect individual animals, but
can they also contribute to long-term structural transformation of
human-animal relations? APOs like the Society for the Prevention
of Cruelty to Animals (SPCA) operate in profoundly challenging
and unjust circumstances—a world in which the killing and exploitation of animals on a massive scale is routine, sanctioned by law,
and woven into the very fabric of modern capitalist societies and
economies. APOs struggle valiantly to create a space that can provide basic care and protection for some of the animals trapped in
this animal-industrial complex[1] and promote policy changes aimed
at blunting the violence. But the prospect of justice in human–
animal relations is remote; APO staff are continuously confronted
with tragic choices and a disheartening sense of being caught up
in scenarios of unending crisis and band-aid solutions rather than
contributing to a longer-term project of meaningful change for
animals.

Indeed, APO staff may feel not only powerless to change these
larger structures, but also at risk of becoming morally implicated
in the very practices they hope to change. Whereas activist animal

Sue Donaldson and Will Kymlicka, *Transformative Animal Protection* In: *The Ethics of Animal Shelters*. Edited by:
Valéry Giroux, Angie Pepper, and Kristin Voigt, Oxford University Press. © Oxford University Press 2023.
DOI: 10.1093/oso/9780197678633.003.0009

rights groups can take an uncompromising stand not to collaborate with unjust practices or institutions, APOs can rarely afford that luxury. To fulfil their mandate, APOs may need to work collaboratively with law enforcement officers to enforce animal cruelty laws even if they view those laws as deeply inadequate and unjust.[2] APOs may also be expected to work with government officials and animal industries in reviewing public policies even if they view these policy reviews as likely to rubberstamp unjust policies.[3] They are also heavily dependent on donations from the general public and may worry that taking a strong public stand against animal agriculture, say, or animal experimentation, is likely to alienate key members of their donor community or damage their reputation with the general public. For all these reasons, APOs often feel they need to moderate their animal rights commitments (or indeed to avoid the language of animal rights entirely), sticking to "safe" campaigns around (noninstitutionalized) animal cruelty and neglect.

Given these constraints, the prospects for APOs to play a transformative role seem dim. Perhaps we should simply recognize that different types of organizations play a different role in the moral division of labor. Whereas radical animal rights activists can advance a transformative agenda, the institutional constraints on APOs may require them to downplay transformative commitments.

Our own view is more optimistic. We believe that most APOs can be part of (or contribute to) a transformative movement, changing the very terms on which human–animal relations are defined and not just patching up cracks in the status-quo that facilitate its ongoing functioning. Indeed, we believe that creating this sense of transformative possibility is important for maintaining staff and volunteer morale.[4] APOs may inevitably be drawn into morally compromising relations with law enforcement, government regulators, animal industries, and donors but, if so, that is all the more reason to find spaces and places where staff and volunteers can act in an uncompromising way in pursuit of interspecies justice.

While institutional constraints may preclude APOs from taking an uncompromising public stand on animal rights,[5] we believe there is scope for APOs to be more transformative in their own internal practices and ethos and through grassroots partnerships. One way to promote transformative change is to engage in "prefigurative" change:[6] even within the current circumstances of profound injustice, one can try to carve out moments or spaces for treating animals the way they should be treated in a (more) just society and establishing the kinds of relationships with animals that would characterize a (more) just society. We move toward this better society by prefiguring it in the present.

There are different visions of what a better society for animals would look like, and this pluralism is undoubtedly reflected among APO workers and across different organizations. Our own view is that justice involves recognizing animals, not just as sentient beings who have rights not to be harmed, but also as agents who have their own lives to lead. In the case of many domesticated animals and others unable to lead lives independent of humans, it means recognizing them as equal members of a shared society who have the right to shape society and their relationships with us. A transformative model of animal protection, then, would attempt to prefigure, at a micro-level, a society in which these animals are seen as embodied agents and as full members of a shared society with humans.

Commentators have discussed three broad reasons why prefigurative politics within a particular site or organization can contribute to transformative change throughout society as a whole. First, we need "laboratories of experience" to help us learn what futures are possible. In relation to animals, we have never asked as a society how animals want to live with us or made any attempt to explore the full range of possible modes of co-existence with them. There is a huge epistemic gap here that prefigurative politics can help overcome. Second, prefigurative politics is capacity-building. In a world where so many of our skills, habits, identities, values, and norms are tied to human supremacism, prefigurative politics enables us to develop new capacities for engaging in interspecies justice. Third, prefigurative politics has demonstration effects, sometimes due to pro-active attempts to diffuse the experience to a wider audience, but also simply from the way that the mere presence of such experiments in society serves to put inherited practices into question. For these and other reasons, many social movements have come to believe that, in addition to engaging in oppositional tactics to contest existing injustices in the larger society, one must also engage in constructive efforts at the micro-level to prefigure justice (Yates 2015).

In previous work, we have explored the prospects for transformative strategies in sanctuary communities for animals rescued from animal agriculture (Donaldson and Kymlicka 2015; Blattner et al. 2020). Not all farmed animal sanctuaries have a transformative agenda: some simply seek to provide decent care to animals so that they can live out their lives in peace and comfort. (We can call this the "safe refuge" model of sanctuary.) But other sanctuaries have a more prefigurative political agenda of the sort we advocate: they view their sanctuaries as sites for humans and animals together to explore the sorts of new relationships that might emerge in a better society. These sanctuaries relate to the animal residents not just as vulnerable individuals who need protection and provision, but also as agents and members working together to create new relationships (which may or may not include humans).[7] We have argued that prefigurative animal sanctuaries—and other forms of "intentional communities," "enclaves," or "counterpublics"—can play an important role in the wider struggle for animal rights.

Can we imagine a transformative model for APOs more generally? As noted, one possible challenge concerns disagreement about what constitutes transformational change. What, exactly, is the goal being prefigured? This chapter offers a fairly radical vision of transformation, with a correspondingly challenging conception of the steps required to move toward it. Some (perhaps many) APOs and their staff will not share this vision, but we believe that the general strategy of prefigurement can apply even if the substantive guiding vision of justice differs and that some of the specific analyses and suggestions might be helpful in a broad range of cases.

This connects to a further challenge: it is not obvious that organizations like the SPCA would even exist in a radically transformed world that takes interspecies justice seriously. Perhaps the idea of an organization devoted to animal "shelter" and "rescue" only makes sense in a society that treats animals as exploitable property.

If so, then perhaps the very terms of the organization and the nature of its mandate preclude it taking on a more prefigurative as opposed to band-aid role. And maybe some APOs' ability to function is premised on maintaining a very modest set of goals of limiting damage within the contours of the existing system, a goal around which staff can rally even if they hold widely divergent ideas of just human–animal relations.

Our view is that even in a much better world there will continue to be a need for animal protection organizations and that prefiguring their role in a more just future is a worthwhile transformative project. This chapter begins by imagining how APOs might operate in such a transformed world. We then turn to the question of how this vision can inform their current operations.

7.2 Imagining APOs in a Better World

As noted, some people might believe that APOs would not be needed in a just society. For example, extinctionist views of human–animal relations are premised on the idea that domesticated animals would no longer exist in a just society and that humans would largely avoid intervening in the lives of all animals and exercising power over them. This view is most notably captured in Francione's claim that the only right animals need is the right not to be property (Francione 2004). We have challenged this view on moral, prudential, and empirical grounds (Donaldson and Kymlicka 2011: chap 4). Humans don't have the right to unilaterally bring about the demise of domesticated animals or expel them from society. Animals have the right to make their own decisions about how they will live, including the extent and nature of their involvement with humans, and, for some animals, living in multispecies communities with humans may be a desirable way to live. Moreover, the idea that humans can seal themselves off from animals, leaving them to get on with their lives without human impact, is untenable in a world in which countless animals gravitate to humans and (ever-expanding) human settlements. Of course there are also many wild animals living in the wilderness who do not gravitate to human settlement, and for them, an approach that creates boundaries and limits on human activity and impacts is essential. But for countless domesticated animals (and for "liminal" urban wildlife animals), sharing space and possibly community with humans is inevitable.[8] The asymmetrical power of humans and the inevitability of human impacts can't be imagined out of existence, and so our goal should be to make the exercise of human power more accountable.

Once we recognize the inevitability of geographic, ecological, and/or social entanglement with animals, it becomes clear that APOs will continue to have a place even under more just circumstances. On the one hand, we can imagine that many current (and indeed expanded) functions of APOs would be incorporated into government and legal institutions—similar to child welfare, health, education, and advocacy—and be properly resourced through public funding. Human–animal relations would be the focus of core public policy development and implementation by democratic governments, not relegated to the periphery of ad-hoc nongovernmental organization (NGO) and volunteer efforts. But even the best public policy is beset by gaps, changing circumstances, and unpredictable events, so a continued role for emergency rescue and attention to emergent issues will persist. Even in a much better world animals will always be vulnerable in their relations with humans, and our relations with them will need to be subject to heightened scrutiny just as for other vulnerable groups within society. APOs, whether inside or outside government, will have a crucial ongoing role in advocacy and monitoring, enforcement, public education, and response to change. And there will be an ongoing requirement for expert crisis care at individual and societal levels (e.g., protection for stray, abandoned, mistreated animals; provision of emergency response to natural disasters, conflict, and social breakdown).[9]

In other words, even in a world dramatically improved in terms of human–animal justice, APOs will continue to exist and play a crucial role. The goal of this chapter is to show that anticipating this future role can help us to prefigure it in the current structure, policies, and relations of APOs, thereby contributing to transformation.

Moreover, it may help make the work of APO staff and volunteers more tolerable and rewarding and less subject to burnout. Enabling them to feel part of a project that goes beyond crisis management and unavoidable compromise with the animal-industrial complex can contribute to a sense of control and provide a welcome opportunity to contribute to and witness animal flourishing, thereby relieving some of the terrible pressure that comes from bearing responsibility for continuous life-and-death decisions in a seemingly unending cycle of animal suffering.[10]

7.2.1 Crisis Care versus Permanent Residency: Different Representation for Different Circumstances

An important distinction in the kinds of relationships APOs have with the animals they serve is between *episodic/crisis care* on the one hand and *permanent home/sanctuary* on the other. Some APOs provide crisis care (rescue, shelter, acute or preventative medical care, food provision) on a temporary or intermittent basis before releasing animals to their "home" (whether that home is in the wild, on the streets, or a new home arranged through adoption by human individuals and organizations). Other APOs themselves provide *permanent homes or sanctuary* to animals whether as part of the APO workplace or in dedicated sanctuaries for formerly farmed animals or rescued/rehabbed wild animals who cannot be released to the wild. And many APOs are in the business of providing both intermittent/crisis care for some animals *and* longer-term sanctuary for others.

We believe that this is a crucial distinction since the forms of power exercised over animals in these situations call for different kinds of accountability. While it is important for animals' agency to be enabled and for their interests to be well represented in both episodic settings and long-term community, the forms of enablement and representation will be different. For starters, the kinds of decisions made about animals' interests in a crisis care setting are more likely to be justifiably paternalistic because animals often require acute care (from injury, abuse, neglect) or other medical interventions (vaccines, etc.) that animals are not in a position to consent to in a fully informed way. This doesn't mean that animals should not be consulted in these decisions, but rather that their preferences are less likely to be decisive (Blattner 2020; Healey and Pepper 2021). Many of the decisions made in animals' permanent homes, neighborhoods, and workplaces, on the other hand, are ones that they can and ought to be able to make their own choices about and shape over time. The stable context and reiterative nature of decision-making make it possible for animals to learn about the options open to them and create new options, learn how to make decisions, and exercise greater control over their environment and relationships (Franks 2019; Côté-Boudreau 2019).

A second distinction between crisis and long-term settings is that the power held by humans over animals in crisis care settings, while affecting crucial interests, is nevertheless of temporary duration. Animals may not have as much power over decision-making in this setting, but this is a short-term suppression of their freedom, not a permanent condition of subordination. The goal of paternalistic crisis interventions is to return animals to settings in which they exercise greater autonomy. In long-term settings, on the other hand, failure to respect animals' participation and self-determination rights is far more problematic because it denies them the exercise of forms of autonomy possible for them and limits their opportunities to contest power and shape mutual relations that govern their daily lives.

The work of most APOs falls more toward the crisis/intermittent care end of the spectrum.[11] Care for stray and abandoned animals put up for adoption; treatment and release of injured liminal/wild animals; trap-neuter-release (TNR) programs; and veterinary clinics for financially strapped families are examples of episodic/crisis care. However, many APOs also provide shelter for animals who are unadoptable or un-releasable (including seized exotic "pets" and farmed animals, injured liminal animals who can't fend for themselves, dogs with behavioral issues precluding adoption, and so on).

All too often, these animals end up being killed because many APOs have no capacity or mandate to provide a permanent home for such animals. Increasingly, however, some APOs are exploring ways to provide permanent care for those animals who need it, either within their own organization or in partnership with other institutions and organizations.

We expect this trend to continue, as many APO staff and volunteers question long-standing practices of killing so-called unadoptable animals and push for a more "no-kill" ethos. However, this trend toward having animals under permanent care raises distinctive challenges. These animals don't just require different kinds of care while under APO responsibility, but also need different kinds of political participation and representation, or so we will argue.

7.2.2 Animals Who Are under Permanent Care with APOs

Regarding animals in the second category (i.e., those for whom an APO is providing permanent sanctuary), it is crucial to find ways for them to be able to contest and shape the environment that is their forever community. The APO isn't just an institutional setting or civil society organization. From the perspective of animals who will live their entire lives within its ambit, the APO is their entire world, their only ecological, social, cultural, and political community. If meaningful agency for humans and animals requires a "holding environment" (Honig 2017), then the APO (and its partners) are that holding environment for long-term animal residents. Diminishments of autonomy and self-determination that might seem acceptable on a short-term basis become completely unacceptable if this is one's whole life.[12] (Consider quarantine and other restrictions under the COVID-19 pandemic and how the duration of these restrictions makes all the difference in terms of our willingness to sacrifice some agency.)

Supporting the agency of animals who become permanent members of an APO community may be very challenging in some

cases. Consider animals who have been abused or inadequately socialized, animals with severe injuries or illness requiring ongoing
treatment, or wild animals who have been irreparably severed from
the free-living communities and habitats in which they could truly
flourish. The opportunity for many of these individuals to live self-
determining lives is deeply compromised. Nevertheless, there may
be important ways in which an APO could support their agency and
their participation in shaping the world they share with humans,
even if it is a second-best world.

In our research concerning formerly farmed animals living in
interspecies communities, we have explored various mechanisms
for supporting animal agency and participation in community with
humans, so that animals can co-author their relationships with us
(Donaldson and Kymlicka 2015; Donaldson 2020; Blattner et al.
2020). These include, first of all, cultivating the ethos that animals
have a right to participation and the expectation that they can be
agents. Agency is relational—created in the relationships between
individuals (and between individuals and environments)—and this
requires that we actively seek out, support and solicit the agency of
others—that we be the "bearers" of each other's agency, in Sharon
Krause's terminology (Krause 2013, 2016). Especially in cases where
an animal's agency has been suppressed or quashed, we must not
take their apparent passivity or lack of initiative or interest or pur-
poseful activity as evidence that they lack the capacity or desire for a
more agential existence.[13]

Soliciting, enabling, and cultivating the agency of animals
requires that they feel secure, that they feel part of a supportive and
stable social community (for social animals), and that they have
sufficient liberty, space, time, and social and environmental stimulation to explore possibilities, make serendipitous discoveries,
and offer proposals for how to organize our lives together. And it
requires ongoing relationships with responsive humans who get to
know animals as individuals and community members and who
are committed to recognizing and supporting their agency. These
must be individuals whom animals like and trust. This support
includes making appropriate adjustments to the social and physical

environment. It means being responsive to animals' proposals and pursuing them.[14] It means scaffolding learning opportunities to help individuals build competences and confidence, allowing animals to gradually explore a wider range of environments, social roles, activities, and relationships.[15] And it means undertaking these steps in deliberate and demonstrable processes that can be reviewed by third parties with expertise in animal ethology, animal ethics, and interspecies democratic processes for achieving participation and co-authorship in community decision-making.[16]

Is there any realistic way that an APO could prefigure this form of democratic community for the seized, injured, abused, and traumatized animals who come under their permanent care? One option is to create relationships with existing sanctuary communities to relocate animals, assuming of course that these sanctuaries are themselves committed to a prefigurative project. (Otherwise, the APO is just punting the responsibility.) This is undoubtedly a practical solution if appropriate sanctuaries exist, especially for farmed animals seized in neglect or cruelty cases. Or an APO could operate its own sanctuary. This would be an expensive option, although siting the sanctuary in a rural area with low property values might be a possibility. (Creating such a sanctuary as part of a deal with government/industry to restore/rewild a former industrial or agricultural area might make it more feasible financially.)

An APO could also take a more direct role in fostering new kinds of community partnerships that could provide the stable, socially and environmentally rich, and participatory framework that we are advocating. A possible inspiration here is the so-called greenhouse school located within a Finnish middle school. It is worth quoting in depth Hohti and Tammi's description from their ethological study conducted at the school. The school

has a greenhouse located in the building's atrium. This is the biggest educational greenhouse in the Nordic countries, complete with all the technology required to create a subtropical climate in the middle of the surrounding arctic environment. First used as a rescue facility for homeless pets, the greenhouse has evolved into an unofficial educational zoo inhabited by both rescue animals and purchased ones. The school is located in a disadvantaged, largely immigrant-background suburb. The establishment of the greenhouse was possible in the early 1990s, when municipality allocated the resources for it following the so-called "positive discrimination" policy. The greenhouse inhabitants currently include approximately 40 bigger animals such as turtles, rabbits, a parrot, a dove, cockatiels, a green iguana, a water dragon, a corn snake, mice, guinea pigs, gerbils, a rooster and a hen. There are also smaller critters such as stick insects, ants, snails, mealworms and flies. Plants include tropical fruit trees, jacarandas, hibiscuses and more. Some animals are moving around on the floor of the greenhouse, some are in their cages and terrariums, or flying and sitting on beams close to the glass ceiling. The doors of the greenhouse are open to visitors, but there is the inner circle of some 20 students (aged 13–16) who like to spend most of their free time in the greenhouse. These greenhouse kids, as we like to call them, come in the greenhouse first thing in the morning, when it is often still dark, and they stay sometimes until the janitor leaves in the evening. Most of these young people have taken a course during sixth grade to qualify as responsible carers of the animals, and they are mentored by two biology teachers, Armi and Taina. Some of the secondary school students lead so-called animal clubs, which are afternoon clubs for smaller children, aged 8–12. Often, we find no adults present in the greenhouse. The young people spend time there on their own, taking full responsibility over feeding, cleaning and other daily tasks related to maintaining the greenhouse and taking care of the animals. (Hohti and Tammi 2019, 170)

It is not a great stretch to imagine that the turtles, rabbits, chickens, parrots, iguanas, and others who find their way into APO care could flourish in such a setting. As currently structured, this Finnish greenhouse school falls within a "safe refuge" model rather than the full "political" model we are advocating. While the greenhouse seeks to ensure good welfare standards, it is not conceived as the holding environment of animal residents' agency: the main responsibility of humans is to provide protection and care, not to solicit and support animals' agency in shaping important elements of their community. As it stands, therefore, one might worry that the greenhouse prioritizes human flourishing and learning through care of animals, rather than directly centering the agency and rights of animals, a concern that we have expressed about some farmed animal sanctuaries (Donaldson and Kymlicka 2015). Other dimensions of the description also raise red flags. Does being "open to visitors" perpetuate a zoo model of animals as entertainment for stranger/voyeur humans instead of a community model of ongoing relationship? And why are some animals "purchased"?

But a community greenhouse model could be reconceived along the lines of an intentional community or counterpublic—the center of a new web of relationships that model different human–animal relations, with the potential to transform all who come in contact with it. At a minimum, this model would stand as an alternative and challenge to the common perception of animals as "commodities" to be bought and sold (or simply killed or abandoned) as it suits the human owner. It would embody a deep moral commitment to the idea that even "non-adoptable" dogs or abandoned backyard chickens or exotic "pets" who are discarded by human owners are nonetheless owed moral concern. But it could also help to challenge the assumption that the best or only way to care for dependent animals is through assigning them to private individuals or families. We need to explore more social or communal modes of living with animals, in which animal residents are attended to and cared for by multiple humans with whom they develop trusting relationships. Building on these new relationships, the greenhouse could experiment with a more political model in which the space becomes the "holding environment" of democratic community and the center of a new idea of "the public" (based on the principles outlined above for soliciting, enabling, and cultivating animal agency and participation in joint worldmaking). In this model of political community, animals aren't owned by humans or positioned as patients in an asymmetrical, institutional "safe refuge" arrangement, but rather are seen as neighbors and co-citizens occupying their own unique spot in a diverse democratic community.

In practical terms, creating such a community would require an APO to partner with a school board, retirement residence, prison, community group (e.g., biodome/botanic garden, food garden/hub), or homeless shelter to create an experimental community where APO animals can live their "second-best life."[17] As noted, the great danger is that this might simply collapse into the familiar scenario in which institutions adopt resident animals solely to alleviate human boredom and loneliness, educate the public, or instill caring behavior in children—rather than exploring the transformative potential of democratic community with animals. So, important groundwork would have to be undertaken to find partners interested in this kind of radical project.

Having said that, we think it is vital to acknowledge the mutuality involved. The fact is, humans *would* stand to benefit enormously from their relationships with animals in such a community. The whole point of shifting from a "safe refuge" model to a "political" model is that it places community members in a relationship of equal, reciprocal citizenship, rather than a hierarchical relationship between care-giving agent and recipient patient. And the mutual benefit is what makes this a realistic aspiration, not a utopian one. Schools, retirement homes, and other organizations with the finances to partner with an APO on such a project aren't going to do so if they don't perceive benefits for the populations they serve. In turn, animals in need of care and community stand to benefit from tapping into human resources of attention, interest, skill, imagination, and concern that are often wasted or frustrated by the structures of mainstream society that too often relegate children, seniors, street people, prisoners, and others to controlled settings of care and control rather than generative settings of participatory democratic community. What we are imagining here is a synergistic relationship in which animals and humans who typically lie outside of mainstream democratic practices become the center of new sites of democratic experimentation and renewal.[18]

It should also be noted that on this model it's not just members of the public who enter into a new relationship with animals, but also staff at the APO. They would maintain a special duty as advocates for the animals transitioning to broader community membership and responsibility centered in the greenhouse community, but they could also, themselves, become part of this new community, this reconstituted "public," in a co-citizenship (and neighbor, friend, acquaintance etc.) relationship with animals and not just as care-giver/advocate. It was striking that, during our short visit with the Montreal SPCA, animals who had been permanently adopted by staff, spending time at the shelter as members of the SPCA family and not just clients/patients, seemed to fill a crucial role in comforting staff and reconciling them to the challenges of their workplace. Even if the total number of animals involved in an enduring greenhouse community initiative might be dwarfed by the numbers of animals cared for on an episodic basis in other APO programs, the opportunity to develop long-term relationships with at least some animals in a community setting that prefigures transformed human–animal relationships could be enormously beneficial for staff well-being.

7.2.3 Animals Who Are under Power of an APO on a Temporary or Episodic Basis

Let us turn now to the second category of animals under APO care: namely, those who are receiving temporary or episodic care. The sort of long-term relationships of attention, trust, and mutual learning that make it possible for humans and animals to jointly co-author a permanently shared community are not possible (and per-haps not necessary or desirable) for animals who are in the power of an APO on a short-term basis. We think it is important to keep the "permanent" model in mind, however, when thinking about tempo-rary or episodic care in order to appreciate the unique dimensions, limitations, and challenges of representation and advocacy in the crisis-type setting. Animals in the temporary care of an APO are very vulnerable individuals, subject to the power of a large and complex organization that is mysterious to them (think of a small child undergoing treatment in a hospital). We know that in hospital settings, for example, patients need advocates. Having a robust framework of legal safeguards, professional ethical guidelines, and ethics review boards is certainly essential to protect patients, but is not sufficient. Crisis care institutions are subject to their own failures (communications breakdowns, bureaucratic mentalities, incompetent or criminal staff, failures of attention and care to individuals, etc.). The policies and procedures of caring institutions are sometimes designed more for the efficiency or convenience of staff rather than the best interests of patients. Despite good intentions, it is easy to fall into patterns of manipulating patients into compliance with rules, practices, and decisions, rather than centering their needs and experience.

So even if an APO operated with a strong commitment to interspecies justice, we should not assume that this means animals would be well represented (just as the legal framework of human rights does not guarantee that human residents/patients are well-represented within hospitals, group homes, hospices, shelters, etc.). We might envisage two broad ways of ensuring better representation of animals. First, animals would need advocates who take on a fiduciary role in relation to particular individual animals (animal "guardians"); and, second, an advocate with an independent/arms-length role within the organization whose sole responsibility is to represent animals' interests (animal "ombudsperson").

Animal guardians would be empowered to speak up on behalf of individual animals whose circumstances they know well and whose interests they can speak to, contesting or influencing APO decisions that affect that particular animal. Staff members at the Montreal SPCA, for example, already do this on an informal basis. They form special interests in or attachments to particular animals and advocate for them. This is sometimes viewed as a problem of partiality (special pleading for certain individuals when decisions should be made on an impartial utilitarian basis). But we would argue, rather, that these special attachments could form the basis of a system of effective guardianship. The problem is not that APO staff form attachments to particular animals under their care and speak up on their behalf. The problem is that not all animals have such a guardian.

This problem can be addressed by formalizing the system. All (or a self-selecting subset of) staff would be assigned a certain number of animals for whom they stand in relation as guardian (selection based on animals' inclinations/indications of trust and attachment, human inclinations/indications of attachment, or random assignment if necessary). Rather than having to justify special pleading for a particular animal, APO staff would be obliged to do this for those individuals under their guardianship. (At the same time, they would be relieved of the burden of feeling they need to advocate for *all* animals under APO care. The burden would be shared.) When decisions affecting the animal are taken, the guardian's input, while not decisive, would hold special weight. The fact of their strong attachment and special relationship to the animal in question, far from being seen as detracting from the possibility of dispassionate decision-making, would rather offer some assurance of the animal's interests being heard as crucial decisions affecting their life are taken.

An *animal ombudsperson* would operate on a more systemic level, continuously reviewing APO policies and procedures with a view to centering the experience, interests and rights of animals and proposing modifications or reforms. The ombudsperson would not face any conflicting priorities (budgets, staff problems, work load, etc.) to interfere with their role as advocate. The key objective here is to create a position for an animal representative that isn't automatically biased or compromised by cost–benefit analyses and other competing responsibilities and perspectives. If someone occupies the role of vet, legal advocate, or adoption coordinator within the organization, it is very hard for this role not to shape their perspective on animals' interests and limit their ability to cast a critical eye on the workings of the institution. A dedicated animal ombudsperson would be in a better position to advance an unbiased and uncompromising form of animal representation, complementing the role of guardians. The role might encompass duties such as developing a bill of rights for animals within the institution or guidelines for decision-making affecting fundamental interests and overseeing the role of guardians. Perhaps most fundamentally, the role of the ombudsperson would be to make explicit the conflicting commitments and agendas within the institution; highlight the inevitable ways in which individual rights and interests can be sidelined by practical, administrative, managerial, and financial exigencies; and, where possible, implement policies to guard against the predictable pitfalls of institutionalized care. Even in short-term care settings, it is important to recognize that animals' interests must be independently represented within any organization—not subsumed under general and professional guidelines of care.

The primary responsibility of animal guardians and ombudspersons in situations of episodic/crisis care is to act as a shield against institutional power—to hold that power to account on behalf of animals who, for a variety of reasons, cannot be effectively agential (e.g., they are held captive; they are often ill, traumatized and/or frightened; they tend to be both overstimulated and understimulated in ways that compromise well-being; and they are completely unfamiliar with the social and physical environment). Despite the best intentions of human caregivers, this is not a good environment for animals or a possible "holding environment" of effective agency. As we have argued, supporting animal agency in meaningful terms is only possible in relation to shaping and appropriating a long-term community environment where animals can indeed feel at home in their permanent residence.[19] This is not to say that agency is irrelevant in captive and crisis settings. On the contrary, even in highly constrained circumstances it is possible to give animals some sense of control over decisions concerning bedding, food, companions, etc., and this should be enabled as much as possible. (Supporting these forms of "micro" agency would be a particular responsibility of animal guardians.) Nevertheless, the primary goal of the animal guardian/ombudsperson is to act as a shield against institutional power and practices, not as an enabler of agency.

This representation is intrinsically important to ensure justice for animals—providing a stronger voice for animals' interests, ensuring that these interests, even if they cannot always be met, are at least not buried under the exigencies of crisis management. But we would suggest that creating these dedicated roles of animal guardians and ombudspersons would also be good for the staff and volunteers.

Currently, staff members bear a terrible burden of being all things to the animals under their care, a burden which could be eased by sharing and formalizing advocacy roles. The guardian role would validate and empower (but also limit) a role that staff already assume informally. An ombudsperson role would significantly remove the burden from staff of trying to be the best possible advocate for animals while carrying out their more immediately pressing duties as administrators, caregivers, medical practitioners, investigators, fundraisers, and public educators. It would also allow staff to feel that they are part of a prefigurative politics, piloting new forms of animal representation and political recognition and empowerment.

7.3 What Difference Would This Make to APOs under Current Circumstances?

We have argued that, even in a (more) just society, something like APOs would still be needed to provide both short-term and long-term care for vulnerable animals. But in such a society, there would be built-in mechanisms to ensure (a) agency/participation for long-term residents and (b) effective advocacy/representation for short-term residents.

To what extent can this vision of a future APO be "prefigured" today? Can an APO today instantiate the kinds of rights and relationships that would characterize a more just society? We have explored a number of possibilities, including

1. Working with partners to seed "alternative communities" for animals in long-term care along the lines of a more radical version of the "greenhouse school" (or existing prefigurative animal sanctuaries).
2. Creating roles for animal guardians/ombudspersons within the APO itself.

We realize that these proposals may seem like they are imposing yet further expectations and burdens on an already overburdened (and underresourced) organization. Viewed from another angle, however, we can see these proposals as lightening the burden on staff, many of whom feel deeply torn between the constraints of their institutional roles and their moral aspirations for a more just world. In a better future, the distance between these constraints and aspirations would be much smaller, but, for the foreseeable future, the distance will be profound. We need to find a way, therefore, to reduce this conflict, and we believe that prefigurative policies can help here. Staff need to know that, notwithstanding the deeply morally compromised day-to-day realities of APOs in the current world, there are times and places where justice can be envisaged and explored, including in alternative communities or in new modes of political representation. This might in turn lead to a subtle reorientation of staff to those animals under their care—by separating the roles of care provider and advocate. It is a common pitfall of caring institutions—whether these institutions are caring for humans or animals—that caregivers take on "monopolies of care" which are unhealthy and unsustainable for both the caregiver and the cared-for.[20]

It is hard to predict how the practices and policies of an APO might change if these proposals were adopted. What sorts of communities would those animals in permanent care try to build with humans? What sorts of priorities would animal guardians and animal ombudspersons establish for those in temporary care? This is impossible to predict. But this is the point of all genuinely transformative animal politics: we can't know in advance what the consequences of enhanced animal agency and improved animal representation will be—we actually have to implement them to find out. And we believe that APOs have a valuable role to play in the process.

Acknowledgments

Thanks to Valéry Giroux, Angie Pepper, and Kristin Voigt for inviting us to be part of this volume and for helpful comments on our initial draft. Special thanks to Élise Desaulniers and the staff at the

Montreal SPCA for sharing their experiences with us so openly and frankly.

Notes

1. The term "animal-industrial complex" originates in Noske (1989). For an update and elaboration, see Twine (2012).
2. As, e.g., when the law limits the SPCA to considering cases of cruelty that fall outside the standard operating procedures of industry and science while preventing them from attending to the vast structural cruelties of the animal-industrial complex. Or, as another example, when the SPCA must comply with an order to kill a dog who has attacked a human even if the behavior originates in human abuse and neglect.
3. As, e.g., in efforts to make incremental improvements to farm animal welfare legislation when the fundamental role of this legislation, arguably, is the authorization of violence against animals, not animal protection (Bryant 2010). APOs may also be expected to cooperate in the creation of guidelines for entities such as the Canadian Council on Animal Care and the National Farm Animal Care Council, two industry-led and unaccountable bodies to whom the government defers on matters concerning the well-being of researched and farmed animals. On how industry has captured these bodies, and sidelined pro-animal voices, see Bradley and MacRae (2011).
4. Insofar as the mandate of most APOs includes a principle of ensuring "protection" or "consideration" for animals, one could argue that a transformative commitment is already implicit in their mandate. However, many APOs explicitly deny that this principle entails repudiating ideologies of the instrumental use of animals. See, e.g., the Ontario SPCA's explanation that it is an "animal welfare" and not an "animal rights" organization (https://ontariospca.ca/who-we-are/faqs/). Philosophically, one might question whether this is a coherent or defensible interpretation of the principle of protecting animals, but it has historically been the predominant view within many APOs, and efforts to move APOs in a more transformative direction have often been resisted by their governing boards and donors. For the purposes of this chapter, therefore, we will assume that APOs are defined first and foremost by their commitment to the immediate rescue and protection of individual animals and that the question of whether or how to supplement that with a more transformative commitment is a matter of ongoing debate.
5. For a discussion of the particular challenges facing APOs when their public pronouncements contradict prevailing social norms, see Chapter 5, this

volume. In this chapter, our focus is less on public pronouncements and more on internal practices and grassroots partnerships.

6. The term "prefigurative politics" originates in Boggs (1977), who defined it as "the embodiment, within the ongoing political practice of a movement, of those forms of social relations, decision-making, culture, and human experience that are the ultimate goal." It has since become a central concept for understanding a wide range of contemporary social movements. For a helpful overview, see Yates (2015).

7. Sanctuaries are diverse and reflect a broad range of what might be deemed prefigurative elements—whether consciously adopted in those terms or more intuitively evolved in caring practice. Part of our goal in this chapter is to contribute analytic tools to identify these elements so that APOs can, if they choose, adopt them with greater intention.

8. On the distinction between "domesticated" animals (who we've brought into our society to live and work alongside us), "liminal" animals (who are not domesticated but live among us as urban or suburban wildlife), and "wild" (or "wilderness") animals (who attempt to live on their own habitat and generally avoid human contact), see Donaldson and Kymlicka (2011).

9. See Pepper and Voigt (2021) for related discussion concerning the future role of zoos.

10. On the high level of stress and burnout among animal shelter staff, see Dunn et al. (2019).

11. Other APOs which fall primarily on the crisis end include wildlife rehab centers. Most of their work is transitory, involving crisis care for injured or orphaned liminal and wild animals who will be released into the wild. But some animals cannot be released safely into the wild, and, where permitted, rescue centers often provide a permanent home to these individuals. A related example is "drop in" forms of sanctuary for free-roaming animals—e.g., sanctuary clinics for village dogs, cows, and donkeys in India, or feral cat support networks— in which humans provide not just crisis care, but also a structure of ongoing supportive intervention. This ongoing support might include constructing shelters, providing food and intermittent medical care, and offering temporary respite from life on the streets. So, the distinction between temporary crisis care and a permanent home/community is a continuum, as is the distinction between more formally organized and informal care networks.

12. Even the conservative field of animal welfare science has awakened to the importance of animal agency and autonomy. See Špinka and Wemelsfelder (2018) and Franks (2019) for recent overviews of studies concerning the inherent importance to many animals of being able to exercise control over their lives, to the point that they will sacrifice material benefits and other welfare outcomes in favor of retaining or achieving greater agency.

13. See Franks (2019) for a discussion of this issue in the context of "choice studies" involving animals. For example, stressed animals in captivity may show little inclination to explore new options, which is sometimes taken as evidence that providing options does not contribute to their welfare. In reality, what this shows is that they are in a state of poor welfare and so unable to take up what would be welfare-improving options.

14. See Meijer (2019) for a discussion of animals making proposals to us (and vice versa).

15. The idea that the capacity for choice requires "scaffolding" is familiar in child psychology. We extend it to animals living in interspecies communities in Donaldson and Kymlicka (2017).

16. In relation to farmed animal sanctuaries, we argue that this scaffolding should even extend to creating the conditions under which animal residents can safely exit community with humans over time, if they so choose. Animals who currently live in close relationships with humans might gradually form their own communities with much reduced interaction with humans. In the VINE sanctuary in Vermont, for example, cows have the option of either leading a more independent semi-feral life on their own in the expansive upper pasture or living in more constant and direct interaction with humans and other animals in the middle pasture (as discussed in Donaldson and Kymlicka (2015) and Blatter, Donaldson and Wilcox (2020). This is unlikely to be a realistic option for the animals falling under permanent care of an APO.

17. We refer to it as "second best" to highlight the fact that it is a life path made necessary/possible by earlier misfortune or injustice. This does not preclude the possibility that this life path leads to a highly valued life, just as human tragedy can sometimes push people onto a new path that they ultimately cherish.

18. See Donaldson and Kymlicka (2016) for a more extended discussion of how prefigurative animal politics can be located within networks of participatory local institutional settings: e.g., having an animal sanctuary as part of complex that brings together a school and a home for seniors.

19. On the importance of animals being able to appropriate their environment to feel at home in it, see Bachour (2020), Bachour, Chang, and Van Patter (2021).

20. On the dangers of monopolies of care, see Gheaus (2018).

References

Bachour, O. (2020) "Alienation and animal labour." In C. Blattner, K. Coulter, and W. Kymlicka (eds.), *Animal Labour: A New Frontier of Interspecies Justice*. Oxford: Oxford University Press, 116–138.

Bachour, O., D. Chang, and L. Van Patter (2021) "Dwelling with Animal-Others: Meaning-Making and the Emergence of Multispecies Community." (under review)

Blattner, C. (2020) "Animal labour: Toward a prohibition of forced labour and a right to freely choose one's work." In C. Blattner, K. Coulter, and W. Kymlicka (eds.), *Animal Labour: A New Frontier of Interspecies Justice*. Oxford: Oxford University Press, 91–115.

Blattner, C., S. Donaldson, and R. Wilcox (2020) "Animal agency in community: A political multispecies ethnography of VINE Sanctuary." *Politics and Animals* 6, 1–22.

Boggs, C. (1977) "Marxism, prefigurative communism, and the problem of workers' control." *Radical America* 11(6), 99–122.

Bradley, A., and R. MacRae (2011) "Legitimacy and Canadian Farm Animal Welfare standards development: The case of the National Farm Animal Care Council." *Journal of Agricultural and Environmental Ethics* 24(1), 19–47.

Bryant, T. (2010) "Denying childhood and its implications for animal-protective law reform." *Law, Culture and the Humanities* 6(1), 56–74.

Côté-Boudreau, F. (2019) *Inclusive Autonomy: A Theory of Freedom for Everyone*. PhD dissertation. Queen's University (Kingston, Canada).

Donaldson, S. (2020) "Animal agora: Animal citizens and the democratic challenge." *Social Theory and Practice* 46(4), 709–735.

Donaldson, S., and W. Kymlicka (2011) *Zoopolis: A Political Theory of Animal Rights*. Oxford: Oxford University Press.

Donaldson, S., and W. Kymlicka (2015) "Farmed animal sanctuaries: The heart of the movement?" *Politics and Animals* 1, 50–74.

Donaldson, S., and W. Kymlicka (2016) "Envisioning the zoopolitical revolution." In Paola Cavalieri (ed.), *Philosophy and the Politics of Animal Liberation*. London: Palgrave, 71–116.

Donaldson, S., and W. Kymlicka (2017) "Rethinking membership and participation in an inclusive democracy: Cognitive disability, children, animals." In Barbara Arneil and Nancy Hirschmann (eds.), *Disability and Political Theory*. Cambridge: Cambridge University Press, 168–197.

Dunn, J., C. Best, D. L. Pearl, and A. Jones-Bitton (2019) "Mental health of employees at a Canadian animal welfare organization." *Society and Animals* 30(1) 51–87.

Francione, G. (2004) "Animals: Property or persons?" In Cass Sunstein and Martha Nussbaum (eds.), *Animal Rights: Current Debates and New Directions*. New York: Oxford University Press, 108–142.

Franks, B. (2019) "What do animals want." *Animal Welfare* 28(1), 1–10.

Gheaus, A. (2018) "Children's vulnerability and legitimate authority over children." *Journal of Applied Philosophy* 35(S1), 60–75.

Healey, R., and A. Pepper (2021) "Interspecies justice: Agency, self-determination, and assent." *Philosophical Studies* 178(4), 1223–1243.

Hohti, R., and T. Tammi (2019) "The greenhouse effect: Multispecies childhood and non-innocent relations of care." *Childhood* 26(2), 169–185.

Honig, B. (2017) *Public Things: Democracy in Disrepair.* New York: Fordham University Press.

Krause, S. (2013) "Beyond non-domination: Agency, inequality and the meaning of freedom." *Philosophy and Social Criticism 39*(2), 187–208.

Krause, S. (2016) "Agency." *Political Concepts: A Critical Lexicon.* Issue 3:5. https://www.politicalconcepts.org/

Meijer, E. (2019) *When Animals Speak: Toward an Interspecies Democracy.* New York: New York University Press.

Noske, B. (1989) *Humans and Other Animals: Beyond the Boundaries of Anthropology.* London: Pluto Press.

Pepper, A., and K. Voigt (2021) "Covid-19 and the future of zoos." *Ateliers de l'éthique/The Ethics Forum 16*(1), 68–87.

Špinka, M., and F. Wemelsfelder (2018) "Environmental challenge and animal agency." In Michael Appleby, Anna Olsson, and Francisco Galindo (eds.), *Animal Welfare,* 3rd ed. Wallingford: CABI, 39–55.

Twine, R. (2012) "Revealing the animal-industrial complex: A concept and method for critical animal studies." *Journal of Critical Animal Studies 10*(1), 12–39.

Yates, L. (2015) "Rethinking prefiguration: Alternatives, micropolitics and goals in social movements." *Social Movement Studies 14*(1), 1–21.

Afterword

Élise Desaulniers

It is astonishing that, almost two centuries after the creation of the first shelters, this work constitutes, to my knowledge, the first real ethical reflection on the stakes of animal protection organizations.

The daily life in a shelter is one of emergencies and unexpected events. The moments when we can sit down and take a step back from what we are doing are rare, if not nonexistent. Meeting with a group of ethicists and reading their recommendations made me realize the complexity of our work and provided a solid and necessary foundation for our reflections and continuous improvement processes.

The Montreal SPCA is the oldest and still one of the most important animal protection organizations in Canada. We take care of 12,000 to 15,000 animals each year. Although it is the main provider of animal services to the City of Montreal, we are funded primarily through donations and self-generated revenue. The Montreal SPCA's mission goes beyond that of most shelters: it is to protect animals from neglect, abuse, and exploitation; represent their interests and ensure their well-being; promote public awareness; and contribute to the development of compassion for all sentient beings.

In addition to shelter activities, the Montreal SPCA also offers a spay/neuter service for low-income families, operates an investigation office that enforces animal protection laws, and works to advance the animal cause in Quebec with its animal advocacy team. The Montreal SPCA is behind the recent modifications to the Civil Code of Quebec, which now recognizes animals as sentient beings. It is due to the Montreal SPCA's efforts that cats, dogs, and rabbits who do not come from shelters can no longer be sold in pet stores across the city, that the ban on certain breeds of dogs has been ended, and that horse-drawn carriages no longer operate in Old Montreal.

Our organization is much more than a traditional shelter. It is one of the leading animal rights groups in Quebec. It is therefore important for us to be exemplary in our ways. We don't just want to adopt best practices; we want to establish them.

The recommendations that have been made (and are reproduced in this volume) will be read and analyzed carefully. Some of them have already been implemented or are in the process of being implemented, such as vocabulary issues or the creation of an ethics committee. Others, such as the creation of a second site, seem difficult to implement in the short term, but they illustrate the difficulties of realizing our ambitious projects in our current facilities. When we talk about organizing the Montreal SPCA into subunits that have discretion over their own budgets, rather than being in ongoing competition for limited resources with several other units, this seems difficult with very limited financial resources. The issue is not so much the distribution of the budget as the size of the budget itself, which forces prioritization. Other recommendations require more thought, such as anything to do with our enforcement powers and our criticism of the Ministry of Agriculture, Fisheries and Food (MAPAQ). We must ask ourselves what is best for the animals in the short, medium, and long term—and, above all, whether one of the problems is not that the SPCA is one of the only groups defending animal rights in Quebec.

A common thread linking all these issues is the fact that in Quebec—as elsewhere in the world—funding for animal protection depends almost exclusively on donations from the public and therefore on public opinion. Deprived of subsidies, organizations like ours spend a good part of their resources on fundraising activities that are necessary to offer basic care to animals—such as shelter and veterinary care—that represent staggering costs. Our organizations do not always have the freedom of other advocacy groups to make bold moves that put their funding at risk. On the other hand, the optimization of scarce resources is a constant concern.

Since the visit of the group of ethicists who wrote these recommendations for our shelter, much has changed at the Montreal SPCA. New programs, especially for cats with ringworm and unweaned kittens, have been implemented and are already being emulated elsewhere in Quebec. Processes have been improved to ensure that all options are truly considered when making decisions about an animal's life. The pandemic has also forced us to rethink and optimize all our services as well as develop a series of community support programs. We now temporarily house the animals of victims of domestic violence and refugees. We have a food bank to provide pet food to those who are going through difficult times. We have helped develop shelters for people experiencing homelessness that now house animals and provide training for street youth to learn proper animal care.

All of this community work is missing from the recommendations but will undoubtedly become more and more important in our work over the next few years. It makes us realize the importance of thinking about our relationships with animals in a broader way. More and more groups are putting forward the concept of One Health: animal health, human health, and environmental health are intrinsically intertwined and interdependent. The health of one affects the health of all. I believe that animal welfare groups like ours will be called on to work in concert with other organizations to help create a more just and sustainable world. Shelters and animal welfare in the broadest sense should no longer be thought of in silos but as part of a larger whole. Of course, all this will certainly lead to other ethical reflections. But it is by fighting for more social justice and by reducing inequalities that we will arrive at a fairer world for animals.

Index

For the benefit of digital users, indexed terms that span two pages (e.g., 52–53) may, on occasion, appear on only one of those pages.